C000183784

THE BUMPER BOOK OF RESOURCES

HOLY WEEK

EDITED BY JOHN COX

kevin
mayhew

www.kevinmayhew.com

kevin mayhew

First published in Great Britain in 2015 by Kevin Mayhew Ltd
Buxhall, Stowmarket, Suffolk IP14 3BW
Tel: +44 (0) 1449 737978 Fax: +44 (0) 1449 737834
E-mail: info@kevinmayhew.com

www.kevinmayhew.com

© Copyright 2015 David Adam, Claire Benton-Evans, Rupert Bristow, John Cox, Peter
Dainty, Nick Fawcett, Michael Forster, Nick Harding, John Hardwick, Mary Hathaway,
Peter Jackson, Gerald O'Mahony, Susan Sayers, David Schofield, Ray Simpson, Ken Taylor,
Stuart Thomas, Pete Townsend, Sheila Walker.

The right of David Adam, Claire Benton-Evans, Rupert Bristow, John Cox, Peter Dainty,
Nick Fawcett, Michael Forster, Nick Harding, John Hardwick, Mary Hathaway, Peter Jackson,
Gerald O'Mahony, Susan Sayers, David Schofield, Ray Simpson, Ken Taylor, Stuart Thomas,
Pete Townsend and Sheila Walker to be identified as the authors of this work has been asserted
by them in accordance with the Copyright, Designs and Patents Act 1988.

The publishers wish to thank all those who have given their permission to reproduce
copyright material in this publication.

Every effort has been made to trace the owners of copyright material and we hope that no
copyright has been infringed. Pardon is sought and apology made if the contrary be the case,
and a correction will be made in any reprint of this book.

All rights reserved. The material on the accompanying CD-Rom may be copied without
copyright infringement, provided that it is used for the purpose for which it is intended.
Reproduction of the contents of the CD-Rom for commercial purposes is subject to the
usual copyright restrictions. No other part of this publication may be reproduced, stored
in a retrieval system, or transmitted, in any form or by any means, electronic, mechanical,
photocopying, recording, or otherwise, without the prior written permission of the publisher.

9 8 7 6 5 4 3 2 1 0

ISBN 978 1 84867 789 0
Catalogue No. 1501484

Cover design by Justin Minns
© Images used under licence from Shutterstock Inc.
Edited by John Cox
Typeset by Chris Coe

Printed and bound in Great Britain

CONTENTS

RESOURCES

MAUNDY THURSDAY

PRAYERS

SERVICES

SERMON IDEAS

ALL-AGE SERVICES

RESOURCES

GOOD FRIDAY

PRAYERS

FOREWORD

This Bumper Book (together with its two companion volumes) draws together material from a wide range of sources and a number of top authors to create an invaluable resource for anyone seeking help with prayers, services, sermon ideas and illustrative material both for general and all-age worship.

The three volumes cover the major festivals of the Christian year:

Volume 1: Harvest, All Saints, All Souls and Remembrance
Volume 2: Advent, Christmas and Epiphany
Volume 3: Holy Week, Easter, Ascension and Pentecost

Each volume is accompanied by a CD-ROM providing activity sheets and illustrations that can be reproduced to enliven learning and interactive worship.

PALM SUNDAY

PRAYERS

General Prayers

Blessed are you, Lord God of our salvation;
to you be praise and glory for ever.
As we rejoice this day
in the triumphant entry into Jerusalem,
may we too be willing to walk the way of the cross.
By our lives may we witness to you
as our Lord and King
and declare your saving love to the world.

David Adam

Blessed are you, Lord God of all creation.
You have created us out of your love and for your love.
Help us to welcome you with songs of 'Hosanna',
knowing that you are our strength and our shield.
Help us to welcome Christ our Lord into our lives
as our Lord and Saviour.

David Adam

Blessed are you, Lord Jesus, for you are our Saviour.
As you were welcomed into Jerusalem,
may we welcome you into our homes and our lives.
Let our lives sing Hosannas to you,
that we may be full of your praise.
As we carry palm crosses
may we know the great sacrifice of love
that you made for us,
Jesus our Lord and King.

David Adam

Lord God,
we hold these palm crosses as signs
of Jesus our King riding into Jerusalem as the Messiah
and of his suffering and dying on the cross.
Bless these palms that they may be to us
a sign of his victory and of your eternal love.
May we who hold them
always accept him as our King
until we rejoice in the kingdom
where he reigns with you and the Holy Spirit,
now and for ever.

David Adam

Lord Jesus Christ,
you entered Jerusalem on a wave of enthusiasm,
greeted by your joyful people,
by shouts of praise and protestations of loyalty on every side.
Yet you knew that the bubble would soon burst,
that the welcome was only skin-deep.
We come today with equal gladness,
but conscious that our commitment,
like that of long ago,
may not be as strong as it should be;
our faith fickle if put to the test,
our loyalty flawed.
Speak to us through the story of that first Palm Sunday,
and through the events that followed,
and so may our hosannas ring out as loudly tomorrow
as they do today.
In your name we ask it.   *Nick Fawcett*

Saviour Christ,
King of kings and Lord of lords,
we want today to offer more than well-intentioned routine,
more than hymns and prayers,
words and music,
preaching and teaching.
We want to offer worship,
praise,
adoration,
bubbling up from within,
welling up,
spilling over,
expressing our love and gratitude,
and offering our lives back to you in joyful response.
Come among us now, through your Spirit,
and reveal your glory.
Fill and thrill us afresh with your grace,
and help us to bless your name,
as you have blessed us in so much.   *Nick Fawcett*
Lord Jesus Christ,
we come to declare your greatness,
to acclaim you as King,
to profess our allegiance
and to seek your will for our lives.
Instruct us through this service,
so that, glimpsing the true meaning of power
and the nature of your rule,
we may commit ourselves more fully to you
and gain a clearer understanding of your purpose for all.   *Nick Fawcett*

Lord Jesus Christ,
we are good at singing your praises when life goes as we want it to,
but it's another matter when our expectations are overturned,

our preconceptions challenged and our faith tested.
We are eager to receive your blessings
but reluctant to take the way of sacrifice.
We are happy to proclaim you as king
but hesitant in offering our service.
So often our commitment is short-lived,
superficial and self-centred,
more about our own well-being than your kingdom.
Forgive us,
and, by your grace,
help us to offer you true allegiance,
whatever you may ask,
to the glory of your name.   *Nick Fawcett*

Lord Jesus Christ,
we are reminded of how you entered Jerusalem
to shouts of joy and celebration.
But we remember too how quickly that welcome evaporated,
how soon the mood of the crowd changed.
Lord Jesus Christ,
we know all too well that we are not so different,
our commitment to you so often short-lived,
superficial,
self-centred.
Help us to welcome you into our lives with true gladness,
and to go on serving you come what may,
now and always.   *Nick Fawcett*

Lord Jesus Christ,
remind us through this day
that you are King, but not of this world;
that you rule, but not through force;
that you invite our respect, but do not demand it;
that you are the Lord of lords, but servant of all.
Give us a deeper understanding of your kingdom
and a firmer grasp of your will.
Teach us the way of humility and the path of love,
so that we may honour you now in worship
and each day in service,
to your glory.   *Nick Fawcett*

Lord Jesus Christ, we come today
remembering how crowds joyfully welcomed you
into Jerusalem,
but remembering also how a mob called there for your death,
the space of a few days making such a difference
to the response you received.
Help us, then, as we greet and acclaim you,

to search ourselves and examine the homage we offer,
so that the faith we profess today will be as real tomorrow and every day
as it is now,
to the glory of your name.   *Nick Fawcett*

Lord Jesus Christ,
you came to our world as the King of kings
and Lord of lords,
yet also as the servant of all.
You came deserving our praise and worship,
yet willingly accepting mockery, rejection and suffering for our sakes.
You came to bring life in all its fullness,
yet you offered your life for the life of the world.
Lord Jesus Christ,
teach us to recognise the values of your kingdom
that turn our world upside down.
Help us to understand that strength lies in weakness,
greatness in humility,
and the secret of life in offering our lives to others.   *Nick Fawcett*

Father,
as the crowds welcomed Jesus and sang your praises,
we welcome you
into our hearts and lives
over the coming year.
We pray for opportunities
to spread your good news and courage to take them.   *Susan Sayers*

Father,
we recall the donkey Jesus rode on,
and we pray for that real humility in our hearts
which treats status and image casually,
and truth and loving service seriously.   *Susan Sayers*

Father,
as the children sang and shouted your praise,
we pray for that same innocent trust in our lives
and the confidence to shout your praises
in our homes, our city and our land.   *Susan Sayers*

Father,
the crowds were responding
to the healing love they had seen in action in Jesus.
We bring to you in our love and imaginations now
all the parts of our lives
which need your healing and help.
Give us comfort and reassurance,
wholeness and hope.   *Susan Sayers*

Father,
we, too, spread our coats on the road
as we express our thankfulness
for all you have done for us
and the amazing extent of your love.
You are our God, we welcome you!   *Susan Sayers*

Clip, clop, clip, clop!
Hosanna! Hosanna!
Hooray for Jesus,
the king on a donkey!
Hosanna! Hosanna!
Clip, clop, clip, clop!   *Susan Sayers*

O God,
when the ride is bumpy
and the world passes us by,
you pour out your life for us,
right to the very end.
When we are edged aside
and doors are shut in our face,
you pour out your life for us,
right to the very end.
When others are out to get us
and our home is not secure,
you pour out your life for us,
right to the very end.
When our lives are but a flicker
in the darkness that encroaches,
you pour out your life for us
right to the very end.   *Susan Sayers*

The One who created us
comes willingly to suffer for us;
let us spread our resolves before him like branches of palm.   *Ray Simpson*

The Almighty comes to us
as one gentle and lowly of heart;
let us put on clothes of humility and praise.
The spirit is willing but the flesh is weak;
let us watch and wait with him.   *Ray Simpson*

As your trial drew near, you looked upon
the city and wept over it, because it did not
recognise its salvation.
Open our eyes, that we may weep with you.
May we weep with you for the blindness of pride

15

that corrodes the dignity of human life . . .
Open our eyes, that we may weep with you.
We weep with you for the mad rush to consume
that tramples down on the Earth and its children . . .
Open our eyes, that we may weep with you.
We weep with you for the lust to control
that imprisons the soul and fragments community . . .
Open our eyes, that we may weep with you.

Ray Simpson

Welcoming the King

Gracious God,
as we remember this day
how Jesus entered Jerusalem to cries of celebration,
help us to welcome him afresh
into our own hearts and lives.
Accept the praise and worship we bring you,
and give us a real sense of expectation
as we look towards his coming kingdom.
Hosanna to the Son of David,
glory in the highest heaven.

Gracious God,
like your people long ago
we do not always see clearly,
our faith shallow and self-centred;
we do not understand as we should,
our praise short-lived and superficial.
But, we ask, take the faith we offer,
weak though it may be,
and deepen it through this day,
so that we may truly welcome Christ as our King,
and worship him with joyful praises,
now and always.
Hosanna to the Son of David,
glory in the highest heaven,
now and always.

Nick Fawcett

Confession

Lord Jesus Christ,
you came to Jerusalem and were greeted by shouts of joy,
welcomed as God's promised deliverer,
the one he had chosen to rescue his people.
But when the nature of your kingdom became clear,
the sort of freedom you offered fully apparent,
so the response changed.
The shouts of 'Hosanna!'
turned to cries of 'Crucify!'

The hands outstretched in friendship
became fists curled up in hate.
The declarations of loyalty
became voices raised in mockery and rejection.
Lord Jesus,
have mercy.

You come to our lives
and we welcome you with gladness.
We have accepted you as our Saviour,
the one who sets us free.
But we too can so quickly change our tune
when you overturn our expectations,
when you do not act as we hope,
when you turn out to have different ideas from our own.
We, too, even while professing faith
and going through the motions of commitment,
can push you aside,
preferring our own way to yours.
Lord Jesus,
have mercy.

Lord Jesus Christ,
on this day we are reminded of how easy it is
to welcome you as King of kings,
but how hard to follow in the Way of the Cross.
Lord Jesus,
have mercy,
for in your name we ask it.

Nick Fawcett

Intercession

Jesus enters Jerusalem as the Prince of Peace, riding on a donkey. At the heart of our rejoicing is the pain he is bound to suffer in redeeming us through unflinching love. Yet we still certainly rejoice, for we know he has won the victory. Jesus is indeed our King.

Fellow pilgrims, as we welcome Jesus
and hail him as our King,
let us offer to God our Father in prayer
the deep concerns and needs
of the Church and of the world.
We bring to your love all who are baptised,
and especially those who have lost their faith
or have stopped praying;
may they be brought back through your love,
and put into contact with those
who can guide and reassure them.

Silence for prayer

Lord, uphold us:
give us your strength.

We bring to your love every meeting,
demonstration, convention and all large crowds;
may they be peaceful and ordered,
inspiring those present for good,
rather than inciting them to violence.

Silence for prayer

Lord, uphold us:
give us your strength.

We bring to your love our own loved ones,
the members of our families, our friends
and especially those from whom we are separated,
either by distance or death;
and all who are missing from their homes;
may your powerful love protect us from all that is evil.

Silence for prayer

Lord, uphold us:
give us your strength.

We bring to your love those suffering
from incurable or life-threatening diseases;
those who need medical care, but are either too poor,
or live too far away to receive it;
make us more ready to help
with our time, money and influence,
so that unnecessary suffering and death are avoided.

Silence for prayer

Lord, uphold us:
give us your strength.

We bring to your love those who have died;
may they rest in the light and joy
of your presence for ever.

Silence for prayer

Father, may we praise you
not only with our voices
but also in the lives we lead.

Silence for prayer

Merciful Father,
**accept these prayers
for the sake of your Son,
our Saviour Jesus Christ.**

Susan Sayers

No Compromise

Lord Jesus Christ,
How easy it would have been for you
on entering Jerusalem
to have taken the easy way.
With the shouts of welcome still ringing in your ears,
the hosannas of the crowd
still fresh in your memory,
it must have been so tempting
to give them what they wanted,
to be the sort of Messiah
they hoped you would be.
But you soon made it clear, if any doubted,
that there would be no compromise,
no watering down of your message
for the sake of popular acclaim.
You stayed true to your calling
despite the inevitable consequences.
Lord Jesus Christ,
we too can try and shape you to fit our expectations.
Help us as we recall those last days leading up to the Cross,
to learn what you expect of us,
and find strength to honour it.

Nick Fawcett

Year A

Hosanna to the King of kings!
Lord, we give thanks that your Son humbled himself on the cross,
yet was exalted in his resurrection.
Your word was fulfilled, through his ordeal and our salvation.
But let us understand and feel the great suffering in this sacrifice,
the tears shed, the pain experienced, the abandonment felt.
May we who hear this story feel stronger for it
and more steadfast in our faith.
Lord, hear us.
Lord, graciously hear us.

As the processions in and around our churches
show to the world that the Easter story lives
and that Jesus' suffering was not in vain,
may that hope spread out into communities across the land.
Give confidence to your Church in its outreach
and in its capacity to draw people in.
Let young and old alike hear this story
and share in the pain and the joy.
Lord, hear us.
Lord, graciously hear us.

As the world looked on at your Son in his journey to the cross,
so may the world today know the extent of your love.
Give us all a glimpse of that sacrifice,
a taste of the degradation of the cross,
an idea of your generosity in the face of rejection.
Let the world know the power of redemption and be grateful.
And where there is oppression today, Lord,
bring your hope to the downtrodden,
remembering especially at this time . . .
Lord, hear us.
Lord, graciously hear us.

In our own community we pray for . . .
Lord, hear us.
Lord, graciously hear us.

In your compassion watch over those
who suffer through illness and pain,
as we pray for those who are in urgent need . . .
Let those who care know your strength and your patience.
Lord, hear us.
Lord, graciously hear us.

Give to those who mourn the hope of your eternal kingdom
as they come to understand that you have taken away
the tears of those who have died
and are now at peace with you, remembering especially . . .
Merciful Father,
accept these prayers
for the sake of your Son,
our Saviour Jesus Christ.

Rupert Bristow

Year B

God our Father, who understands suffering and loss,
help us to appreciate the enormity of your generosity
in sending your Son to minister to us
and bring us back from the brink.
As we cry 'Hosanna' and join the crowds
in strewing the path with palms,
we look ahead to the crown of thorns awaiting him.
May we recognise the glory to come in the way of the cross.
Give us the strength to survive our own moments
of doubt and testing,
of challenge and pain,
knowing that we can never suffer as he suffered.
Lord, in your mercy
hear our prayer.

Let your Church 'do justice, love kindness and walk humbly' with you, our God.
As we approach the glory and joy of Easter,
we pray for the state of the Church,
so that your word can be spread
and your love can be known more widely.
Nurture and challenge our faith, Lord,
at this time in the church year
when we walk with your Son and watch with his mother,
knowing the glorious outcome, but recognising the pain of the cross.
Lord, in your mercy
hear our prayer.

Just as your Son was aware of the needs of those around him,
even in his final agony, so may we be aware
of the needs of the world.
Grant to us the perception and the imagination
to identify the places and people we should help,
remembering especially at this time . . .
May we respond generously to cries for help
and may the right ways to bring hope and relief be shown to us.
Lord, in your mercy
hear our prayer.

In our own community we pray for . . .
Lord, in your mercy
hear our prayer.

We pray for the sick and all those who bring comfort, care
and professional skill to the relief of pain and treatment of illness.
We remember those in urgent need of our prayers . . .
Lord, in your mercy
hear our prayer.

We pray for those who have passed through the veil
and are now at peace with you, especially . . .
Comfort family and friends who mourn
and let fond memories wipe out the tears.
Merciful Father,
accept these prayers
for the sake of your Son, our Saviour Jesus Christ.

Rupert Bristow

Year C

Lord, we have all denied you,
knowingly or unwittingly, as Peter did.
We give thanks for your Son's choice of ordinary people
as apostles and disciples,
so that we may all identify with them in our failings
as well as seek to emulate them
in the way we share the Christian story.

As we benefit from the forgiveness
and redemptive power of your Son,
so may we acknowledge the way
to encourage and empower the growth of faith,
whatever the imperfections
and human frailties within us and around us.
Lord, hear us.
Lord, graciously hear us.

We pray for archbishops, bishops, and priests throughout your Church,
as they rededicate their ministry
and reach out through baptism to a receptive world.
Bring to congregations an appetite for learning
and a desire to share ministry and mission.
Help us to seek new ways to sustain our church
in ministering to the needs of the community.
Lord, hear us.
Lord, graciously hear us.

May we reach out to the needs of the world
in all we say and do as Christians.
Just as the centurion at the cross knew that Jesus was innocent,
so there are many who look to the Church for values and meaning,
in the midst of anger and suffering.
Deepen our commitment to God in the world.
Help us to see you in the darkness of conflict
as well as in the beauty of creation,
so that we can share your hope with those who seek it.
We pray especially for the people of . . .
Lord, hear us.
Lord, graciously hear us.

In our own community we pray for . . .
Lord, hear us.
Lord, graciously hear us.

We ask for your healing powers to be at work
in bringing relief to those who are sick, especially . . .
Let those who care know
that you are standing alongside them in their compassion.
Lord, hear us.
Lord, graciously hear us.

We give thanks for the lives of those who have died
and now rest with you in your eternal kingdom, remembering . . .
Give comfort to those who mourn and sustain them as they grieve.
Merciful Father,
accept these prayers
for the sake of your Son,
our Saviour Jesus Christ.

Rupert Bristow

Praise – The King of Glory

Lord Jesus Christ,
we greet you today as the Word made flesh,
before all,
beyond all,
within all –
the one in whom all things have their being,
yet entering our world of space and time,
sharing our humanity,
experiencing the joys and sorrows of flesh and blood,
living and dying among us
so that we might share in the joy of your kingdom.
Blessed is the king who comes in the name of the Lord!
Hosanna in the highest heaven!

We greet you as the Messiah,
the Son of David,
King of Israel –
Servant of all,
Saviour of all,
anointed for burial,
crowned with thorns
and lifted high on a cross –
your kingdom not of this world.
Blessed is the king who comes in the name of the Lord!
Hosanna in the highest heaven!

We greet you as Lord of the empty tomb –
the risen Christ,
victorious over death,
triumphant over evil,
the one who has gone before us,
whose Spirit walks with us now,
and who will be there to greet us at our journey's end –
Jesus Christ, the pioneer and perfecter of our faith.
Blessed is the king who comes in the name of the Lord!
Hosanna in the highest heaven!

We greet you as the King of kings and Lord of lords,
the ascended and exalted Lamb of God,
ruler of the ends of the earth,
enthroned in splendour,
seated at the right hand of the Father,
worthy of all honour and glory and blessing – the King of Glory!
Blessed is the king who comes in the name of the Lord!
Hosanna in the highest heaven!

Lord Jesus Christ,
we greet you today with joyful worship and reverent praise.
Hear our prayer
and accept our homage,
for we offer it in your name and to your glory.

Nick Fawcett

23

Confession – the King of Love

Lord Jesus Christ,
we claim to be your followers,
and we declare that you are the Lord
and King of our lives,
but all too often our actions deny our words.
When you look at our lives,
the weakness of our faith
and the frailty of our commitment,
you must grieve over us
as surely as you wept for Jerusalem long ago.
You offer us salvation,
joy, peace and fulfilment,
yet we so easily let it slip through our fingers.
King of Love,
have mercy upon us.

We thank you that your kingdom is not of this world,
that you rule not as a dictator but as a servant,
winning the hearts of your people,
inspiring devotion through who and what you are.
If you dealt with us as we deserve,
then our future would be bleak,
none of us able to stand before you,
for day after day we break your commandments,
betraying your love,
ignoring your guidance, our faith fickle,
our allegiance poor.
King of Love,
have mercy upon us.

Forgive us all the ways we fail you,
through thought, word and deed.
Forgive our limited understanding of your greatness
and the narrowness of our vision.
Forgive our inability to grasp the values of your kingdom,
still less to base our lives upon them.
We want to bring honour to you, but so often we do the opposite.
King of Love,
have mercy upon us.

Lord Jesus,
we come before your throne,
throwing ourselves upon your grace,
and asking you to receive our worship,
despite its weakness;
to accept our service,
despite our many faults.
Rule in our hearts

and use us for your glory.
King of Love,
have mercy upon us.
In your name we ask it.

Nick Fawcett

Petition and Intercession – the Prince of Peace

Lord Jesus Christ,
you came not as a king mighty in battle,
but as the Prince of Peace,
the promised deliverer,
sent to heal and restore our broken world.
So now we pray for peace and unity between nations.
Your kingdom come,
your will be done.

We thank you for signs of hope in the world today –
for the desire to make this planet a safer place,
for initiatives that have been taken
to reduce nuclear and conventional arms,
for the breaking down of seemingly insurmountable barriers,
and for a willingness to engage in genuine dialogue
rather than empty rhetoric.
Prosper all such efforts,
and grant that a spirit of trust and co-operation
may develop among all.
Your kingdom come,
your will be done.

We pray for those places where tension continues –
where there is still hatred,
division,
violence
and slaughter.
We pray for all those caught up in the awfulness of war –
those maimed and injured,
those who have lost loved ones,
those for whom life will never be the same again.
Break down the barriers which keep people apart –
the prejudice and intolerance,
greed and envy,
injustice and exploitation
which continue to scar our world.
May your Spirit of love overcome
all that causes people
to take up arms against one another.
Your kingdom come,
your will be done.

Lord Jesus Christ, Prince of Peace,
come again to our world
and bring the unity that you alone can bring.
May the day come when swords
shall be beaten into ploughshares,
and spears turned into pruning hooks;
when nation shall not lift sword against nation,
neither learn war any more;
a day when no one will hurt or destroy
on all your holy mountain.
Your kingdom come,
your will be done.
For your name's sake.

Nick Fawcett

SERVICES

A Palm Sunday Procession

Processions form a significant part of the witness and worship of Palm Sunday. Local situations will determine how elaborate or simple they are. In some places the procession will involve a walk around the village or neighbourhood and include an actual donkey. Elsewhere this will not be practical but there will be a procession around the church itself, either outside or inside or both. The theme of procession, acclamation and humility might well be given a quite different kind of expression with the Christ figure riding a bike and followers waving scarves. The detailed arrangements are up to local decision.

The service offered here is an outline that could be adapted for any of such settings. It incorporates readings, movement, singing and prayers. It is intended to be a resource rather than a fixed blueprint. Different voices could be used to lead at each station.

Station 1 – Gathering

We gather in the name of the Lord, the Christ, the King of Glory.
We gather as the followers of the Prince of Peace, the Servant of all.
We gather not knowing what he will ask of us,
not always understanding what he will do in us.
We will follow the One who comes in the name of the Lord.

While Jesus was going up to Jerusalem, he took the twelve disciples aside by themselves, and said to them on the way, 'See, we are going up to Jerusalem, and the Son of Man will be handed over to the chief priests and scribes, and they will condemn him to death; then they will hand him over to the Gentiles to be mocked and flogged and crucified; and on the third day he will be raised.' *(Matthew 20:17-19)*
We will follow the One who comes in the name of the Lord.

Jesus said: 'If any want to become my followers, let them deny themselves and take up their cross and follow me. For those who want to save their life will lose it, and those who lose their life for my sake will find it.' *(Matthew 16:24, 25)*
We will follow the One who comes in the name of the Lord.

Hymn

Will you come and follow me?

During the singing of this hymn palm crosses are distributed.

Prayers

Lord Jesus, you set your face to go to Jerusalem and told your disciples what would happen there. Grant us a trust like theirs, that we may follow you whatever is asked of us and wherever you may lead. Grant us through your Spirit the knowledge of your presence with us, to sustain us and guide us, to encourage and to challenge us, that we may witness to your truth and your love in all we do and say and are. In your name we ask this.

We hold the palm of acclamation.
May we always be bold in our witness to you, our King.
We hold the cross of sacrifice.
May we always be courageous in following your way of service to others, whatever the cost.

Further prayers of praise and commitment may be offered.

Lord Jesus, you are the Way we would follow, the Truth we would know, the Life we would experience and the King we would serve. Enable us by your Spirit to fulfil our intentions, to be steadfast in our loyalty and courageous in our actions.

The procession moves to its next station.

Station 2 – Preparation

Rejoice greatly, O daughter Zion!
Shout aloud, O daughter Jerusalem!
Lo, your king comes to you;
triumphant and victorious is he,
humble and riding on a donkey,
on a colt, the foal of a donkey. *(Zechariah 9:9)*
We will follow the One who comes in the name of the Lord.

When they had come near Jerusalem and had reached Bethphage, at the Mount of Olives, Jesus sent two disciples, saying to them, 'Go into the village ahead of you, and immediately you will find a donkey tied, and a colt with her; untie them and bring them to me. If anyone says anything to you, just say this, "The Lord needs them." And he will send them immediately.' *(Matthew 21:1-3)*
We will follow the One who comes in the name of the Lord.

Hymn

We have a king who rides a donkey *(verses 4 and 5 may be omitted)*

If a donkey is to be used it should be brought in during this hymn.

All creatures give praise to the Lord,
for he has wonderfully made you and all are in his care.
None is too humble for the King to use.
None is too lowly for the Lord to call to his service.
We will follow the One who comes in the name of the Lord.

Lord, you call us to your service.
May we be prompt in our response and willing in our obedience.
We will follow the One who comes in the name of the Lord.

Lord, you invite us to share in your work of love.
It is not a burden to serve you but a joy;
it is not a hardship but a privilege.
We will follow the One who comes in the name of the Lord.

Lord Jesus, King of all, you sought the help of others in your needs and met the needs of others. We pray for all who are in special need: the hungry and the lonely, the lost and the forsaken, the oppressed and all victims of violence and abuse. May we be generous in our giving, sensitive in our helping and loving in our supporting.

Further prayers of intercession for the needs of the world and of individuals may be offered.

The procession moves to its next station.

Station 3 – Enthronement

The Lord is king; let the peoples tremble!
He sits enthroned upon the cherubim;
let the earth quake!
The Lord is great in Zion;
he is exalted over all the peoples.
Let them praise your great and awesome name.
Holy is he!
Mighty King, lover of justice,
you have established equity;
you have executed justice and righteousness in Jacob. *(Psalm 99:1-4)*
Blessed is the king. Hosanna in the highest!

The disciples went and did as Jesus had directed them; they brought the donkey and the colt, and put their cloaks on them, and he sat on them. A very large crowd spread their cloaks on the road, and others cut branches from the trees and spread them on the road. *(Matthew 21:6-8)*
Blessed is the king. Hosanna in the highest!

Hymn

All glory laud and honour
or You are the king of glory

If practicable, coats and branches could be laid down in front of the procession.

Lord, you are king,
enthroned in majesty,
come and rule in our hearts.
Blessed is the king. Hosanna in the highest!

Lord, you are king,
the ruler of nations,
bring peace to our world.
Blessed is the king. Hosanna in the highest!

Lord, you are king,
worshipped by angels,
accept our praise.
Blessed is the king. Hosanna in the highest!

Lord of lords and King of kings, we pray for all who have the responsibility of leadership in the nations of the world. Grant them integrity in all their dealings and decisions, and a desire to serve that is stronger than a desire for personal power. In Jesus' name.

Further prayers for the leaders of the nations may be offered.

The procession arrives at the church door or, if it has been taking place inside the church, moves to the back. The procession is met by people waving palm branches.

Station 4 – Acclamation

Blessed is the one who comes in the name of the Lord!
We bless you from the house of the Lord.
The Lord is God and he has given us light.
Bind the festal procession with branches
up to the horns of the altar.
Blessed is the One who comes in the name of the Lord.

The great crowd that had come to the festival heard that Jesus was coming to Jerusalem. So they took branches of palm trees and went out to meet him, shouting, 'Hosanna! Blessed is the one who comes in the name of the Lord – the King of Israel!' (*John 12:12, 13*)
Blessed is the One who comes in the name of the Lord.

The crowds that went ahead of him and that followed were shouting, 'Hosanna to the Son of David! Blessed is the one who comes in the name of the Lord! Hosanna in highest heaven.' (*Matthew 21:9*)
Blessed is the One who comes in the name of the Lord.

The whole multitude of the disciples began to praise God joyfully with a loud voice for the deeds of power that they had seen, saying 'Blessed is the king who comes in the name of the Lord! Peace in heaven, and glory in the highest heaven!' (*Luke 19:37, 38*)
Blessed is the One who comes in the name of the Lord.

The procession moves through the church to the front during the singing of the hymn.

Hymn

Ride on! Ride on in majesty!

The palm branches are held up and waved.

Glory and honour, praise and adoration,
we offer to Jesus our King.
With crowds adoring,
we greet his coming.
He is our Lord and our God.
Hosanna in the highest!

The palm crosses are held up.

Glory and honour, praise and adoration,
we offer to Jesus our Saviour.
The cross will bring true victory;
the sacrifice of God's lamb will bring our peace.
Hosanna in the highest!

Reflection or Address

Prayer

Heavenly Father,
we have joined in the acclamation of your Son,
echoing the words of the crowds.
Forgive us when our praise grows silent,
when our acclamations give way to apathy.
Forgive us the times we ask for the wrong things
and look only to our own wants.
Forgive us the times when we hide from your demands,
and want your power but not your love.
Go with us through this coming week,
that we may accompany you on your road to the cross
and so discover the joy and the wonder of your resurrection.
We ask this in the name of our King and our Saviour.

Hymn

Praise to the Holiest

Blessing

May the Lord of Glory bless you and keep you.
May the Son of David bless you and keep you.
May the humble King bless you and keep you
on this day of acclamation,
through this week of trial and execution
and in the wonder of his resurrection.   *John Cox*

You Only Have to Ask

Mark 11:1-11; (Matthew 21:1-11; 19:28-40; John 12:12-16)

Opening Prayer

Hosanna!
Blessed is he who comes in the name of the Lord.
Hosanna in the highest.

31

Blessed is he who comes as King.
Hosanna in the highest.
Peace in heaven and glory in the highest.
Hosanna in the highest heaven.

Hymn

All glory, laud and honour

Praise

Come, O Lord, and save us we pray.
Come, O Lord, send us now prosperity.
I will give thanks to you,
for you have become my salvation.

Blessed is he who comes in the name of the Lord;
we bless you from the house of the Lord.
I will give thanks to you,
for you have become my salvation.

You are my God and I will thank you;
you are my God and I will exalt you.
I will give thanks to you,
for you have become my salvation.

O give thanks to the Lord, for he is good;
his mercy endures for ever:
I will give thanks to you,
for you have become my salvation.   *Psalm 118:25, 26, 28, 29*

Confession

A brief time of silence

Lord, have mercy.
Christ, have mercy.
Lord, have mercy.

Christ, have mercy.
Lord, have mercy.
Christ, have mercy.

Lord, have mercy.
Christ, have mercy.
Lord, have mercy.

The Lord our King
comes in peace,
to welcome sinners
and to forgive you your sins.

Reading

Zechariah 9:9, 10
Rejoice greatly, O daughter Zion!
Shout aloud, O daughter Jerusalem!
Lo, your king comes to you;
triumphant and victorious is he,
humble and riding on a donkey,
on a colt, the foal of a donkey.
He will cut off the chariot from Ephraim
and the warhorse from Jerusalem;
and the battle-bow shall be cut off,
and he shall command peace to the nations;
his dominion shall be from sea to sea,
and from the River to the ends of the earth.

Hymn

We have a King who rides a donkey

Prayer

Lord Jesus,
you entered Jerusalem on a donkey's back,
amidst shouts of praise and triumph;
come to us with your rule of peace
that we may rejoice in the glory of the cross
and in the triumph of your resurrection.

Story

I'd never met Jesus before that day. It was my cousin who knew him really. He took up with him a year back, gave up his job and travelled round the countryside with some of the other followers. He was never one of the inner group but he said there was something really special about Jesus. He reckoned big things were going to happen that could make all the difference for us Jews, and even for the Gentiles as well.

He visited us once and told us some of the stories that Jesus used when he was teaching the people. They were about all sorts of things – some were just about people like you or me, country stories about farming and fishing, and there were others about kings and important folk, even some about Samaritans. They explained what God's kingdom was like – coming unexpectedly, in small ways that would grow and grow, with an invitation to everyone, and an urgency you shouldn't ignore. Anyhow that's what I made of it, best as I could. And then there were the healings – the blind and the lame. He told me Jesus would even go up to lepers and touch them to make them better. Now that's not something you see every day. It obviously made a big impression on my cousin, and he's nobody's fool.

I couldn't leave the farm or I would have gone and seen this Jesus for myself. But, as I told my cousin, if ever they were this way and there was anything they needed, all they had to do was ask. To be honest I didn't expect anything to come of it – but I meant it all the same. And when they did come it was quite a party, I can tell you.

The first I knew about it was this row going on outside in the street. I'd planned to take the donkeys up to the other fields and I'd just popped in the house to tell the missus, leaving the creatures tied up outside. When all of a sudden there was all this shouting. Such a carry on. I could hear Zechariah, my neighbour, having a right go at someone, so I dashed out. And there was my cousin and another bloke about to lead one of my young colts off. 'What do you think you're doing?' Zechariah was shouting. 'You northerners think you can do what you like at festival time. Clear off!'

'What's going on?' I asked. 'It's the Master,' my cousin said. 'He needs an animal to ride on and he told us to come and fetch an untried colt. He'll send it back later. You always said we could have anything we needed.' I said it was fine and Zechariah calmed down after that. Apparently Jesus and some of his followers were on their way to Jerusalem for the festival and Jesus had decided he wasn't going to be like the other pilgrims, go in on foot, but he would ride. It didn't really make sense to me so I asked my cousin what was going on.

'The way I see it,' my cousin told me, 'Jesus is making some kind of statement. I think he sees himself as the king that has been promised. He keeps telling us to read the scriptures and then we would understand. But I'm not too sure about it myself. I just hope people don't get the wrong message. He keeps saying he's coming to bring peace but I've also heard him say he's come with a sword, not that I've ever seen one, apart from the one Peter has. He's certainly acting like a king – he as good as told us to requisition this colt of yours. But you don't go to war on an ass, so I suppose he really does mean he wants a kingdom of peace. We'll just have to see, but I don't think the Romans will be too happy.'

To be honest, I'm not sure I understood what he was on about but it intrigued me. So I left the rest of the animals where they were and followed my cousin and his friend.

We found Jesus and the others just outside Bethany on the road into Jerusalem. There was quite a crowd. Some of the disciples had stripped off their coats and they put them on the colt's back for Jesus to climb on. It looked uncomfortable to me, the way they had piled them up, like a throne, someone said. Others were putting their coats on the road. It was as though they were putting themselves at the king's disposal. A sign of their obedience to him. There was a lot of cheering and people were getting very excited. They began chanting and shouting hallelujah. And they waved branches they'd stripped off the trees by the roadside. It's like what we do at the Feast of Tabernacles during the recitation of the Exodus Psalms. It all seemed to make good sense then and I joined in the shouting: 'Hosanna! Blessed is he, blessed is the king who comes in the name of the Lord.' We wanted a king and here he was, riding to his city, the city of David and we didn't care if the Romans were going to be upset. It felt good.

I followed all the way into Jerusalem and then things sort of fizzled out. Jesus and his disciples went off to the temple and I took the colt home. The Romans did get upset. They killed Jesus and that would have been the end of it but my cousin is convinced he's alive again and that he now knows that Jesus really is a king. I don't quite get it. But then I'm just an owner of donkeys.

Take time to reflect on/discuss the story

Prayers

Let us come to the King,
who came to us and is with us now,
who showed us the way of peace and humility,
and who prays for us to the Father.

Lord Jesus,
we pray for all peace makers and peace keepers,
for the United Nations and its Secretary General;

for the leaders of the nations,
for our own government and all members of parliament;
Lord, hear our prayer
and let our cry come unto you.

Lord Jesus,
we pray for your church throughout the world,
that it may be united in obedience and praise,
faithfully witnessing to your kingly rule;
Lord, hear our prayer
and let our cry come unto you.

Lord Jesus,
we pray for all who suffer from injustice and oppression,
for those who are exploited and unfairly imprisoned,
for the victims of violence and greed,
for the dispossessed and the powerless;
Lord, hear our prayer
and let our cry come unto you.

Lord Jesus,
we pray for ourselves,
that we may serve you with love
and our neighbours with unselfishness,
following the example of your own self-giving,
and sharing your resurrection life;
Lord, hear our prayer
and let our cry come unto you.

The Lord's Prayer

Hymn

Ride on ride on in majesty!

Blessing

May the peace of Christ the King rule in your hearts.
May the humility of Christ the King rule your lives.
May the glory of Christ the King surround your way.
And the blessing of God almighty,
the Father, and the Son, and the Holy Spirit,
be with you now and always.

John Cox

35

Palm Sunday – The Star

Preparations

- Order palm crosses from Africa from your usual supplier or from www.africanpalms.co.uk or ask people the previous week to bring small branches or banners to wave.
- Create a display in your church or meeting place to stay in place until 3.00pm on Good Friday. For example, a rough wooden cross fixed to the back of a chair, with a royal red robe draped over part of the cross and the chair; a hammer and large nails on the chair seat.
- You may wish to project a picture of a donkey on to a screen.

Introduction

'All the world's a stage' said William Shakespeare, and the life and death of Jesus has been called 'The greatest story ever told'. Jesus never did anything just for show. He was the real thing – Reality Incarnate. Yet he deliberately staged his last entry into his capital city in the last week of his life.

Today we shall relive that last Sunday in Jesus' life on earth. First let's join with the crowds in singing 'Make way, make way'.

Hymn

Make way, make way

Reflection

It was the first day of the Jews' working week, but in their capital city of Jerusalem crowds were gathering for their annual Passover festival. At this festival they recalled the time when, as refugees pursued by the military forces of superpower Egypt, the seawater inlet known as the Red Sea unexpectedly ebbed for just enough time to allow them to pass over to freedom. At this festival they slew lambs as sacrificial offerings to God, to signify that a response was needed from them for that merciful act of God in their history.

At that particular Passover the networks – all by word of mouth – were full of rumours about a prophet, teacher and miracle worker named Jesus who might or might not be coming south for the festival. Some said he was the messiah; others said he could not be, because he refused to take up arms, and how else could anyone overthrow the Roman occupying forces? Tensions were mounting, too, among the religious establishment. They were opposed to Jesus lest a people's uprising toppled their system of control.

Into this volatile situation Jesus made a striking entry – pregnant with paradox. He rode into the city centre on a donkey! Why did he do this?

Reading: Zechariah 9:9, 10

Preface the reading with the following:

In 536 BC, about sixteen years after the first return to Israel of Jewish exiles from Babylon, a prophet named Zechariah inspired his beleaguered compatriots with the following visionary words:

Reflection

Rabbis collected a series of prophetic sayings about a future messiah and repeated them to their hearers.

So, although Zechariah's words may not have been in the front of people's thinking, they were there in the background memory of some.

Jesus was making an unstated statement. He did not say he was the messiah, but he did something that a messiah would do.

Perhaps there was another reason why he chose to make his entrance on a donkey. Donkeys are small, lowly animals. They can be stubborn. They are neither as splendid nor as highly trainable as a horse. Yet we all love a donkey. Children like donkey rides on the beach. So the people's hearts went out to the man who rode on a donkey. Jesus was among the people, not above them. If he was a star, he was a people's star.

Reading

When fishes flew and forests walked
and figs grew upon thorn,
some moment when the moon was blood
then surely I was born.

With monstrous head and sickening cry
and ears like errant wings,
the devil's walking parody
on all four-footed things.

The tattered outlaw of the earth,
of ancient crooked will;
starve, scourge, deride me:
I am dumb, I keep my secret still.

Fools! For I also had my hour;
one far fierce hour and sweet:
there was a shout about my ears,
and palms before my feet.   *'The Donkey', G. K. Chesterton (1874-1936)*

Hymn

Ride on, ride on in majesty

During this hymn, palm crosses are given to each person, unless they were given as they entered the building.
The leader invites everyone to hold up their palm cross in one hand during the last verse.
During the last verse four people form a V, two each side, in the direction of the focal point or altar. They represent four types of people in the crowd and/or now.

FIRST MEMBER OF THE CROWD (JESUS WEPT OVER THE CITY)
Steps forward holding up the palm cross; returns to seat after the intercession.

I was walking into town from Bethany and found myself behind Jesus' lot. As they came to the brow of the hill and the city came into view, he wept over it. That's all I can think about.

He said: 'If only you had recognised – and it was possible, even for you – the things that make for your wellbeing. Now it is too late. The time will come, within the lifetime of people here, when this city will be surrounded by military forces and be put under siege. And your buildings will be razed to the ground.'

Adapted from Luke 19:41-44

Later I heard him say in the temple precincts: 'Jerusalem, Jerusalem, how often have I longed to gather you to me as a mother hen gathers her chicks, but you refused me.'

Matthew 23:37

Intercessions

We pray for a sense of the holy in our commerce and public services, in our treating of the sick and our transporting of people to work, in our provision of goods and in the joy of sport, in our designing of buildings and tending of the landscape leading us to create sacred space at the heart of it all.

Hymn

All glory, laud and honour

SECOND MEMBER OF THE CROWD (JESUS SAID THE STONES WOULD SPEAK)
Steps forward holding up the palm cross in one hand and a stone in the other; returns to seat after the intercession.

I heard some Pharisees shout at him. 'Tell your fan club to keep quiet; they are disturbing the peace.' And Jesus said: 'I tell you, if these became silent the very stones would shout out.'

Luke 19:39, 40

I love nature. I have always felt that God nods and beckons to us through every stone and star. Jesus knows this. He knows that even the stones would clap and cheer if everyone stayed as sour faced and closed of heart and lip as these people who should know better.

Intercessions

We pray for a sense of the holy in the trees that line our street, in the way we eat the earth's produce and treat our rubbish, in the way we learn from the birds and the elements and the sky.

THIRD MEMBER OF THE CROWD (THE BIGOTS)
Steps forward holding up the palm cross; returns to seat after the intercession.

I am a modern person. I am angry. I found myself in a group of religious bigots who think they have a divine right to run religion. I read in the Bible Jesus' prediction that this world's empires would come to nothing, including the little religious empire of his day and the temple in Jerusalem. I think of the pride and glory of empires, and of their decline and fall. The trouble is, each generation gets rid of one lot of tyrants and then behaves like tyrants themselves. If I'm really honest, there's a tyrant in me, too. Which is why we need big doses of penitence in our prayers.

Intercessions

Lord, have mercy on me, a sinner.
Lord, have mercy on me, a sinner.
Christ, have mercy on me, a sinner.
Christ, have mercy on me, a sinner.
Lord, have mercy on me, a sinner.
Lord, have mercy on me, a sinner.

Music

Kyrie, eleison . . .

FOURTH MEMBER OF THE CROWD (THE DONKEY)

Steps forward holding up the palm cross; returns to seat after the intercession.

I couldn't stop thinking about the donkey. What a surprise! It's not how you expect a VIP to make their entrance, sitting on an everyday, dumb little animal like that, but it's beautiful really. What I really think, deep down is – the man on that donkey has a beautiful humility. A noble humility. Respect. He respects the people in the streets. I say to myself, 'I don't know what he's going to do next, but whatever it is it will be true, and I want to follow someone like that.'

Intercessions

Children sing your praises.
But we have gone our own way.
A donkey gladly bears your weight.
But we have gone our own way.
A thief will cry to you for mercy.
But we have gone our own way.

We pray for children, who if adults were dumb would not be silenced. May the song and the love and the talent in every child's heart be unlocked, and may they flower into adults whose lives are a symphony that Jesus conducts.
We pray for stones, sacred repositories of memory, which remain sentinels to their Creator in fair weather and foul. We pray for rocks and minerals and seas – may we not do to them what we did to Jesus.
We pray for a sense of respect for family, neighbours and fellow citizens. A sense of the holy in the colour of someone's hair or skin, in the play of a child and the wrinkles of an old person. A sense of awe for the mystery and majesty of Jesus himself.

Reflection

It has been suggested that on Palm Sunday Jesus should be given the title Avatar – since he is Deity taking flesh, and connects energies of the unseen Spirit world to everyday human networks. But he is so much more even than that. So we have called him the Star. Not a star, but the Star. Not just the star of the truest and greatest story ever told, but the night star who, when death and deepest darkness engulfs all that we see and know, remains to shine and accompany us. Majesty shining through meekness.

Hymn

Meekness and majesty

Blessing

Be a bright star to guide us through the coming darkness.
Jesus, King of the universe
ride on in humble majesty,
ride on through conflict and debate,
ride on through sweaty prayer and betrayal of friends,
ride on through mockery and unjust condemnation,
ride on through cruel suffering and ignoble death,
ride on to the empty tomb and your rising in triumph,
ride on to raise up your Church, a new body for your service;
ride on, King Jesus, to renew the whole earth in your image.

A prayer from India

Ray Simpson

The Opening Days of Holy Week

Introduction

Waiting, we say, can be the hardest part, especially when we're facing the prospect of something frightening or unpleasant about to befall us, and no doubt that was as true for Jesus as for any. He rode into Jerusalem to the acclaim of the crowds, yet he knew that just a few days later he would face a very different reception, an altogether contrasting fate. From the start of his ministry he'd lived with the knowledge that it would lead to a cross; to suffering, sorrow and death; and now the moment had arrived, the time when he would be asked to make the final sacrifice. He could so easily have turned back, putting himself before others, but he didn't; he continued instead on his chosen path to the very end. Today, we reflect on the final stages of his journey to Calvary – on the enormity of his courage, the extent of his sacrifice and the depth of his love. Remember, and give thanks.

Opening prayer

Father God,
speak again in this Holy Week of your love in Christ,
of your surrendering all for our sakes.
Speak of his faithfulness to your call,
of his selfless service and awesome sacrifice,
and help us to remember what it cost both him and you.
Give us similar courage to give and go on giving,
love and go on loving,
so that we, like him,
may be enabled to put you first,
others second,
and self last.
Meet with us now
and teach us your way,
through Jesus Christ our Lord.

Hymn

Give me joy in my heart

Reading

John 12:12-16

Comment

There's a curious paradox about Holy Week. It starts in celebration, recalling the entry of Jesus into Jerusalem, and ends solemnly, even mournfully, with the remembrance of his suffering and death. Yet the joyful mood of that first Palm Sunday turned out to be a false dawn, the welcome Jesus received from the crowd proving more apparent than real, swift to dissipate once expectations were not met, whereas apparent defeat on the cross proved in reality the greatest of victories, a death that brings life to all. What did the apostles make of the palm-waving multitude? Were they carried along by the euphoria of the moment, or were they already starting to look deeper?

Meditation of Simon the zealot

I think they've got it,
finally understood who Jesus is,
for look at the welcome they're giving him:
the joy in their faces,
laughter in their eyes.
They're tearing down palm branches in their excitement,
shouting themselves hoarse:
'Hosanna!
Blessed is the one who comes in the name of the Lord!'
They surely realise at last that he's the Messiah,
the one sent by God to redeem his people.
Or do they?
For what is it they're calling him now:
the King of Israel.
That would have been music to my ears not so long ago,
for it's what I longed to see:
a ruler coming to drive out the Romans,
to restore our earthly fortunes,
to establish a new era of plenty and prosperity –
with our people at the centre –
and God's kingdom here on earth.
But having walked and talked with Jesus,
having heard his message and seen the difference he alone can bring,
I realise now that what we need is a change
not to the regime or system,
but to people's lives,
to who and what we are.

That's where he wants to reign:
in human hearts rather than on an earthly throne.
Have they understood that?
Have any of us?
They're welcoming him with open arms,
proclaiming their devotion,
but if he fails to deliver what they want
will their commitment hold,
their allegiance stay true?
Will they still salute him as king if his kingdom's not of this world?
Time, I suppose, will tell.

Silence

Prayer

Lord Jesus Christ,
teach us what it means to honour you,
to enthrone you in our lives.
Help us to understand that true commitment
involves more than declaring our loyalty,
however sincere that may be;
more than homage offered with our lips,
however eloquent it may sound.
Teach us to acclaim you from the heart
with lives consecrated to your service,
seeking your will and walking your way,
so that we may truly acknowledge you as Lord
and work meaningfully for the growth of your kingdom,
on earth as it is in heaven.

Hymn

What kind of greatness

Reading

John 12:1-11

Comment

If Lazarus had the spotlight in John chapter 11, being astonishingly raised to life, here that honour moves to his sister Mary as she impulsively anoints Jesus' feet with her hair in a spontaneous gesture of love. Yet there's a third family member involved in this story, albeit passing almost unnoticed as she unobtrusively gets on with her work behind the scenes. Martha's may have been a less eye-catching ministry than her sister's, but it was just as sincere and equally valuable.

Meditation of Martha, sister of Mary and Lazarus

What's that you say?
Still serving at tables?
But of course! –
wasn't that the least I could do?
Jesus had raised my brother, remember –
somehow brought him out of the tomb,
just weeks earlier, alive and well,
when by rights his body should have been rotting into dust.
The resurrection and the life, Jesus called himself,
and I'd seen for myself it was true,
the power of the grave defeated,
death put to flight.
No words could sum up how we felt,
for, through his awesome power,
he'd transformed our world,
turning darkness to light,
despair to hope,
sorrow to joy –
and we couldn't thank him enough.
But I had to try,
had to show him in some way how grateful I was.
So yes, I was serving again,
glad to play my part in the way I knew best.
But that's not the half of it,
for I'm resolved also to offer service of a different sort –
to walk his way and give him, as best I can,
my love,
my life,
my all.

Silence

Prayer

Loving God,
speak to us again of the new life you offer,
new beginnings in Christ.
Speak of the fresh start you daily make possible in this world –
the opportunity to put the past behind us and set out again,
the slate wiped clean,
the future open.
Speak of life beyond the grave,
eternal,
lived for ever with you,
unlike anything we can know now or ever imagine.
Remind us of your renewing, redeeming power,
and help us to respond in grateful service and joyful praise,
through Jesus Christ our Lord.

Hymn

I know that my redeemer lives

Reading

John 2:13-22

Comment

A red rag to a bull – that's what Jesus' actions in the Temple must have seemed like to his followers as he stormed through its precincts, overturning the stalls of those trading there. What was he thinking of? Surely he knew that the religious establishment was already out to get him, and that provocation such as this would only increase their hostility. So why court controversy? Why deliberately cause offence and hasten his own demise? What was so important to Jesus that he felt it necessary to make a stand, no matter what the cost?

Meditation of Nathanael

Why was he so annoyed, we wondered?
Alright, so those money-changers and the like were charging top whack,
but there was nothing new in that –
any trader would do the same.
Business is business, as they say –
we all have to make a living.
Yet, as we came eventually to realise,
it wasn't the prices Jesus objected to,
nor the idea of selling goods in God's house;
it went much deeper than that,
to the very heart of our faith.
He was challenging the whole system,
the idea that God's pardon depends on anything we might do.
No, he said,
that's not how it works:
God forgives because it's in his nature to do so,
because he simply can't help loving,
our part being simply to respond and receive.
No need for sacrifices, whether doves, pigeons or anything else.
Whatever was asked for, he would do on our behalf.
Faith, in his eyes, is as extraordinary and simple as that.
Yet there in the Temple
people were expected not only to perform the required ritual
but to pay for the privilege of doing so,
as though God's favour is something that can be bought and sold.

Those traders were stunned, I can tell you,
when he stormed in and overturned their tables like that,
but not half as stunned as we were
when we realised what he was getting at –
that the whole law is summed up by the command to love –

for we'd been brought up to believe
that following every commandment to the letter is vital,
the key to salvation.
He showed us instead a better way,
too wonderful for words.
We can't earn God's blessing,
still less deserve it.
It's his gift,
generous beyond measure,
offered freely to all,
depending not on anything we might do
but entirely on what he has done!

Silence

Prayer

Almighty God, forgive us,
for we are false and faithless in so much.
Through ignorance,
weakness
or wilful disobedience
we abandon your way,
resisting and rejecting your guidance.
We lose sight of what you really want
and of what you offer to all –
a life lived in the light of your love –
turning faith instead into outward show,
a matter of observing rules and regulations
rather than of enjoying a right relationship with you.
In your great mercy,
show us the error of our ways,
and teach us joyfully to receive
the blessings you long to lavish upon us,
through Jesus Christ our Lord.

Hymn

Come, let us sing of a wonderful love

Reading

John 12:20-33

Comment

If Holy Week points to one thing in particular, it is surely sacrifice – Christ's offering of himself on the cross. For three years his life and ministry had been leading up to this point:

the moment when he would give his all for the sake of the world. He'd understood that cost from the beginning, but as the moment of truth drew near so the immensity of what was being asked of him hit home. But he continued nonetheless, refusing to be deflected from his chosen path. Far less is asked of us, but there are times when we too must be ready to deny ourselves, to look beyond this world to the things of heaven. Have you understood how much Jesus gave for you? And are you ready to give him something back in return?

Meditation of Andrew

'Hate their life in this world'?
What does he mean by that?
It sounds so negative,
hardly a great advert for Christianity –
as though the main criterion for following Jesus
is to be so thoroughly disenchanted
that you want to end it all!
He can't mean that, surely,
and I don't think he does,
for he's spoken repeatedly of the joy he brings,
the blessings he wants to bestow,
not just in some distant future,
but here and now.
I don't hate life in this world, that's for sure,
but I do hate certain aspects:
those things that wound, damage and destroy,
scarring relationships and demeaning people as objects
to be used, exploited, ignored,
and yes, I hate my own culpability in its hurt and heartache,
for none of us are whiter than white,
untarnished by such faults.
Is this what Jesus had in mind?
That we must renounce this life if it leads us astray?
That we must be ready to make sacrifices,
even perhaps the greatest sacrifice of all,
in order to confront what we know to be wrong
and make a stand for good?
I can make sense of that,
strive towards it,
though I can't help feeling it's an ideal,
always out of reach,
for who among us would completely turn their back on self
for the sake of others,
surrendering all for their sake?
It would take incredible courage,
unparalleled love.
Could anyone, I wonder –
even Jesus –
show devotion such as that?

Silence

Prayer

God of all, give us a proper perspective on life.
Help us to celebrate the good things you have given –
to rejoice in the beauty of this world
and the blessings you daily shower upon us.
But help us also to grieve over whatever scars your creation,
denying your love and thwarting your purpose.
Teach us to stand up against such things,
irrespective of the cost to us,
recognising that true fulfilment and our ultimate destiny
lie not here on earth but in your eternal kingdom,
where, by your grace, we will savour life indeed
for evermore.

Hymn

May the mind of Christ my Saviour

Reading

Mark 10:35-45

Comment

'Make way', run the words of a popular modern hymn: 'make way, for the King of kings; make way, make way, and let his kingdom in.' It's a statement of faith and outpouring of praise, looking forward to the time when Christ will finally be all in all. But, of course, the crowds in Jerusalem did not finally make way, or acknowledge him as king, instead calling for his death, then watching him die. The glory of Jesus was to prove very different to that of this world, displayed not on a throne but on a cross. Many of his followers were to tread a similar path, giving their lives in his service, paying the ultimate price. Holy Week brings the challenge: how much does our faith mean to us? What, if anything, are we ready to surrender for the cause of Christ?

Meditation of James and John

James	We did know what we were asking,
	or at least we thought we did.
John	We wanted a share of the spoils,
	to be identified with Jesus,
	when he came into his kingdom,
	as his right-hand men,
	his loyal followers,
	sharing in the limelight,
	basking in his glory.
James	Only that's not what his glory meant.
John	We hadn't fathomed it at all,
	both of us still thinking in terms of human values,
	the approbation of this world.

James   And we couldn't have been more wrong,
for the crown he would wear was one of thorns,
his lifting up to be on a cross
and his victory to be won through death.

John   Would we have asked to share that glory
had we known what it involved?

James   Would we have taken the way of service and sacrifice,
of costly commitment?

John   I don't think so,
for though we'd followed Jesus for years,
we'd still barely grasped what he'd come to do.

James   I tell you what though, we grasped it later,
for we saw him suffer,
watched him die,
his life freely offered as a ransom for many.

John   He's enthroned now, of course,
but his kingdom is in heaven,
not on earth,
and he, the King of kings and Lord of lords, rules there as servant,
the one who surrendered all to make us his.

James   It's my turn now to take up my cross,
and for me that's not just a figure of speech;
it's meant literally,
for I too now must give everything.
I asked for glory,
and I've got it,
though not of this world.
It's been an honour, Lord, to serve.

Silence

Prayer

Lord Jesus Christ,
we try to see beyond this world,
but we struggle to do so,
for the here and now is what we know best,
the context in which we play out our daily lives.
Though we strive to do otherwise,
automatically we assess things from a human point of view,
from what popular opinion counts as success.
Help us instead to grasp the values of your kingdom,
in which defeat is victory,
the last are first,
the weak are strong
and death brings life –
to recognise that glory, as you understand it,
is not about lording it over others but about selfless service,
about giving rather than receiving,

a cross instead of a crown.
If we would share you glory,
teach us first what it truly means.

Hymn

You laid aside your majesty

Closing prayer

Lord Jesus Christ,
inspire us through your dedication,
your willingness to take the costly path of sacrifice
in order to make us whole.
Though we will always fall short,
give us something of your courage and commitment,
your selfless love for all.
Keep our eyes,
like yours,
fixed on the joy set before us,
the things you have kept for us in heaven,
so that we may walk faithfully in your footsteps,
running the race with perseverance to our journey's end.

Nick Fawcett

Affirmation of God's Presence

Today we share in the joys and sorrows of our Lord. We remember his joyful entry into Jerusalem with the waving of palms. But our palms are in the shape of a cross for we move through the events of Holy Week to the Passion and the crucifixion of our Lord.

Palm crosses are given out either as people enter the church or at this point.

Invitation to worship

We are in the presence of God the Father our Creator,
of Christ the King our Redeemer,
of the Holy Spirit who empowers us.
The Lord is here.
His Spirit is with us.

Blessing of the Palms

Ask the people to hold up their crosses as this prayer is said.

God our Father,
whose Son our Saviour entered Jerusalem as the Christ
to suffer and to die for us all,

bless these palm crosses.
May they remind us of all that Christ has done for us.
May we welcome him into our lives and homes.
Grant that we who welcome him as King
follow in his way until we come to the fullness of life eternal.
We ask this in the name of him who is our King and Saviour,
Jesus Christ our Lord.
Hosanna to the Son of David.
Blessed is he who comes in the name of the Lord.
Hosanna in the highest.

The Gospel
Year A Matthew 21:1-11
Year B Mark 11:1-11
Year C Luke 19:28-40

Hymn
All glory, laud and honour
(If possible there should be a procession of all who are holding the palm crosses during this hymn.)

Prayer
Lord Jesus,
as you were welcomed when you entered into Jerusalem
with palms and shouts of praise,
we rejoice in your coming to us this day
and pray that you may enter into our lives
and the life of our community
as our Lord and King;
to you be all glory and honour,
who lives and reigns with the Father
and the Holy Spirit,
One God, now and for ever.

Silence

Ministry of the Word

Old Testament
Isaiah 53:4-9

Hymn
Ride on, ride on in majesty

Gospel readings from the Passion of our Lord and Saviour

After each reading, sing a hymn, verse of a hymn or keep silence.

Jesus is betrayed

Year A Matthew 26:30-56
Year B Mark 14:32-50
Year C Luke 22:39-53

Hymn

It is a thing most wonderful

Jesus is denied

Year A Matthew 26:69-75
Year B Mark 14:53-54, 66-72
Year C Luke 22:54-61

Hymn

My God I love thee

Jesus is condemned

Year A Matthew 27:1, 2, 11-26
Year B Mark 15:1-15
Year C Luke 23:1-4, 13-25

Hymn

O my Saviour lifted

Jesus is crucified

Year A Matthew 27:32-50, 54
Year B Mark 15:22-39
Year C Luke 23:26, 32-47

Silence

Hymn

Glory be to Jesus

Creed

Confession

Thanksgiving

Thanks be to you, my Lord Jesus Christ,
for all the benefits you have won for me,
for all the pains and insults you have borne for me.
O most merciful Redeemer,
Friend and Brother,
may I know you more clearly,
love you more dearly,
and follow you more nearly, day by day.   *St Richard of Chichester 1197-1253*

Intercessions

Praise to you, King of eternal glory,
we rejoice with all who welcome you
into their hearts and homes.
Bless your Church,
may it be an instrument of peace,
and in praising you lead others to know you.
We remember all who preach and teach in your name,
and all who are seeking to follow you faithfully.
Jesus, Lamb of God,
hear us and help us.

Praise to you, King of eternal glory,
we rejoice with all who are aware of you
in the midst of the city,
in the midst of commerce and trade.
Bless all who witness to you through fair dealing and justice,
through striving for freedom and in the caring for others.
We remember before you Jerusalem and all its troubles,
and long for peace in our world.
Jesus, Lamb of God,
hear us and help us.

Praise to you, King of eternal glory,
we rejoice with all who reveal your presence through love.
Bless our families and friends and all our community.
We remember all who feel that they do not belong anywhere,
especially any who are scorned, persecuted and rejected.
Jesus, Lamb of God,
hear us and help us.

Praise to you, King of eternal glory,
we rejoice with all who proclaim you as their Lord and Saviour.
Bless all who give their lives in the service of others,
especially those who seek to relieve pain and suffering.
We remember those who are ill and who have sorrow,
especially any who are despairing and losing faith.
Jesus, Lamb of God,
hear us and help us.

Praise to you, King of eternal glory,
we rejoice with all who have remained faithful to you even to death.
Bless our loved ones departed,
that they may know you as their God and Saviour.
We remember all who have died this day and all who mourn:
may we all know that in you, and you alone, is life eternal.
Merciful Father,
accept these prayers for the sake of our Saviour, Jesus Christ.

Collect

Almighty Father,
look with mercy on this your family
for which our Lord Jesus Christ
was content to be betrayed
and given up into the hand of sinners
and to suffer death upon the cross;
who is alive and glorified
with you and the Holy Spirit, one God,
now and for ever.   *Common Worship Collect for Good Friday*

The Lord's Prayer

Silence

Hymn

There is a green hill

Blessing

The cross of Christ
defend you from all evil,
strengthen you in your love for him,
keep you firm in the faith,
give you comfort in your sorrows,
and rescue you from death:
and the blessing of God Almighty,
the Father, the Son and the Holy Spirit
be upon you and your loved ones,
now and ever more.   *David Adam*

SERMON IDEAS

A Royal Welcome

After they had brought the colt to Jesus and spread their cloaks over it, he sat on it. Many among the crowd spread their cloaks out on the road, while others cut down branches from the fields and spread those likewise. Those in the vanguard of the procession and those bringing up the rear cried out, 'Hosanna! Blessed is the one who comes in the Lord's name! Blessed is the coming kingdom of our forefather David! Hosanna in the highest heaven!' (Mark 11:7-10)

Coming in with a bang, going out with a whimper – in the eyes of many that could be said to describe the last days of the life of Jesus leading up to the cross. One moment he was accorded a positively rapturous welcome as he rode into Jerusalem, and, the next, people were baying for his blood, declaring that they had no other king than Caesar. It's a truly breathtaking turnaround in his fortunes, and a reader coming to the story for the first time could be forgiven for thinking that those who greeted Jesus as their king on Palm Sunday were sadly mistaken – misguided if not deluded. To a point they'd be right, for any hopes the crowds may have had that Jesus was intending to stage some kind of political coup in order to establish an earthly kingdom were to be thoroughly quashed in the week ahead. But it was precisely through all that followed – the mocking and flogging, the crown of thorns, the agony of the cross – that he took up his throne, opening the way to a kingdom beyond this world.

The betrayal, arrest and crucifixion of Christ were not some unfortunate error that was somehow rectified at Easter but were the fulfilment of God's purpose: Jesus established his rule through surrendering his all. That is the Lord we worship – the one who came to serve rather than conquer, to bring life through enduring death. That is the Saviour we seek to honour. If we see him as sovereign yet not as servant, as raised high without also being brought low, then we, too, like so many who welcomed him on that first Palm Sunday, will have altogether missed the point.

Nick Fawcett

Palm Sunday – Year A

Aim
To join in welcoming Jesus as our Saviour and King.

Readings
Liturgy of the Palms
Matthew 21:1-11
Psalm 118:1, 2, 19-29

Liturgy of the Passion
Isaiah 50:4-9a
Psalm 31:9-16
Philippians 2:5-11
Matthew 26:14–27:66 or Matthew 27:11-54

Let the dramatic readings of the Passion narratives replace the sermon today. Allow the Scriptures to speak for themselves. Use as many people as possible to share in the readings. I have provided ideas for the Liturgy of the Palms rather than comment on the Passion. I hope Holy Week will be used to do that.

Thought for the day

It is near the Passover and the last events in the life of Jesus begin in great drama. Everywhere is crowded. It is estimated that over 2 million people could make their way to Jerusalem to celebrate the Passover. Already there is a plot to take Jesus and put him to death. Jesus must be careful because it is dangerous for him to enter Jerusalem. Let us look at the courage, the claim and the call of Jesus.

We see the courage of Jesus. He was aware of the hostility and the danger. He knew he was likely to be put to death. But he did not go into hiding. He made a public declaration by his entry into Jerusalem. Jesus challenged the authorities – and does to this day. In many ways the riding into Jerusalem was an act of defiance. Yet he was not foolish. When he sent for the donkey and colt, a password is used: 'The Lord needs them.' Matthew alone talks of two creatures, a donkey and colt. He wanted to show how Jesus literally fulfilled what the prophet said:

'Tell the daughter of Zion.
Look, your king is coming to you,
humble and mounted on a donkey,
a colt, the foal of a donkey' *(see Zechariah 9:9).*

Even in this passage, the double mention of donkey and colt does not imply two creatures but one. It must be remembered that the donkey was considered a noble beast and was sometimes the choice of a king when he rode into a city in peace. To witness to this, the people welcomed him like a king by spreading their cloaks on the road and branches from the trees. Jehu, when he was proclaimed king, was welcomed in this manner by his friends (2 Kings 9:13) and so was Simon Maccabaeus when he entered Jerusalem after a notable victory (see 1 Maccabees 13:51).

So in his entry into Jerusalem we see the claim of Jesus. This is the entrance of a king and of the Messiah. Jesus is the Christ, the One who comes in the name (in the power and presence) of God. It is likely that he is proclaiming to be the cleanser of the Temple as Judas Maccabaeus had done 200 years before. Then people waved branches in the same way and this is the next act of Jesus (see 2 Maccabees 10:7 and Matthew 21:12-14). The cry of the people 'Hosanna' means 'save us now' and is a cry for help. It is a call for deliverance to their Saviour and their King.

The call of Jesus is not one for earthly kingship; it is for the hearts of people. Will we accept him as the Christ, our Lord and Saviour? Will we let him rule in our hearts? His rule is one of peace and love, and yet many still turn away. Will you acknowledge his claim and hear his call to you?

Illustration

In a time when in some areas even the wearing of a cross is forbidden, and when the media are often pro-other faiths and anti-Christian, one Anglican bishop made a telling comment. He was asked why the Christians did not threaten with bombings and reprisals as some did. The bishop replied simply, 'We are not allowed to react like that: we follow the Prince of Peace.'

David Adam

Palm Sunday – Year B

Aim

To share in the joy of the triumphal entry into Jerusalem, and in the sorrow for the events that followed.

Readings

Liturgy of the Palms
Mark 11:1-11 or John 12:12-16
Psalm 118: 1, 2, 19-29
Liturgy of the Passion
Isaiah 50:4-9a
Psalm 31:9-16
Philippians 2:5-11
Mark 14:1–15:47 or Mark 15:1-39 (40-47)

Let the dramatic readings of the Passion narratives replace the sermon today. Allow the Scriptures to speak for themselves. Use as many people as possible to share in the readings. I have provided ideas for the Liturgy of the Palms rather than comment on the Passion: I hope Holy Week will be used to do that.

Thought for the day

It would seem that Jesus had planned ahead for this visit to Jerusalem. The donkey was where Jesus said and the password 'The Lord needs it' would allow the disciples to take it. The fact that the colt had never been ridden made it especially suitable for religious purposes. The cart on which the ark of the Lord was carried had never been used for any other purpose (1 Samuel 6:7).

Jesus was received like a king as he approached Jerusalem. People spread their cloaks in front of him. This is what the friends of Jehu had done when he was proclaimed king (2 Kings 9:13). People waved palm branches as they did when Simon Maccabaeus came to Jerusalem after a great victory (1 Maccabees 13:51). The words of welcome came from today's Psalm 118, which was used to welcome pilgrims to the feast. The word 'Hosanna' means 'Save us now': people used it when addressing their king or their God.

The prophet Zechariah talked of the king to come entering Jerusalem upon an ass. Jesus is fulfilling a Messianic prophecy. The ass was seen as a noble animal but not an animal to ride to war with. Jesus was coming to conquer but with love and not by force. The ass was seen as an animal of peace and Jesus enters in peace. He comes not to destroy or condemn but to set free and to encourage. He will not force himself upon the people: love will be his restraint. In the days ahead we will see how people edge him out of their lives, out of their city and out of their world. We need to welcome him into our lives and into the world in which we move. *(The readings replace the sermon and illustration.)*

David Adam

Palm Sunday – Year C

To rejoice at the entry of Christ into Jerusalem and to share in the Passion story.

Readings

Liturgy of the Palms
Luke 19:28-40
Psalm 118:1, 2, 19-29

Liturgy of the Passion
Isaiah 50:4-9a
Psalm 31:9-16
Philippians 2:5-11
Luke 22:14–23:56 or Luke 23:1-49

Let the dramatic readings of the Passion narratives replace the sermon today. Allow the Scriptures to speak for themselves. Use as many people as possible to share in the readings.

Thought for the day

Jesus was travelling from Jericho to Jerusalem, about 20 miles and uphill nearly all the way. This was a rocky and dangerous road, more dangerous for Jesus because the leaders of the church had already outlawed him. There was a price on his head (John 11:57).

Jesus would not be swayed from coming to celebrate the Passover in Jerusalem. It was all planned. He had made arrangements for the ass and the password was 'The Lord needs it'. Bethphage and Bethany were favourite places of Jesus and here he was well known and liked. These places were on the southeast side of the Mount of Olives and were counted as part of Jerusalem for festivals. Here Mary had anointed Jesus. Here he stayed at the house of Lazarus, Mary and Martha. Here he raised Lazarus from the dead. It was also where he had stayed at the house of Simon. And on this hillside was the Garden of Gethsemane. The Palm Sunday events started from here.

Jesus could have slipped into Jerusalem unseen but he confronted the authorities by his action. Many people rode donkeys. The donkey was counted a noble beast. Kings rode horses to war or when they wanted to emphasise their might. When they came in peace they rode upon a donkey. Jesus would enter Jerusalem as the Prince of Peace, the promised Messiah. People would be given the choice to accept him or reject him, as is still the case. Already groups were polarising for or against Jesus. Jesus refused to be a puppet king who would dance at the whims of people. He refused to be a warlord and lead them to battle. He refused false dignity and pomp. Yet he would rule in the hearts of those who would allow him to.

Jesus rode on the donkey to fulfil the prophecy of Zechariah 9:9, 10 (read these verses out). He is your King. Will you accept him? It is by living his way that God's kingdom comes on earth.

David Adam

Changing Our Tune

As he rode, people carpeted the road with their cloaks. Then, as he started the descent from the Mount of Olives, the whole multitude of the disciples began loudly and joyfully to praise God for the mighty deeds they had seen, saying, 'Blessed is the king who comes in the name of the Lord! Peace in heaven, glory in the highest heaven!' Some Pharisees in the crowd said to him, 'Teacher, rebuke your disciples and tell them to stop.' He answered, 'I tell you this, if they were to keep silent, the very stones would shout out.' As he caught sight of the city, he wept over it, saying, 'If only you recognised this day the things that make for peace! Instead, though, they are hidden from your eyes!'
(Luke 19:36-42)

It was only a children's story but it made the point well. 'Who will help me sow my seed?' asks the chicken. 'Not I,' comes the answer. 'Who will help me reap the harvest?' 'Not I,' comes the answer again. 'Who will help me grind the flour . . . knead the dough . . . bake the loaf? 'Not I . . . not I . . . not I.' Then, finally, the all-important question: 'Who will help me eat the bread?' and, immediately, a change of tone: 'Me! Me! Me!' It is an illustration, of course, of the fickleness of human nature, our friendship and loyalty so often depending on what's in it for us.

So it was on that first Palm Sunday as Jesus entered Jerusalem to the acclaim of the crowds; only this time the story is in reverse. 'Who will welcome me as king?' his actions seemed to be saying, and the answer was 'Me!' Who wants to share in the kingdom of God?' and again the answer is 'Me!' Yet, just a few days later when the crunch question comes – 'Who will follow the way of the cross?' – the response from many is so very different: 'Not I!' – or, to put it more accurately, 'We have no king but Caesar. Crucify! Crucify! Crucify!' Palm Sunday is a day that challenges us concerning our loyalty, asking how ready we are to follow when faith is demanding and the going gets tough. Thank God, it is also about the one who, however often we may change our tune, stays faithful to us to the point of death.

Nick Fawcett

ALL–AGE SERVICES

Palm Sunday

Leader

Your attitude to one another should arise out of your life in Christ Jesus, who, though he was in his very nature divine, did not grasp at equality with God but made himself nothing, taking the form of a servant.

Silence

Leader

Lord Jesus, Son of David and Son of God, you humbled yourself by taking our humanity and obediently accepting death on a cross. Now you are exalted to the highest place and have the name which is above all other names, to which every knee must bow. As we offer ourselves to you in worship, may we also follow your example of humility and obedience so that in dying to sin, we may rise with you to eternal life.

Song

You are the king of glory

Leader	We do not preach the Gospel with words of human wisdom, lest the cross of Christ be emptied of its power. The message of the cross is folly to those who are perishing,
All	but to us who are being saved it is the power of God.
Leader	God has made foolish the cleverness of the wise man, the scholar and the philosopher,
All	for the world cannot know God through wisdom.
Leader	Through the folly of what is preached
All	God is pleased to save those who believe.
Leader	The Jews demand signs, while the Greeks seek after wisdom,
All	but we preach Christ crucified.
Leader	The cross is a stumbling-block to the Jews and folly to the Gentiles,

All   to those who are called, whether Jew or Gentile, it is the power and wisdom of God.

Leader   The foolishness of God is infinitely wiser than human wisdom,

All   his weakness is infinitely greater than human strength.

Reading

As they approached Jerusalem and came to Bethphage on the Mount of Olives, Jesus sent two disciples, saying to them, 'Go to the village ahead of you, and at once you will find a donkey tied there, with her colt by her. Untie them, and bring them to me. If anyone says anything to you, tell him that the Lord needs them, and he will send them right away.' This took place to fulfil what was spoken through the prophet: 'Say to the daughter of Zion, "See your King comes to you, gentle and riding on a donkey, on a colt, the foal of a donkey."'

The disciples went and did as Jesus had instructed them. They brought the donkey and the colt, placed their cloaks on them, and Jesus sat on them. A very large crowd spread their cloaks on the road, while others cut branches from the trees and spread them on the road. The crowds that went ahead of him, and those that followed shouted, 'Hosanna to the Son of David! Blessed is he who comes in the name of the Lord! Hosanna in the highest!' When Jesus entered, the whole city was stirred and asked, 'Who is this?' The crowds answered, 'This is Jesus, the prophet from Nazareth in Galilee.'

Jesus entered the temple area and drove out all who were buying and selling there. He overturned the tables of the money changers and the benches of those selling doves. 'It is written,' he said to them, '"My house will be called a house of prayer", but you are making it a den of robbers.'

Matthew 21:1-13

Meditation

Although Jesus knew he was entering Jerusalem to face certain death, nothing could have seemed less likely than his crucifixion only a few days later. Many people would have identified his entry into the city on a donkey with Zechariah's prophecy, and so they acclaimed him as their king, the one who would restore the Davidic monarchy and challenge the authority of the Romans. The cheering and celebration of the crowds are in marked contrast to the jeering and humiliation which greeted him so soon afterwards. It would have been easy for Jesus to bask in the popular acclaim, but he knew how quickly this could change, and didn't allow it to deflect him from his mission. Immediately he went to the Temple, and banished the traders in the courtyard, issuing a direct challenge to the corruption and rottenness which were debasing the whole system of religion. Popularity can seem very attractive in the short term, but it doesn't last long and usually gets in the way of achieving anything worthwhile. Jesus kept his mission in full view, never moving away from it or allowing himself to be distracted. How important is popularity to you, and what lengths will you go to in order to achieve it? On what issues would you risk unpopularity with your family, friends or colleagues? Where can you challenge the prevailing corruption and evil, and how might you go about it? Ask God for courage to resist the attractions of short-term acclaim and to oppose everything which is contrary to his kingdom.

Leader   We stand in the presence of Jesus our Saviour, who for our sake willingly followed the path of suffering and pain to the cross, and we ask for strength to share that way with him.

Group A   For the times when we are tempted to take the broad path of popularity and acclaim which leads to destruction, Lord give us your will.

Group B   For the times when we are tempted to turn aside from the narrow road of service and obedience, Lord give us your resolve.

Group A   For the times when we find ourselves in conflict with evil and corruption, Lord give us your anger.

Group B   For the times when we are called to uphold your standards of righteousness and justice, Lord give us your zeal.

Group A   For the times when we are confronted with fear and despair, Lord give us your hope.

Group B   For the times when we see misery and pain all around us, Lord give us your compassion.

Group A   For the times when the road ahead of us seems rough and impassable, Lord give us your courage.

Group B   For the times when we hear you calling us onwards in our pilgrimage, Lord give us your vision.

Leader   Help us so to walk with you in the way of the cross, that in this world we may find joy and peace in faithful service, and in the world to come eternal life, for your holy name's sake.

Song

I, the Lord of sea and sky (Here I am, Lord)

Leader   In quietness and trust we find our strength. As we wait on the Lord we commit to him the way ahead of us, praying for guidance to know where we should be going, and confidence that he will lead us in the right paths.

    Silence

Leader   We pray for all Christian leaders both within the church and in other fields, that they will fulfil their duty to defend the truth and lead us in the pilgrim way. Lord, by your mercy,

All   keep them faithful.

Leader   We pray for all governments and authorities, that under your guidance they will fulfil their responsibilities fairly and rule us justly. Lord, by your mercy,

All   keep them righteous.

Leader   We pray for all aid-workers and carers, that they will tend those to whom they minister with compassion and devotion. Lord, by your mercy,

All	keep them kind-hearted.
Leader	We pray for all teachers and those who work with young people, that they will nurture them in your ways and guide them with your love. Lord, by your mercy,
All	keep them strong.
Leader	We pray for all whose pilgrimage is hard and unrewarding, that they will not lose faith in you but trust you to see them through. Lord, by your mercy,
All	keep them hopeful.
Leader	Keep us steadfast in faith and firm in hope as we run the race before us with our eyes fixed on Jesus, who taught us to pray:
All	Our Father . . .
Leader	For strength for today and bright hope for tomorrow, let us bless the Lord.
All	Thanks be to God.

Stuart Thomas

Jesus Finds a Donkey

Reading
John12:12-16: Jesus enters Jerusalem

Equipment:
flip chart and marker pen
music and lyrics
palm cross
paper and pens

Announce to the group that you are going to a party during the week and you are a bit unsure what to wear. Can the group make any suggestions? Ask the group what they would wear if they were going to a really smart party. Make a list of the types of outfits and accessories. What kind of vehicle would each member of the group like to arrive in at the party? Would they invite the press and photographers to record the event of the year? Which magazines or newspapers would they like to see themselves in?

(Allow 10 minutes for this activity)

A lot of people make up their minds about who and what we are from the way we look. But things are not always what they seem.

Take a look at 'The happy song' by Martin Smith or 'O sacred King' by Matt Redman. You can use a different piece of music with a similar theme. Try and have a copy of the lyrics available.

(Allow approximately 5 minutes)

Discuss the piece of music with the group. What did the lyrics have to say about Jesus and/or God?

Read John 12:12-16

The Passover Feast was an important part of Jewish culture. At least once in their life each male Jew would try and attend the Feast in Jerusalem. There would have been several hundred thousand people gathered in Jerusalem The atmosphere would have been one of great expectancy and excitement.

Jesus rode into Jerusalem to be met by a huge crowd of people all shouting and waving palm branches. It must have been an amazing sight!

Immediately before arriving in Jerusalem, Jesus had performed yet another miracle by raising Lazarus from the dead. The chief priests were already plotting how to get rid of Jesus. They were also trying to figure out how to kill Lazarus!

Two main features of the entry into Jerusalem stand out:

Firstly, Jesus rode into Jerusalem as a wanted man. Not wanted as a liberator or saviour by the priests but wanted by them as a criminal. Even the disciples were taken up with the idea that Jesus had at last come to claim his place as King of the Jews. The people greeted Jesus with a cry of 'Hosanna' or 'hooray', which roughly translates as 'please save us'. This was a shout of praise to God but it would have made the chief priests even angrier than before, as it was also a shout acknowledging that Jesus was in some way connected with God; worse, that he was a 'saviour'.

Secondly, Jesus rode into Jerusalem on a donkey. This act fulfils the prophecy from the Old Testament book Zechariah (9:9-10). Zechariah writes that everyone in Jerusalem should celebrate and shout 'your King has won a victory and he is coming to you . . . riding on a donkey' (verse 9). We may not think that riding a donkey gives the impression of a king! In Old Testament times, if a king were going to war, he would ride a horse. But if the king rode a donkey it meant he came in peace. Jesus made a significant statement. He rode into Jerusalem as a king of peace; not to liberate the world by force but by peace.

Even though Jesus knew that he was considered a threat to the chief priests (see verse 19) and that he would die a criminal's death, he rode a donkey to make the most profound statement.

God didn't send his Son into the world to condemn its people but to save them (see John 3:17). The Prince of Peace rode a donkey knowing that he would die a violent death at the hands of soldiers for a crime he didn't commit.

Ask the group to consider the entry of Jesus into Jerusalem. Picture the scene with the excited crowds all waving palm branches and shouting.

- What do they think the disciples and followers of Jesus thought?
- Did they think a major change was about to take place?
- Did they think that Jesus was going to cause a revolt against the Romans?

(Allow 5 minutes for this task)

Place a palm cross in the centre of the room. Give each member of the group a piece of paper and a pen. Ask them to write on the piece of paper an issue or situation that is causing trouble or giving them concern. The issue or situation may or may not involve the group member directly. When each member has written an issue or situation which they are concerned about, ask them to fold the paper and place it by the palm cross.

When everyone has placed their piece of paper by the cross, read the following prayer:

Lord, trouble seems to have a habit of getting under my skin.
It itches and aggravates,
and the more I scratch it, the more it itches.
How does trouble find me?
I certainly don't go looking for it,
it seems to find me wherever I am.
It's not always my fault,
well, sometimes maybe, but not every time!
Please help me to see things your way,
because my way sometimes misses the point
or makes the trouble worse!
I need to see things your way,
because I have the knack
of sometimes missing the obvious
or making up my mind
without knowing all the facts.
You seemed to know what you were doing
on the way into Jerusalem.
Even though others thought it odd
that a king should ride a donkey.
But you had other thoughts in mind,
beyond what could be imagined
by your closest friends.
Prince of Peace, take my troubles
and bring your peace instead.

Pete Townsend

The Servant King

Focus of service:

Jesus entering Jerusalem on a donkey. The Servant King facing rejection and death to free us from everlasting death.

Mood:

Bitter/sweet. Rejoicing and yet heavy with the shadow of the cross. Fresh awareness of our own human fickleness.

Possibilities for worship:

- Purple hangings. Plain cross draped with cloth, the base in among stones.
- Symbols of Jesus' death brought to the cross during the offertory – nails, hammer, dice, rope, coins thrown down from a bag, thorns, a tall reed.
- Palm branches, any branches, streamers and flags for the procession, preferably outside. Songs that everyone can sing at a pitch they can reach, during the procession. Even a donkey, perhaps?

- Dramatised choral reading of the long Gospel; involve the whole gathered people. Or try a recorded version.
- Where there are Stations of the Cross, walk in procession around these as the story is narrated. Or make a 'Way of the Cross' outside and all around the church with the Gospel read as everyone walks it together.
- At some point in the worship, encourage everyone who can to kneel, even if this isn't usual practice.
- For the time of Penitence, place on the floor a cross of lit candles in sand.
- Projected images of the Crucifixion through art.

Prayer areas:

- Stones and thorns, with soundbites from the Gospel narrative printed among them.
- Focus on the crosses around the building,
- Provide tiny crosses to hold and place in the prayer areas. Different images of Christ projected or displayed.
- Suggestions for prayer: Pray for the world to want God's kingdom; pray for God's peace which the world cannot give; pray for those imprisoned who are innocent; pray for better discernment to recognise propaganda for what it is and hold firm to the truth.

Susan Sayers

The Joy of Palm Sunday

Aim

To capture the joy of the entry into Jerusalem.

Readings

Liturgy of the Palms
Matthew 21:1-11
Psalm 118:1, 2, 19-29

Liturgy of the Passion
Isaiah 50:4-9a
Psalm 31:9-16
Philippians 2:5-11
Matthew 26:14–27:66 or Matthew 27:11-54

Teaching

If the children have taken part in a Palm Sunday procession, talk about it; if not, have a procession. Let the children wave streamers or palm branches and sing the chorus from 'Give me oil in my lamp'.

Show a picture of a donkey. Ask how many of them have seen a donkey or even ridden one. Has anyone noticed that there is a dark line down a donkey's back and across its shoulders? (Draw the shape for them to see.) What shape does it make? It is a cross. Where have you seen a cross? Is there one in church? Why do we have a cross? We have it because Jesus died on a cross. But let me tell you what happened a few days before that, when the people wanted Jesus to be their king.

Jesus wanted to go into Jerusalem – and he wanted people to know he was their king. Sometimes kings used to ride a donkey. Jesus asked someone to lend him a donkey. He said he would send his disciples to get it. He told the man he would give them secret words to say. They would say, 'The Lord needs it.' (Let us say, 'The Lord needs it.')

Once they had the donkey, the disciples put a cloak on its back for Jesus to sit on. As they came near to Jerusalem there were lots of people and they were very excited. They believed that Jesus was sent by God, and they shouted 'Hosanna' (let us shout it), which means 'Save us' (now let us shout that).

The people started to make a carpet for the donkey to walk on. They took off their cloaks and spread them on the ground. They cut branches off the palm trees and laid them on the ground. Some waved palm branches in the air (get the children to wave streamers or palm branches – or their palm crosses). It was all very exciting. They wanted Jesus to be their king.

Let us invite Jesus to be our King. Jesus will look after us and save us because he is our Saviour.

Activity

Today the main activity is the Palm procession. Re-enact this at the end of the lesson. Get the girls to shout, 'Hosanna', and the boys to shout, 'Save us'. Let them pretend to lay cloaks on the ground. Give them something to wave. Let them all shout, 'Welcome to Jesus our King.'

Prayer

Jesus, you are our King and Saviour.
We welcome you and we shout,
'Hosanna – save us.'
We know you love us
and we give our love to you
today and always.

Song

Give me oil in my lamp
(chorus only)

Colour the picture of Jesus riding into Jerusalem

For parents and children to pray together:
'Jesus, as the people of Jerusalem welcomed you, may we welcome you into our homes and our lives as our King.' Amen

David Adam

Palm Sunday – Red Carpet*

Resources

- A volunteer dressed in white, with bare feet, carrying a large wooden cross
- Leaders should be wearing something red so that they can start off the 'red carpet'.

Leader

When Jesus entered Jerusalem, he was treated like a celebrity. The people cheered and laid down palm leaves to cover his path: this was their equivalent of laying down the red carpet for him. If Jesus came here today, would we give him the red-carpet treatment? What would we lay down for him to walk on? Today we will reflect on this as we pray an active prayer. Here we have our representative of Jesus with his cross: in a moment of quiet, consider what you will lay down for him to walk on. Will it be your coat or scarf? Will it be a bag or a hat? If it is red, then so much the better for making a red carpet, but it could be anything of any colour which you would willingly lay down.

Prayer action

The people lay down their things in the aisle and 'Jesus' walks barefoot across them to take his cross up to the altar.

Closing words

Living Lord,
what will we give you?
Will we lay out the red carpet for you?
What will we lay down before you
as you walk into our lives?

(Pause.)

Come, Lord Jesus.

Claire Benton-Evans

If I Were a King!

Aim

To show what good leaders should be like. Christians believe that Jesus is king, but he is very different from other kings.

Song

Come on, let's celebrate
or Sing hosanna, shout hooray

---

* This prayer is the work of many hands. The original inspiration came from a symbolic action suggested by the Iona Community (*Stages on the Way*, Wild Goose Publications, 1998, p.73). It was changed and developed by the all-age worship team at St John's, Ivybridge and I have further adapted the form we used there to create this version.

Puppet sketch

(Micky is asleep in his bag, so everyone calls for him. Micky wakes up not knowing where he is.)

Micky   Where am I?

John   You're at *(name of venue)*.

Micky   I can't be!

John   Why?

Micky   Because I'm a king, that's why.

John   A king? Hardly, you're our mate, Micky.

Micky   You're joking. Don't say I was only dreaming!

John   You were only dreaming.

Micky   Oi! I said don't say I was only dreaming. Oh, what a shame. It was a wonderful dream. I – yes, I – was a great, powerful king, dressed in fine clothes and wearing a crown.

John   You?

Micky   I had lots of servants that I could boss around.

John   I bet you enjoyed that!

Micky   Servants who did my housework for me. Servants to fan me and keep me cool. Servant girls dropping grapes into my mouth. What a life!

John   Dream on!

Micky   I intend to! I had a Rolls-Royce to go shopping in, a golden shopping trolley, a bit like a chariot, and adoring crowds waving and bowing to me! No waiting in queues for me, *and* I had millions of bananas. I love being king!

John   Micky, kings do more than just boss everyone around all day.

Micky   What?

John   There's more to being a king than just wearing fine clothes, riding around in chariots and waving to your adoring crowds! It's about wanting the best for your people, making sure they have good homes and plenty to eat.

Micky   I'm still tired! I'm going to go back to sleep in my bag and enjoy being a king again. Bye!

Bible story

Matthew 21:1-11

There's a story about a king in the Bible.

The crowds were waving and cheering, but he didn't have fine clothes, or servants to boss around. He had great power and he used his power for the good of his people. He fed them and healed them.

He wasn't rich – in fact he was poor. He didn't have a horse – he had a donkey! No fine clothes and no crown!

But the people didn't care! They knew he was a true king; a loving, kind king, a servant king. They cheered, they sang, they waved palm branches. A wonderful king. The King of kings. King Jesus.

Round-up

Being a rich and powerful king doesn't mean he's great. He is only great if he treats his people well. Being rich, famous or powerful doesn't make someone great. A great person is someone who is kind and cares for others.

Prayer

Lord, thank you
that Jesus is a wonderful king;
powerful but kind,
not rich but generous;
a servant king.
King of kings.

John Hardwick

Discovering the Kingdom

Reading

Luke 19:29-40

Aim

To show that Jesus is a different type of king, ruling over a different kind of kingdom.

Preparation

From silver or gold card, make thirteen simple crowns, and on the front of each one stick a large label with the name of one of the following:

Tutankhamen
Nebuchadnezzar
Julius Caesar
James VI

Henry V
Louis XIV
Philip II
Genghis Khan
Frederick the Great
Montezuma
Nicholas
Boadicea
Jesus

Now, on coloured pieces of card or paper, cut out thirteen large contoured shapes, representing countries. On each of these write the name of one of the following countries:

Egypt
Babylon
Rome
Scotland
England
France
Spain
Mongolia
Prussia
Aztecs (Mexico)
Russia
Iceni

Using sticky tack, stick these 'countries' around the front of the church, on walls, the lectern and choir stalls.

Talk

Ask the congregation if they have ever wondered what it must be like to be a king? Tell them that, for a few lucky volunteers, today is their opportunity to find out, because for five minutes you are going to give them the chance to rule a country. Ask for thirteen volunteers, give each one a crown to wear, and then ask each 'king' to discover their kingdom and hold it up for all to see.

The correct countries are:

Tutankhamen	Egypt
Nebuchadnezzar	Babylon
Julius Caesar	Rome
James VI	Scotland
Henry V	England
Louis XIV	France
Philip II	Spain
Genghis Khan	Mongolia
Frederick the Great	Prussia
Montezuma	Aztecs (Mexico)
Nicholas	Russia
Boadicea	Iceni
Jesus	?

All of your 'kings' should quickly be able to find their kingdoms except for the one whose crown bears the name 'Jesus'. Arrange the 'kings' in a line with 'Jesus' on one end; then, starting at the other end, announce the name on each volunteer's crown and country, and ask whether these have been paired correctly (exchange if necessary). Continue along the line until you reach the volunteer wearing the crown with the name 'Jesus'. Why has no country been found to match?

When Jesus entered Jerusalem on what today we call Palm Sunday, it was to be welcomed as king by the crowds who had gathered there to greet him.

'Blessed is the king who comes in the name of the Lord!', they shouted. (Luke 19:38)

So what kind of king was Jesus; and where was, or is, his kingdom? The obvious answer, of course, is that he was king of the Jews, or the king of Israel. And that is exactly what many people at the time hoped he had come to be, what others feared he intended to be, and what the Roman authorities suspected he claimed to be.

Then Pilate asked him, 'Are you the king of the Jews?' (Luke 23:3)

But the answer Jesus gave was very different.

'My kingdom is not from this world. If my kingdom were from this world, my followers would be fighting to keep me from being handed over to the Jews. But as it is, my kingdom is not from here.' (John 18:36)

Those are words we need to remind ourselves of today. When we talk about Jesus being our king, when we sing hymns with words like 'You are the King of Glory', 'Majesty', or 'Rejoice, the Lord is King', we are not saying he is a king like any of these others we have looked at today. For Jesus was not a king in the sense of ruling a single country many years ago. Rather he came as the servant of all, the one who laid down his life for his people, the one who put others before himself, yet the one raised up by God as ruler over all, the King of kings and Lord of lords, now and for all eternity. Here we glimpse the kind of kingdom God has in store for us and all his people and the sort of king Jesus will be. In the words of the hymn, 'This is our God, the Servant King'.

Finish with the hymn *From heaven you came* (The Servant King).

Nick Fawcett

Not What Was Expected!

Reading
Matthew 21:1-11 : Jesus enters Jerusalem

Equipment:
pen and paper for each group member
music and lyrics

Activity 1
Give everyone a pen and piece of paper. Tell them that they have just been given £1,000 to spend. Ask them to write what would be on their spending spree list.

After they've done this, apologise and say that the money was not for them but to be spent on people who they consider to be in need of financial help (they are not to consider themselves in this!).

Once they've completed the second task, ask them how they felt when they were told that the money wasn't actually for them.

(Allow 10 minutes for this activity)

Activity 2

Our expectations are sometimes altered in ways that we'd rather not experience.
Take a look at 'Love songs from heaven' or 'O sacred King'.

(Allow 5 minutes for this)

Activity 3

Sometimes what we expect and the reality are not quite the same. Ask the group what their expectations are, based upon the lyrics of the chosen song.

Read Matthew 21:1-11.
In Jerusalem expectations were running high. For the priests and religious leaders it was a time of celebrating the Passover and, possibly, they might at last get their hands on the one person who was a real pain to them: Jesus.

For the ordinary people the Passover was also a time of celebration but their expectations were even higher than normal. They had seen and heard all of the things that Jesus had done recently and they'd heard of his being referred to as the 'Son of David' (see Matthew 20:31). The term 'Son of David' was a title which the Jewish people understood to mean the messianic king, a new ruler who would liberate his people from foreign rule. Even the Mount of Olives was significant as the prophet Zechariah had spoken of the Messiah making a stand there against all of God's enemies (see Zechariah 14:4).

All the evidence pointed to something exceptional, something of the utmost importance. The crowds gathered and welcomed Jesus as he entered Jerusalem on a donkey (a king would ride a donkey as someone who came in peace). Yet within a week this Messiah, the 'Son of David' was dead.

The priests and religious leaders were content. Order had been restored and this nuisance, Jesus, had been dealt with. The Jewish people's hopes had been dashed against the wood of the cross. Expectations seemed to count for nothing where death was concerned.

Just as Jesus had shown time and again, death had no power over him. His mission was to act as the ultimate sacrifice, once and for all, so that the relationship could be finally restored between God and the people. It was obvious that the majority of people hadn't really understood what Jesus had been saying. The freedom he offered and the authority that he'd shown were not to deal simply with Roman rule but to end the rule of evil.

Sometimes our expectations are limited to what we can see immediately in front of us. Perhaps we should try to see things from God's perspective?

Ask the group to discuss what their expectations are for the future. For example: qualifications, jobs, marriage, health and possessions. Try and encourage the group to consider their expectations from God's point of view. Look at what the Bible might have to say about each of their ideas.

(Allow 5 minutes for this task)

Activity 4

Ask the group to spend a few moments reflecting on their ideas for the future while you read the following:

You have looked deep into my heart, Lord,
and you know all about me.
You know when I am resting or when I am working,
and from heaven you discover my thoughts.
You notice everything I do and everywhere I go . . .
look deep into my heart, God, and find out everything I am thinking.
Don't let me follow evil ways,
but lead me in the way that time has proved true.   *Psalm 139:1-3, 23-24*

Pete Townsend

Palm Sunday

For most people Palm Sunday marks the start of the Easter season, at least in practical terms, as schools break up, holiday plans are made and extra food purchased. In liturgical terms, while Easter Day itself is still seven days away, the activities and events of Holy Week have to lead up to the great climax of Easter morning and also set it in the wider context of God's saving purposes for humankind. Occasional churchgoers may well understand it more as a dramatic twist in the tail, a totally unexpected 'happy ending', than as the culmination of all that God had been accomplishing in and through his Son (indeed, throughout the history of his dealings with his people).

A procession marking Jesus' triumphal entry into Jerusalem has always been part of the Palm Sunday tradition, and if circumstances permit this can be an excellent opportunity for the Christian community to witness more widely to its faith. Many churches, at least in urban areas, can gain access to a suitable local venue, from which the procession can make its way to the main worship centre, although the distance should not be excessive, and more elderly or less mobile members of the congregation allowed to go straight to the destination venue (or offered a lift). A nearby school is sometimes a possible start point, and using this may help build links with the wider community, though a hall or other public place will work as well. Better still, why not co-operate with a local church of another Christian tradition and move from one building to the other? Failing all else the procession can simply circumnavigate the building, though this is unlikely to have as wide an impact.

If you are planning a procession, remember to arrange a wet-weather alternative, as March and April aren't always the most clement months, and if a busy road is to be crossed the police need to be informed – they are usually pleased to help if they can, and will generally offer a crossing patrol. Musical facilities may well be limited at the starting venue, and if there's to be singing en route, an instrumental group should be placed somewhere in the middle of the procession – though beyond a certain length it will be near impossible to keep everyone singing together. Palm branches to wave are very effective, and uniformed organisations often enjoy walking with their flags and banners, though give them plenty of notice as they will need to get written permission for young people to take part.

Palm Sunday is marked by the great contrast between the excited crowds who welcomed Jesus as he entered Jerusalem, and the baying mob who howled just a few days later for him to be crucified. Common Worship retains the tradition of two Gospel readings, one for each venue (or before and after the procession). *Lent, Holy Week* and *Easter* contains dramatised versions of each Evangelist's Passion narrative and in many churches this replaces the sermon: There are considerations of audibility; and where the dramatised reading isn't possible (or even as an addition to it) an alternative address outline is included. Whatever kind of service is held on Palm Sunday, it will be the springboard for the rest of Holy Week and enable those who worship to enter into that journey through the pain and suffering which bursts into glorious new life on Easter morning.

Hymns

Traditional

- All glory, laud and honour
- A man there lived in Galilee
- My song is love unknown
- O dearest Lord, thy sacred head
- Ride on, ride on in majesty
- When I survey

Contemporary

- From heaven you came
- Hosanna, hosanna
- I will enter his gates
- Make way, make way
- Meekness and majesty
- You are the king of glory

Chant

- Stay with me

Children's song

- We have a king

Readings

Year A, B and C: Isaiah 50:4-9a; Philippians 2:5-11
Year A: Matthew 21:1-11; Matthew 26:14-27, 66
Year B: Mark 11:1-11 or John 12:12-16; Mark 14:1–15:47
Year C: Luke 19:28-40; Luke 22:14–23:56

Confession

We kneel in penitence before the King of kings
to seek his forgiveness, saying:
Merciful Lord,
forgive us and cleanse us.

Sometimes we sing your praise,
but often our lips will not own you.
Merciful Lord,
forgive us and cleanse us.

Sometimes we bow to you as Lord,
but often our hands will not do your will.
Merciful Lord,
forgive us and cleanse us.

Sometimes we welcome you gladly,
but often our hearts will not find a place for you.
Merciful Lord,
forgive us and cleanse us.

Sometimes we hail you as King,
but often our lives show little evidence
of your reign.
Merciful Lord,
forgive us and cleanse us,
bring us back to the Cross
and fill us anew with your great love,
for the sake of your holy name.

Absolution

God, our heavenly Father,
have mercy on *you*,
grant *you* pardon from all *your* sins,
peace in *your* hearts
and assurance of his eternal love,
through Jesus Christ our Lord.

Prayer

We stand in the presence of Jesus our King
and ask his blessing on the world, saying,
King Jesus, we welcome you,
come and reign among us.

We ask you to bless this world
which you created,
and invade with your peace
the places where hatred and violence rule,

where lives are scarred with fear and misery . . .
King Jesus, we welcome you,
come and reign among us.

We ask you to bless this community,
and bring the joy of your salvation
to those whose lives are filled
with darkness and despair,
who feel rejected or exploited . . .
King Jesus, we welcome you,
come and reign among us.

We ask you to bless your worldwide Church,
and fill with your power
all who worship and serve you,
who show your compassion
and bring peace and relief in your name . . .
King Jesus, we welcome you,
come and reign among us.

We ask you to bless our homes and loved ones,
and reassure us of your presence
as we share our lives . . .
King Jesus, we welcome you,
come and reign among us.

We ask you to bless anyone who is suffering
or in distress, . . .
to heal them in body, mind and spirit,
and strengthen their confidence in you, . . .
King Jesus, we welcome you,
come and reign among us,
fill our lives with your joy
and our hearts with your love
as we cry 'Hosanna in the highest!'
to our Saviour Jesus Christ.

All-age address

The primary reason why Jesus was rejected and executed by the authorities is that he did not conform to their expectations about the promised Messiah. Instead of associating with the status quo and upholding tradition he mixed with the poor and needy, and challenged the whole basis of established religion. If you're looking for an alternative to the dramatised Passion Gospel the following idea is very effective at conveying the ways in which Jesus confounded expectations and stood against religious hypocrisy and self-righteousness. In effect, it's a tableau and will need thorough preparation and probably rehearsal for those participating. The main figure is a king who changes through the address, with the support of a number of other characters.

There's no dialogue, so you'll need to keep the narrative moving so that the participants know when to do their bit.

1) At the outset the king should be regally attired – in purple cloak, crown, and anything else you can find which looks royal! He needs a retinue of servants, a cheering 'crowd' as he enters, and suitable props to suggest that a palace might be his usual residence. Explain that this is a proper king, powerful and revered, feared by his subjects and enemies alike, who dresses the part and lives in the appropriate style. If you can find a couple of trumpeters to provide a fanfare (or persuade the organist!) it will add to the effect. This is what we all think royalty should be like. But although Jesus was a king, he was a very unexpected one. He didn't live in a palace (pause for a moment while the trappings of palatial grandeur are removed); he didn't wear expensive clothes or accessories (remove the cloak, crown and any other royal touches); he didn't have servants to run round after him (at this point they leave); he didn't have much to do with the aristocracy (they too leave); in fact, he lived like the ordinary folk and at first glance you wouldn't know there was anything different about him. He was a completely unexpected king.

2) The trouble was that people were looking for a king who'd look impressive, who'd lead their army and fight for independence – the government could do without a troublemaker who'd been born into an ordinary family, had no money, got his support from the lower classes, and fought against corruption and evil. So they wouldn't have anything to do with him and tried to find ways to get rid of him (bring the retinue back, looking as though they're discussing and plotting how to cause his downfall). Ordinary people still flocked to hear his teaching (get them to crowd round him), much to the disgust of the hierarchy (who can look suitably disgusted at this point). Because he was an unexpected king, he became a rejected king.

3) He wasn't just rejected. Because he was a threat some people wanted him dead, and eventually they found a way to get him arrested, by bribing one of his friends (this can be mimed). He was tried (stand the king before a mock judge), and sentenced to death, before anyone realised what was happening (again this is easily staged). So he died like a criminal, and everyone thought that was the end. But it wasn't. When this king died he fought the battle himself, against evil and death, on behalf of everyone; and because he loved his people enough to do this, his Father raised him to life three days later. Now he still reigns in the hearts of those who accept him as king, and is Lord of the whole universe – greater than any monarch who lives in a palace, surrounded by wealth. He's the exalted king, before whom all other kings must bow.

Stuart Thomas

From Praise to Passion

Theme

Christ's entry into Jerusalem and the story of his Passion

Scripture

Luke 19:28-40; Luke 23:1-49

Resources

NB Advance preparation needed!

- Worship flags (*see note 1*) for:
  - Jesus
  - two Pharisees
  - Pilate
  - Herod

  Equipment for making the crowd's flags (*see note 2*)
  - thin white fabric, cut into long triangles with a sleeve sewn at one end
  - green and blue fabric pens, paints or crayons
  - balsa wood sticks (sold by craft suppliers as candy floss sticks)
  - pattern templates (*see note 3*)

Leaders

Minimum: 3
- Leader
- Jesus
- Dancer

Optimum: 9+
- Leader *(Introduction and Conclusion)*
- Storytellers 1 and 2
- Jesus, in traditional dress
- Music Leader
- Explorer
- Activity Leader(s), also responsible for the Welcome activity
- Prayer Leader
- Dancer

Suggestions for additional music

- Give me joy in my heart
- Hosanna, hosanna
- I cannot tell

Welcome

As people arrive, invite them to make a flag for use during the service. Find volunteers to carry the special flags for the Storytelling and explain to them briefly what they will be doing (they don't need to remember it all, as the Storyteller will cue them in).

Today is the beginning of Holy Week: it is Palm Sunday, when we celebrate Jesus' triumphant entry into Jerusalem. Let's tell the story together. I need you to stand and hold your flags ready: you are the crowds in the streets of the city. Listen to the story and you'll hear what to do.

Storytelling 1

Jesus arrived in Jerusalem like a king.

Jesus – starting at the back of church – waves his white flag with the gold crown and starts to walk down the aisle.

Although he rode on a humble donkey instead of a white steed, he was surrounded by adoring crowds who cheered him on his way.

Encourage everyone to cheer.

People waved palm leaves in celebration. They blessed Jesus, declared peace in heaven and shouted words of praise: 'Hosanna!'

Encourage everyone to shout 'Hosanna!' and wave their white flags with palms and doves. Keep cheering and waving as Jesus walks to the front of church. As he arrives at the front, two Pharisees enter, waving a black flag with a red cross and a red flag with a black crown of thorns. They block Jesus' path.

Not everyone cheered. Some wanted to silence Jesus and his crowds of followers. The Pharisees said, 'Order your fans to be quiet!' But Jesus said, 'Listen, if they stopped yelling, the rocks all around us would cheer instead!'

The Pharisees sweep down the aisle with their red and black flags. The crowd continues to wave their white flags.

The crowd was unstoppable! People filled the streets of Jerusalem, singing God's praises.

Activity

That is exactly what we are going to do now. We will take our flags, go out into the streets and sing.

Jesus leads the Palm Sunday procession out of the church and into the street, taking a circular route that leads back to the church. Remind everyone to take their hymn books and flags so that they can sing and wave as they go.

Music

We have a King who rides a donkey
Clap your hands, all you people

Storytelling 2

People are now back in their places in the church.

After the celebrations of Palm Sunday, the story of Holy Week continues with those who wanted to silence Jesus forever.

The Pharisees enter at the front with their flags. In between them stands Pilate with his red flag bearing the black Roman motif.

79

The chief priests plotted to get rid of Jesus. They bribed his friend to betray him and then they arrested him. They took him to Pilate, the Roman Governor.

Jesus with his flag kneels before Pilate.

Pilate sent him to Herod, the local king.

Pilate leaves and Herod enters, carrying a black flag with a red crown.

Herod sent him back to Pilate in disgust.

Pilate returns and Herod leaves.

Pilate wanted to let Jesus go but the chief priests stirred up the crowds to shout, 'Crucify him! Crucify him!'

Encourage the Pharisees to lead the shouting of 'Crucify him! Crucify him!' Everyone stands.

The people turned against Jesus.

Encourage everyone to throw down their flags in the aisle.

So Pilate condemned him to death.

Pilate leaves. The Pharisees raise their flags up high and wave them triumphantly until the end of the story.

Jesus was tortured and nailed to a cross. He died and was buried in a borrowed stone tomb.

Jesus lowers his flag and lies down with his arms outstretched. The Storyteller covers Jesus' face and upper body with the flag. Pause for a moment.

Exploring

In Holy Week, we remember the events that led to Jesus' death on the cross. Our flags have reminded us that there was a battle going on between the light and life of Christ and the power of darkness and death. In our retelling of the story, Jesus carried the white flag of peace with the crown of a king, and the crowd waved white flags with the dove of peace and the palms of victory; the powerful people who put Jesus to death carried red and black flags, the colours of death and darkness. By the end of today's story, only those flags were waving, like the flags of a victorious army at the end of a battle. When Jesus died on the cross, it looked as though he had been well and truly beaten. No one knew then that Easter morning would be his final victory.

For our prayers today, a dancer will help us reflect on this battle between life and death, good and evil, which is known as Christ's Passion.

Prayer action

As the tune of 'I danced in the morning' is played slowly and thoughtfully, a dancer performs with flags: one is Jesus' white flag with the gold crown, the other is the black flag with the red cross.

Let us pray.
God of light and life,
for us you took on the power of death
and won.
May we follow you wherever you lead.

Music

I danced in the morning

Conclusion

Lord Jesus,
as we celebrate with palms today
and remember your Passion,
we look forward to celebrating your Easter victory.
May we be faithful witnesses.

Notes

1. Worship flags

These are beautiful resources for worship and well worth making or buying. For each one you will need:

- A piece of dowel
- A semicircle of shiny, floaty fabric – e.g. organza, polyester shiny fabrics, lycra foil, metallic lamé, poly habotai

For this service, the flags need to be particular colours. Each features its own emblem, which should be sewn on as a motif or drawn on with fabric pens:

- Jesus: white flag with a gold crown
- First Pharisee: black flag with red cross
- Second Pharisee: red flag with black crown of thorns
- Pilate: red flag with black laurel wreath and/or Roman eagle
- Herod: black flag with red crown

For the large size, the fabric should be 180cm long and 90cm wide; the dowel should be 90cm long.

Fold over slightly less than half the length of the fabric to form a narrow hem. Sew it across the top and down the side, leaving it open at the bottom so it forms a sleeve for the dowel. Insert the dowel and make sure that there is enough left sticking out of the end of the sleeve for you to hold.

These flags are at their best when in motion. They can be quite spectacular when used in dance, like this:

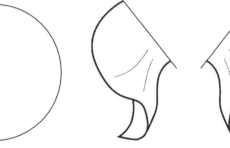

For further pictures, information and videos of dancing with flags, search the internet for 'worship flags'. See especially www.wingsofpraise.com. A UK supplier I can recommend is Kingdom Dance Resources: see www.kingdomdance.co.uk.

2. Equipment for making the crowd's flags

These will be triangular pennants. Prepare beforehand by cutting and hemming the triangles; then fold over the base of each triangle and sew it along two sides to form a narrow sleeve for the stick. Leave it open at the bottom.

People will use the templates to help them decorate their pennants with either a dove (outlined in blue) or a palm leaf (coloured in green). Then they will insert the balsa wood stick in the sleeve to complete their flag.

3. Pattern templates

Make a few copies of each.

Claire Benton-Evans

Cheers and Jeers (For pre-school age to 5 years)

Thought for the day

Jesus rides into Jerusalem cheered by the crowds. Days later crowds will be clamouring for his death.

Readings

Liturgy of the Palms:
Matthew 21:1-11
Psalm 118:1-2, 19-29

Liturgy of the Passion:
Isaiah 50:4-9a
Psalm 31:9-16
Philippians 2:5-11
Matthew 26:14-27:66 or Matthew 27:11-54

Aim

To welcome Jesus, the king on a donkey.

Starter

If your church has a Palm Sunday procession, then the children will be joining in with this. Provide them with branches to wave, cut from evergreen trees, and ask for one of the hymns to be one the children can cope with, such as *Hosanna, hosanna!* or *Rejoice in the Lord always.*

   If the church doesn't organise a procession, have one for the children, and take a portable CD player with you so that everyone can sing and play along with it.

Teaching

Tell the children the story of Jesus coming into Jerusalem on a donkey, either using your own words based on a careful reading of the Bible text, or one of the versions available for young children. As you tell the story, get the children to join in with all the actions, such as miming the untying of the donkey and leading it to Jesus, the waving of palm branches and laying coats on the road, and shouting 'Hooray for Jesus!'

Praying

Clip, clop, clip, clop!
Hosanna! Hosanna!
Hooray for Jesus,
the king on a donkey!
Hosanna! Hosanna!
Clip, clop, clip, clop!

Activities

Use the pattern on the sheet to make palm branches from green paper. There is also a road drawn on the sheet and a donkey to cut out and lead along the road into Jerusalem. Children will need assistance with the cutting. For very young children have the donkey already cut out.

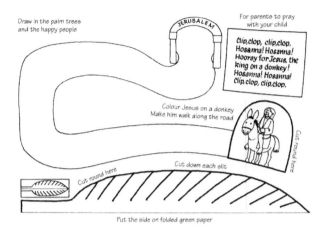

Susan Sayers

Riding to Rejection (For 6 to 10 years)

Thought for the day

As the Messiah, Jesus enters Jerusalem, knowing that he rides towards rejection and death in order to save his people.

Readings

Liturgy of the Palms:
Mark 11:1-11 or John 12:12-16
Psalm 118:1-2, 19-24

Liturgy of the Passion:
Isaiah 50:4-9a
Psalm 31:9-16
Philippians 2:5-11
Mark 14:1-15:47 or Mark 15:1-39 (40-47)

Aim

To understand that Jesus is making a Messianic statement as he enters Jerusalem.

Starter

If possible, let the children join in with the all-age procession, playing their instruments, dancing and singing as they go. Or gather all the age groups and take them on a Palm Sunday procession, preferably outside. Take a portable music player so they can all sing along with the songs.

Teaching

Bring along a little olive oil and a cloth, a crown, and this notice: 'Anointed as God's chosen one = Messiah (in Hebrew) = Christ (in Greek).'

Put the notice, the olive oil and the crown in the centre, and remind the children of when David was a shepherd boy and God chose him to be the future king. To show he was chosen (choose a volunteering child), David was anointed with olive oil. *(Pour a little oil on the volunteer's head and wipe it with the towel, so they understand what being anointed means.)* David was God's chosen king, and when he grew up, he became the king of Israel. *(Place the crown on the same child's head.)*

Long after King David had died, everyone looked back to those wonderful days when he had been their king, and they also looked forward to the time when God would send his anointed, chosen One to be King over all the world for ever. They knew this anointed one would be from King David's family. They called this anointed One the Hebrew for 'anointed' – which is 'Messiah'. We usually call it 'Christ' which is the same thing in Greek, the language the Gospels were written in.

Many, many years later, Jesus was born, of David's family. Gradually people began to realise that this was the Messiah, the son of King David who would reign for ever. When Jesus rode a donkey into Jerusalem, they all got really excited, and cheered and shouted and sang their hearts out. The prophets had even said the Messiah would enter Jerusalem riding on a donkey, and here Jesus was, doing it! 'Hosanna! Hosanna!' they all shouted. 'Hosanna to the Son of King David! Hosanna for the glorious kingdom he's going to bring us!' *(One of the leaders can be a donkey and one of the children can ride the donkey while the others all shout their Hosannas and wave their streamers.)*

What the people didn't quite understand was that Jesus' kingdom was not like a country on a map, but was a kingdom of love, joy and peace in people's hearts and lives. Jesus is the Christ, the Messiah, and reigns as King in our hearts now, just as he can reign in the hearts of anyone, living anywhere, at any time.

Praying

Lord Jesus,
King and Lord of all,
we welcome you and shout 'Hosanna!'
We praise and worship you.

Activities

The different strips on the sheet can be mounted on card and fixed together to form the star of David, so that the children sense the drawing together of all the Law and the prophets in Jesus.

Susan Sayers

Prince of Peace (For 6 to 10 years)

Aim

To show Jesus wants us to accept him as our Prince of Peace.

Readings

Liturgy of the Palms
Luke 19:28-40
Psalm 118:1, 2, 19-29

Teaching

The Chief Priest and the Pharisees had made Jesus an outlaw. They had put a price on his head, which meant if anyone told them where he was, they would be given money. Do you know who betrayed Jesus? Sadly, it was one of his friends, a disciple called Judas. But that is another story.

Jesus wanted to go to Jerusalem but he knew it was dangerous for him. Some people were trying to capture him. At first he stayed with some friends, Lazarus and his sisters. Do you know the names of the sisters? Mary and Martha. Maybe no one knew that Jesus was staying there. Then he decided he would go to Jerusalem. Some of the disciples tried to persuade Jesus not to go, or if he went, to go quietly and well covered up so that no one would notice him. But Jesus was not afraid and he would not sneak into Jerusalem. In fact, he would come to Jerusalem like a king, cheered on by his friends and others.

Jesus planned to do this some time before. Now he was able to say to two of his disciples, 'If you go over to that house, you will find a young donkey tied. Loose it and bring it here. If any one asks you what you are doing, just say, "The Master needs it."' This was the secret password to the owner, and if he heard these words, he would let the donkey go with the disciples. When the disciples were loosening the donkey the owner said, 'What are you doing?' Tell me what the two disciples said. ('The Master needs it.' Let us all say it together). When the passwords were said, the owner allowed them to take the donkey to Jesus.

Now Jesus was ready to enter Jerusalem. He would not sneak in but he would ride in like a king. Not on a warhorse but on a donkey. Kings in the land where Jesus lived rode on donkeys when they came in peace to a place. Jesus wanted to enter the city called the 'Possession of Peace' (which is what the word Jerusalem means) as the Prince of Peace. The disciples put some of their cloaks on the donkey for Jesus to sit on. Now they set off. People became excited when they saw Jesus riding the donkey. They cut down branches from the palm trees and laid them on the ground like a carpet; some even laid their cloaks on the ground for the donkey to walk over. They were welcoming the Prince of Peace. Soon a shout was heard. The people wanted to thank God for all the deeds of power they had seen. 'Blessed is the king!' Many took up the shout 'Blessed is the king who comes in the name of the Lord.' Let us all say it: 'Blessed is the king who comes in the name of the Lord.' The people were shouting, 'Peace in heaven and glory in the highest.' Others still were cheering and shouting, 'Hosanna', which means 'God save us'.

Jesus entered Jerusalem as the Prince of Peace. Many welcomed him. But the Pharisees were not pleased. They tried to stop him. Before the week was out they would cause his death. We all have to decide whether we are for Jesus or against him, whether we welcome him or reject him. Let us welcome him today by praising him and saying 'Hosanna'.

Activity

The main activity is to be part of the Palm Sunday procession. After the lesson let the group re-enact the movement of Jesus from Bethany to the entry into Jerusalem. Encourage them to know why things were done and how they fulfilled the words of Zechariah.

Prayer

Jesus, we welcome you with joy
and with shouts of Hosanna
for you are our King and the Prince of Peace.
Through you, may we have peace
in our hearts, in our homes and in the world.

Song

Give me joy in my heart

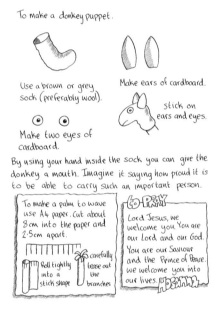

To make a donkey puppet.

Use a brown or grey sock (preferably wool).

Make ears of cardboard.

Stick on ears and eyes.

Make two eyes of cardboard.

By using your hand inside the sock you can give the donkey a mouth. Imagine it saying how proud it is to be able to carry such an important person.

To make a palm to wave use A4 paper. Cut about 8 cm into the paper and 2·5cm apart. Roll tightly into a stick shape carefully tease out the branches

Let us Pray
Lord Jesus, we welcome you. You are our Lord and our God. You are our Saviour and the Prince of Peace. We welcome you into our lives. Hosanna!

David Adam

Holy Week Events (11 plus)

Aim

To get the young people to understand the events leading up to Good Friday and Easter.

Readings

Liturgy of the Palms
Mark 11:1-11 or John 12:12-16
Psalm 118: 1, 2, 19-29

Liturgy of the Passion
Isaiah 50:4-9a

Psalm 31:9-16
Philippians 2:5-11
Mark 14:1–15:47 or Mark 15:1-39 (40-47)

Let the dramatic readings of the Passion narratives replace the sermon today. Allow the Scriptures to speak for themselves. Use as many people as possible to share in the readings. I have provided ideas for the Liturgy of the Palms rather than comment on the Passion: I hope Holy Week will be used to do that.

Teaching

If you were keeping a file on Jesus, the entry into Jerusalem would not necessarily come as a surprise. Jesus was popular with many of the people. Let us list the things that made him popular:

- Healing miracles
- Feeding miracles
- Storytelling (parables)
- Forgiveness (Zacchaeus, Mary Magdalene)
- Actions (cleansing the Temple, stilling the storm)

He cared for people and showed God's love. People saw him as the Messiah, their Saviour. They shouted, 'Hosanna', meaning 'Save us now'.
Some saw him as a revolutionary to drive out the Roman army.
Let the young people offer the reasons for popularity and only use the above as a prompt. Let each write a sentence to express a reason why Jesus was popular.
Then let the group explore the reasons for the events that led to the crucifixion.

Much was due to what Jesus said:

- He spoke against evil.
- He spoke against injustice.
- He spoke against hypocrisy.
- He spoke against the Scribes and Pharisees: he upset the established Church.
- He overturned the tables of the moneychangers.
- He healed on the Sabbath.

Some wanted him to use force and lead an army, and they were angry that he chose an animal of peace to ride on into Jerusalem. Instead of pomp and power, he came in peace and poverty.
Some wanted him to lead them to freedom from the Romans; others feared he would cause a revolution. Some were just jealous of his popularity.
The authorities easily manipulated the crowds.

Activity

There should be as much involvement as possible in making palm crosses, sharing in the procession and in the readings for the day. Instead of a sermon, one group of the young people could put forward ideas why Jesus was welcomed on his entry to Jerusalem. They should have no more than a sentence or two at the most. Others could express reasons for his capture and crucifixion. Keep the sentences crisp and simple. After each sentence there could be a waving of palm leaves and cries of 'Hosanna'.

Prayer

Blessed are you, Lord Jesus,
for you are our Saviour.
As you were welcomed into Jerusalem,
may we welcome you into our homes and our lives.
Let our lives sing Hosannas to you,
that we may be full of your praise.
As we carry palm crosses
may we know the great sacrifice of love
that you made for us,
Jesus our Lord and King.

Song

Hosanna, hosanna

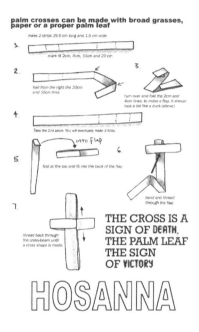

David Adam

Heading for the Cross

Bible base

Matthew 26–27

Aims

- To look at the events of the week leading up to Jesus' crucifixion.
- To identify areas where we might let our friends down and try not to.

Preparation

Ask for specific prayer support as you prepare for this session. The things that you say will have a big impact on the young people, but rather than be daunted by this look upon it as a great opportunity.

Strengthened by the knowledge that your prayer support team is pulling out all the stops, you can prepare and deliver with authority.

Knowing that others will be praying for you always adds a great feeling of being part of a team. In American football they call on the special team to fulfil certain tasks such as kick-offs and 'point after' attempts and it's no exaggeration to call you and your prayer supporters the special team this week. Go for it!

Read

Matthew 28:16-20

Yes, you know this is a potentially tough week to be leading, but rest assured that if you feel a big challenge lies ahead, you are in very good company.

The Bible has many examples of people who protested their unsuitability, only to be proved wrong: Moses, Jeremiah, Amos; and every other reluctant preacher is the same – God says that you're to trust in him, because he'll give you the words and give your listeners the ears to hear him.

So go ahead and do it.

The Great Commission of Matthew 28:16-20 inspires and reminds you why you are where you are today. You have been called to be a fisher of men and women, albeit young ones, on this occasion.

Jesus says: 'All authority in heaven and on earth has been given to me. Therefore go and make disciples of all nations . . . and surely I am with you always, to the very end of the age.'

Pray

Ask for God's authority and power and ask for exactly the right words to minister to your group of young people. Rejoice in the opportunity to share in this special time.

You will need

For the Opening activity
- A tray with around 20-25 small items on it. This should be covered with a cloth until needed, and be able to be covered up again.
- Paper and pencils for each child.

For the Presentation
- A cup and a small plate (or borrow the items used for Holy Communion in your church).
- A free-standing cross.
- Three cards, with the words 'A poor friend – Judas', 'Poor friends – his disciples', 'A poor friend – Peter'.

For the Project time
- Ice-lolly sticks. You will need a long one and a short one for each child. Experiment with the sizes and cut the short sticks in preparation.
- Twine or strong cotton (and scissors to cut it).
- Modelling clay or pieces of polystyrene.
- Fine felt pens for writing on the sticks.

Worship

Spend time worshipping God by thinking of some words that express gratitude for people who are good friends.

Write out words like *Loyal, Trusted, Patient, Unselfish*, and so on, and lay them on the floor in the middle of your group as you sit in a circle.

Explain that you are going to worship God by talking to him and saying what you think of Jesus.

Then start by saying: 'Jesus, thank you for being . . . loyal,' and encourage others to make similar statements using the words in front of them. If they can think of others, then that's great.

Sing one of the following:

Jesus is my friend

Friend of sinners

Pastoral time

Remind the group about the excitement of the crowd on Palm Sunday. Has anyone ever been in a large crowd? Encourage them to share how they felt about it.

Has anyone ever found it hard to stop doing something when they've been in a group doing something not particularly good (maybe picking on someone at school or doing something behind a teacher's back – use other examples if you can think of better ones).

Round off this time by reassuring them that although it's tough going against the crowd, the effort is worth it.

Opener

Play 'Kim's game' (so called after Rudyard Kipling's character in *The Jungle Book*). Gather the children around the tray, and explain they have just one minute to look at the tray before it is covered up again. Then they will try and write down a list of what they saw. There are different variations on this game if you wish to try something different, e.g. two leaders throw 15 (not so small) objects to each other whilst the children watch.

Presentation

We use different things to remind us of important events. Many people have a diary to write down dates and times. Ask what other things we use to remind us about important events.

This is a very important time of the year for Christians, because we remember the most important events of Jesus' life.

On Palm Sunday we remembered the people crowding into Jerusalem. They were there because it was an important feast. After the people of Israel were led by Moses from Egypt, God told them not to forget what he had done, and to gather together to celebrate with a feast on this particular day each year – an anniversary, like a birthday.

It was one of three important feasts, and it was called the Feast of Unleavened Bread, in which the Passover meal was an important part. You may remember that God told Moses that on one special day, everyone had to have a lamb or young goat for a meal. The bread they were to have with the meal was to have no yeast, or leaven, in it. God told the Israelites they had to eat the meal quickly, ready to leave at a moment's notice. They had to put some of the blood from the meat on the doorposts of their houses. Then, when the angel of death came, if the angel saw the blood, he would 'pass over' that house. That terrible night someone died in every Egyptian home, and so Pharaoh told Moses to take the people and leave Egypt at once!

God told Moses: 'Always remember this day. For all time to come, you and your children after you must celebrate this day as a feast in honour of the Lord' (Exodus 12:14).

So Jesus celebrated the Passover meal with his friends, but he did something different. Instead of looking back to the sacrifice of a lamb thousands of years before, he gave the meal a new meaning *(produce the cup and plate)*. That is why Christians have Holy Communion. Some call it a different name, and do it in a different way, but it is something Jesus told us to do to remember what he was going to do.

During that supper, one of Jesus' friends, called Judas Iscariot, left the room, watched by Jesus. He had already agreed to hand Jesus over to the chief priests and others who were jealous of Jesus and thought he was dangerous. The Bible tells us they offered to give Judas 30 silver coins for betraying Jesus. Later that night, the opportunity came, because after supper they went into a kind of garden, called Gethsemane. Knowing it would be dark, and to make sure they arrested the right person, Judas said, 'The one I kiss is the man.' *(Show the first card)*

But Judas was not the only friend to let Jesus down. When the men came and arrested Jesus, there must have been a lot of noise and confusion. The Bible says that all the disciples left him and ran away! *(Show the second card)*

It became even worse. Jesus was taken to the house of Caiaphas, the high priest, where he was interrogated and abused. Peter followed a little later, to see if he could find out what was happening to Jesus.

In the courtyard, three times he was asked if he was a friend of Jesus, and because he was scared of being arrested himself, each time Peter denied even knowing Jesus! *(Show the third card)*. Poor Peter cried, because after the third time, a cock crowed, and he remembered that Jesus had said that is just what would happen.

The next day, as we know, it got even worse for Jesus, and around midday, he was taken outside the city to a place called Golgotha (sometimes called Calvary). There he was executed in a very cruel way by Roman soldiers. It was something they did to all bad people, and as far as they were concerned Jesus was just another criminal. He was nailed to a cross and left to die, watched by anyone who passed by *(Show the cross)*.

Some people wonder why we have so many crosses. Why do we remember the cruel way they killed the person we love most? And the answer is that although this was so very cruel, and Jesus suffered so much, it was the greatest act of love. In a way we don't really understand, because Jesus allowed his life to be taken in this way, it made it possible for us to be forgiven and become God's friends.

This is such a sad story, but we know it wasn't the end, and that's what we'll be thinking about next week.

Response

Play some suitable music, and invite the children simply to stand in silence looking at the cross. Tell them to be aware of the thoughts that may come into their minds, the things God might be showing them or reminding them of.

This may only be a short silence, but be sensitive. Some may want to spend more time in quiet than others.

Memory verse

No one has greater love than the one who gives his life for his friends.

John 15:13

Project time

Using the ice lolly sticks, make small crosses. The two pieces can be tied together, winding twine or strong cotton round and round. After practising on scrap paper, get the children to write the first few words of today's Memory verse on their cross. Push the cross into a base of modelling clay or polystyrene.

Conclusion

Jesus knows that all of us, like his friends the disciples, will sometimes get things wrong – that sometimes we'll be weak even when we want to be strong. He recognises that and still loves us, so that even though Jesus' death was very sad, it was a very important part of God's plan for you and me.

Dear Lord Jesus,
Thank you for forgiving us for all the times we let you down. We want to follow your example and care about all God's children, so please help us to be thoughtful and forgiving to everyone we meet this week.
Amen.

To do

Think of three other important events in Jesus' life. What 'reminders' can you think of or make about these events?

(The Big Ones)

The Crowd

Background

Crowds can be exciting and encouraging, or frightening and threatening, depending on whether they are friendly or angry! Some people love being part of a crowd, while others will do anything to avoid them.

The Gospels are full of crowds, and so Jesus was no stranger to them. But even for him there were times when he got away from them, and one of those times was when he went into the wilderness. He knew that later on he would be faced with crowds of demanding people who would welcome him, but who would also want him to do things for them.

Bible

The disciples went and did as Jesus had instructed them. They brought the donkey and the colt, placed their cloaks on them, and Jesus sat on them. A very large crowd spread their cloaks on the road, while others cut branches from the trees and spread them on the road. The crowds that went ahead of him and those that followed shouted, 'Hosanna to the Son of David!'

Matthew 21:6-9

Jesus was welcomed into Jerusalem with huge crowds of adoring people, but they didn't realise what he was going to do for them. They wanted a leader to raise an army and remove the occupying Roman army, but Jesus would be a different kind of leader and king, giving his life to save all people. As he spent the following days in Jerusalem, Jesus said things that many people, from the religious leaders to the ordinary people in the crowd, didn't want to hear. Very soon the crowd had changed its mood, and was no longer shouting a welcome to Jesus, but calling for him to be crucified instead of a criminal.

So when the crowd had gathered, Pilate asked them, 'Which one do you want me to release to you: Barabbas, or Jesus who is called Christ?'

Matthew 27:17

Actions and Activities

- Talk to someone else about how you feel about being part of a crowd. Are you comfortable being with many other people? Do you find it a bit scary to be in a crowd?

- Imagine you are in the crowd that is shouting a welcome to Jesus as he rides on the donkey. Write down all the chants, calls and comments you hear from those around you in the crowd. Ask yourself these questions:

  Why did they welcome Jesus?

  What did they think he would do?

  Did all the crowd know what was happening?

- *Crowd Confessions*

  Ask each person to think about times when they have gone along with the crowd rather than doing what they knew was right. Ask any who are brave enough to tell the rest of the group about it.

- Spend some time in a crowd at a concert, shopping centre or football match. What makes it feel good to be in a crowd? Why do some people dislike the crowd experience?

- Have a look at the following comments. Which of these do you think explain why some of the crowd changed their minds about Jesus and moved from welcoming him to rejecting him?:

  He wasn't the army leader we wanted.

  He talked about peace instead of war.

  Our religious leaders told us to hate him.

  Others changed their minds, so I did too.

  He didn't say things we wanted to hear.

- Reflect on times in the past when you've continued to act as part of the crowd when God has been calling you to act and behave differently. Ask God to forgive you for not standing up for him, and not being brave enough to stand against the crowd.

Pausing and praying

- *Dear God, the crowd was happy when things were going well, and they didn't ever want things to change.*

Help me to be open to you changing my mind and my plans.
Dear God, the crowd were convinced by the religious leaders that Jesus should die.
Help me to be open to what you have to say to me, and not listen to lies.
Dear God, the crowd didn't really understand what they were doing.
Help me to always do what you want me to do.

- Think about all the different parts of your life and all the things you do. After you have thought of each one in turn say:

Jesus, I welcome you into that part of my life.

Nick Harding

The Way to the Cross

Have the London Underground map printed out on the weekly sheet, or have some larger versions available to show everyone.

Look at the plan and talk about the way it is simple sign language to help us make sense of a huge complicated network of rails and tunnels criss-crossing under the streets. The whole thing is so enormous to understand that we need this simple map.

But when we travel on the underground it only works because, as well as the simple map in our hand or on the station wall, the real massive tracks are laid in all those dark tunnels, and the electrical power is surging through all the thick cables, and the tilers have been busy fixing tiles on the station walls, and the computers are busy checking where each train is so that they don't bump into one another, and those moving stairs, the escalators, are well oiled and running smoothly. Although all this doesn't show up on our plan of coloured lines and blobs, we only have to look at it and we know that all the real stuff is right there.

In a way the cross shape is like one of those plans. Draw people's attention to the crosses they can see around them in church. It is only a simple shape, and we can all make it ourselves by placing one index finger across the other. (Do that now.) When people say 'fingers crossed' what do they do? (Ask some people to show this.) Today it usually means hoping we'll be lucky, but a long time ago it was people making the sign of the cross as they prayed about something they were worried about. (We could go back to using the sign that way!)

Now if the shape of the cross is like the underground train plan, what is all the real, deep stuff that the cross reminds us of? Ask everyone to find or make a cross and look at it, as you tell them about the deeper meaning: God loves the world so much that he was willing to give up everything, and come and live with us in person as Jesus. That loving led him to a cross where he gave up his life for us, taking all the selfishness and sin on himself, and stretching out his arms in welcome and forgiveness, because he so longs for us to be free.

All-age ideas

- The reading of the Passion can be sung by the choir, or dramatised using different voices, with the whole congregation joining in the crowd's words.
- A drama group could prepare a short mime to bring out the meaning of the crucifixion.
- Rather than having set movements to follow, give them some familiar religious keywords to pray about, unpack and express, such as Saviour, Redemption or Justification.

Nick Fawcett

The Difference a Week Makes!

Reading

Luke 19:28-40

Aim

To demonstrate the contrast between the fickleness of human nature and the faithfulness of God, each so powerfully displayed in the events from Palm Sunday to Easter Sunday.

Preparation

You will need a large sheet of paper pinned to a board, or a white-board, and a marker pen. Across the top of the board write the following:

LOVE   CHEER   WAVE   JOY   PALM   KING

Talk

Tell the congregation that you want to talk about change, and to help illustrate what you mean you need their help. Show them the letters at the top of your display board, and tell them that you want to change the words in as few stages as possible to very different words: 'Love' to 'Hate'; 'Cheer' to 'Cross'; 'Wave' to 'Mock'; 'Joy' to 'Woe'; 'Palm' to 'Harm'; and 'King' to 'Kill'. Invite suggestions as how best to do this, and write these down beneath the relevant word until the change has successfully been made. If the ways below are faster (or you can do better!), demonstrate afterwards.

LOVE	CHEER	WAVE	JOY	PALM	KING
COVE	CHEEP	RAVE	TOY	PALE	PING
CAVE	CHEAP	RACE	TOE	HALE	PINT
HAVE	CHEAT	RACK	WOE	HARE	TINT
HATE	CHEST	ROCK		HARM	TILT
	CREST	MOCK			KILT
	CRESS				KILL
	CROSS				

Point out that in a relatively short time it was possible to change the word you started with into a word very different in meaning. But if changing the words so easily seems remarkable, more remarkable still is the fact that the changes you have made actually happened. What day is it? Palm Sunday. What day will it be next Friday? Good Friday.

Palm Sunday and Good Friday: two very different days reminding us of very different events, yet there is less than a week between them. In less than a week, love changed to hate, cheering changed to a cross, the joyful waving of crowds changed to mockery, the joyful hurling of palm branches turned to the hurling of insults and attempts to harm Jesus, the shouts welcoming him as King turned to shouts demanding he should be killed; a day of joy turned to a day of woe. In just a few days, each of these changes took place.

An astonishing turnaround; but thankfully there was to be another more astonishing still, for on Easter Day Jesus was to change it all back again! Hate was replaced by love, the tears after the cross were replaced by cheers following the Resurrection, the mocking of the crowds gave way to hands waving in happiness, woe was replaced by joy, the one who had been killed was worshipped as Lord of lords and King of kings!

Palm Sunday reminds us how quickly people can change, ourselves included; how short-lived our love and faithfulness can be. But it reminds us also that the love of God shown in Christ never changes; that whatever may fight against his will, and however faithless we may be, his love and purpose will endure for ever!

Nick Fawcett

RESOURCES

Palm Sunday

The final week of Lent – Holy Week – begins with Palm Sunday, a remembrance of Jesus' triumphal entry into Jerusalem which is recorded in all four Gospels. Jesus entered Jerusalem riding on a donkey and the crowds laid their cloaks and scattered palm branches on the road before him.

It is significant that Jesus rode a donkey. In the ancient Middle East it was seen as a sign that a king was coming to wage war if he was riding a horse, but he was coming in peace if he rode on a donkey. It was also customary to cover, in some way, the path of someone who was thought worthy of the highest honour. In the Synoptic Gospels, the crowds spread branches and cloaks on the road, but St John's Gospel specifically mentions palm branches. The palm branch was a symbol of triumph and victory in Jewish tradition and may have indicated that this occurred at the Feast of Tabernacles rather than Passover. Most scholars agree that Jesus was making a messianic claim in acting out the prophecy of Zechariah 9:9.

In the Mediaeval Church, processions were formed on Palm Sunday and were led by a representation of Christ – either a Gospel book, a crucifix or a wooden figure of Jesus on a donkey. Very occasionally the procession was led by the Blessed Sacrament. It would process from one church to another.

Where a procession is formed outdoors in present-day practice, the image of Christ is often replaced by a real donkey being ridden or led by someone representing the person of Jesus. If the procession is indoors in a church where processional candles are used, the candles may be replaced on Palm Sunday by palm branches.

Most churches distribute crosses made of palm leaves as reminders of the Passion. The shape of the cross reminds recipients of the suffering of Christ upon the cross and the palm leaf acts as a reminder of his victory of Easter Day. In some churches these palm crosses are blessed, and in others they are merely distributed. Any palms left over from the previous year are used to make the ash for use on Ash Wednesday the following year.

David Schofield

Matthew 21:1-11

In Jerusalem expectations were running high. For the priests and religious leaders it was a time of celebrating the Passover and, possibly, they might at last get their hands on the one person who was a real pain to them: Jesus.

For the ordinary people the Passover was also a time of celebration but their expectations were even higher than normal. They had seen and heard all of the things that Jesus had done recently and they'd heard of his being referred to as the 'Son of David' (see Matthew 20:31). The term 'Son of David' was a title which the Jewish people understood to mean the messianic king, a new ruler who would liberate his people from foreign rule. Even the Mount of Olives was significant as the prophet Zechariah had spoken of the Messiah making a stand there against all of God's enemies (see Zechariah 14:4).

All the evidence pointed to something exceptional, something of the utmost importance. The crowds gathered and welcomed Jesus as he entered Jerusalem on a donkey (a king would ride a donkey as someone who came in peace). Yet within a week this Messiah, the 'Son of David' was dead.

The priests and religious leaders were content. Order had been restored and this nuisance, Jesus, had been dealt with. The Jewish people's hopes had been dashed against the wood of the cross. Expectations seemed to count for nothing where death was concerned.

Just as Jesus had shown time and again, death had no power over him. His mission was to act as the ultimate sacrifice, once and for all, so that the relationship could be finally restored between God and the people. It was obvious that the majority of people hadn't really understood what Jesus had been saying. The freedom he offered and the authority that he'd shown were not to deal simply with Roman rule but to end the rule of evil.

Sometimes our expectations are limited to what we can see immediately in front of us. Perhaps we should try to see things from God's perspective?

Pete Townsend

Introduction and Reflection

Introduction

Although Matthew's account of the Triumphal Entry into Jerusalem draws heavily upon Mark's Gospel, he makes several changes, some of them more significant than others. A small point is the omission of Bethany as one of the two villages Mark mentions. This may simply have been because Matthew realised that Mark had made a geographical error in putting Bethphage before Bethany because it is actually situated after Bethany on the road from Jericho to Jerusalem, the route Jesus would have taken.

The Mount of Olives was understood in Jewish eschatology to be the place of the appearance of the Messiah, which may account for its explicit identification in these events. Matthew gives less space than Mark to the conversation of the two disciples sent to fetch the 'donkey', not because he wishes to deny Mark's point that this revealed the supernatural nature of Jesus' insight regarding the donkey but because he conveys that point in a different way – through scriptural quotation.

It is typical of Matthew that he sees this major event, like other events, as a fulfilment of passages of Scripture that provide the vital key to how the event is to be understood. One of those passages results in a problem for scholars. Zechariah 9:9 states 'Lo, your king comes to you; triumphant and victorious is he, humble and riding on a donkey, on a colt, the foal of a donkey.' Matthew emphasises that the two disciples are to find and take to Jesus both a donkey and a colt. Cloaks were put on them and Jesus sat on them. It is suggested that Matthew misunderstood the nature of Hebrew parallelism whereby two similar words are used but with the intention of conveying only one reality. Thus 'donkey' and 'colt' are used but just one animal is referred to. Others have said this is plainly silly. Matthew would not have made that mistake, nor was he foolish enough to suggest that Jesus rode two animals. He sat on the cloaks (them) on one of the animals.

Such details are of much less importance than what Matthew is doing in using this quotation and the way it provides the thrust of the whole account.

First, he is pointing out that Jesus came as King. It has been suggested that in recalling the details of how the donkey was obtained, Matthew is neither interested in any prearrangements that Jesus may have made with the owner, nor concerned with some supernatural knowledge Jesus may have had about their availability. Rather he is showing Jesus acting as a king. In other words, Jesus was commandeering the animal(s).

Luke makes this same point by stating that the colt had never been ridden – it was forbidden for anyone but the king to ride on the king's horse. This was reinforced by the action of the disciples in putting their cloaks on the donkey and colt. What they were doing was to create a throne for him to sit on. In placing cloaks on the ground the crowd may have had in mind the account in 2 Kings 9:13 that records the occasion of Jehu being announced as king and the people laying their cloaks on the bare steps or ground.

In addition, the crowds cut branches and laid them on the ground. This may reflect the prophetic idea of the way of the Lord being made smooth (Isaiah 40:3). It is only in John's Gospel that the branches are identified as being from palm trees and that the crowds wave them. The use of branches signifies a festival – either the Feast of Tabernacles or Hannukah – and puts a question mark against the Feast of the Passover as the occasion of Jesus' death. However, this came to be associated with the events of Maundy Thursday and Good Friday through theological reflection on Jesus as the saving Lamb of God effecting the true Exodus of the people of God from their slavery to sin. Hannukah was the feast recalling the dedication of the Temple (1 Maccabees 13:51 or 2 Maccabees 10:7) when, amidst praise and rejoicing, palm branches were waved. The incident of the so-called cleansing of the Temple, to which Matthew refers immediately after the account of the Triumphal Entry, may have had especial relevance had it occurred during the Hannukah celebrations. People travelling into Jerusalem for the festival would have cut branches for use later on; they would have been expensive and difficult to obtain in the city itself.

Secondly, Matthew indicates what he came to see as Jesus' alternative view of kingship, namely that he was the king of humility rather than of power. This was highlighted in the quotation from Zechariah. The disciples only comprehended this view of kingship after Jesus' death and resurrection. This is in line with the position each of the Gospels takes but expresses differently – the failure of the disciples to grasp the meaning of Jesus' words and actions (see John 12:16).

Both the crowd that was ahead of Jesus and that which followed began to shout their great acclamation. The distinction between the two crowds may be that those ahead were pilgrims heading for the festival while those that came behind were 'followers' of Jesus. What Matthew records again picks up an Old Testament quotation, this time from Psalm 118:26 – one of the Hallel psalms (Psalms 113–118) used at the festival of Tabernacles – 'Blessed is the one who comes in the name of the Lord.' 'He who comes' may well have become a Christian Messianic title for Jesus picked up from this psalm.

The greeting of 'Hosanna', which had originally meant 'Save now', had come to be simply a shout of praise or a greeting similar to 'Hail'. For Matthew, the acclamation of Jesus as Son of David emphasised his role as the ideal king in the line of David. Luke underlines the kingship by making the acclamation, 'Blessed is the king who comes in the name of the Lord.' It is also Luke who makes explicit the aspect of Peace which marks the arrival of the Messianic age in the person of Christ. He does so by echoing the words of the angels who appeared to the shepherds at the time of Jesus' birth. Matthew's 'Hosanna in the highest' is not easy to interpret and may mean 'God bless him' – 'highest' being a way of referring to God.

By the time of the writing of the Gospels, the entry of Jesus into Jerusalem had acquired enormous significance. It was realised that the Passion and the resurrection had been determined by God to take place in the city (see Jesus' prediction in Matthew 16:21), and their full meaning had only gradually been understood as the disciples reflected on them under the guidance of the Holy Spirit. As they came to be seen as central to the purposes of God in his saving activity in Christ, so the start of that holy week gained in importance. This may account, at least in part, for the way the Gospels speak of crowds acclaiming Jesus as king yet the authorities failed to take any notice of what would have been seen as an act of insurrection, and no reference is made to the entry event in the accusations against Jesus at his trial. It would also account for the apparent dispersal of the crowd, sometimes put down simply to disappointment in Jesus' failure to build on the crowd's adulation and start an armed takeover. In reality, the crowd may have been quite small, largely made up of disciples and followers from Galilee whose enthusiasm amidst the sentiment and emotion of the festival led them to acclaim their leader.

Reflection

There are people whose entry into a room will turn heads. It may be on account of their reputation, their celebrity rating or just personal charisma. Sometimes it is their own heads that get turned. Making a big entry can be dramatic, good for publicity, or just the way things turn out. By all accounts Jesus' arrival in Jerusalem at the start of what we have come to call Holy Week was a big entry. The preacher from Galilee was acclaimed as king.

In the technique of telling Bible stories with groups of children, known as Godly Play, each session concludes with the leader saying: 'I wonder how so-and-so in the story felt . . . I wonder how you would have felt.' We might well wonder what was felt on the day of procession and acclamation, on that Palm Sunday. What was Jesus feeling? What did the disciples feel? How did the crowds feel about it all? How do we feel?

The disciples were geared up for something. Jesus had made it plain on a number of occasions that he was heading for Jerusalem and that his visit on this occasion would be critical. They had been dismissive of his talk about suffering at the hands of the authorities and Peter had earned a stern rebuke for his reaction to such ideas (Matthew 16:23). They didn't understand what Jesus was saying (Luke 18:34) but they knew that Jerusalem would be special. Some of the followers had left, perhaps fearful of what would happen, not wanting to get involved in anything too political.

The atmosphere among the disciples became more charged. They were meeting crowds on the road going up to Jerusalem for the festival (Tabernacles or Dedication) and Jesus seemed to be making arrangements of his own. Their heads would have been increasingly full of sayings and stories from the Jewish Scriptures and their expectations were rising. Their journey had taken them from Jericho and along the road to Bethany where Lazarus lived with his two sisters, Mary and Martha. It was a place of special personal significance for Jesus and his friends. As they came to the Mount of Olives they were aware that this was a place of national significance – a place of Messianic promise; the place where, it was said, would be the general resurrection when God established his kingdom of the new age.

Jesus had sent two of their number to a village with instructions about getting a donkey for him to ride. That was unusual in itself – Jesus normally walked everywhere. The excitement was mounting and they felt that this was going to be the great moment. Their leader was more than just a rabbi; he was the people's leader, the one they had been looking for, the one who would bring in God's new age. They got carried away with it all. As they put their cloaks on the donkey they led the shout of acclamation: 'God bless you, you come as King, in the name of the Lord.' This was what Jesus meant to them, this was what he deserved – the acclamation as leader, as king.

The crowds, too, were caught up in the excitement of the festival. They had cut branches from the trees to take into the city and once the shout went up about a king they waved them and laid them down in front of this figure who was being acclaimed as king. Some of them (according to John) had been amazed by what Jesus had done at Bethany in bringing Lazarus back from the dead, and they added to the shouts of acclamation. Did they know what they were shouting? Was it more than a bit of hysteria in the excitement of the moment? It may well have seemed real at the time but once they got into the city with its narrow streets and the watchful eyes of the soldiers, it all fizzled out. They had to be careful. The Romans were touchy at festival time and brought in extra troops to man the garrison. A man on a donkey wasn't really going to achieve that much. Perhaps he wasn't the king they had shouted for after all. When the Messiah really came he would come with an army and with power.

Jesus, we might imagine, saw all this very differently. Through his times of prayer and struggle he had come to believe that God required him to go to Jerusalem and face whatever that would bring. He knew he had stirred up opposition among the authorities. He had become convinced that it would involve suffering and no doubt his death. He believed he had no choice if he was to be obedient to his Father's will.

That he was a leader, he did not shrink from. That in some way the new age was indeed being brought in, he did not doubt. He knew he had a special role in that. But he had such a different view of the nature of his leadership, the type of kingdom that would be established. The people wanted a powerful leader to overturn the regime of Roman power and to restore Israel's stature as a nation, its independence, its power. Their vision was in the end too narrow, too parochial, too self-seeking. They had not learnt the lesson of the prophets that being God's people was a privilege for service, not for dominance. The Servant of God was for the freeing of all nations, not just the Jews. Jesus was key to the Big Story of peace, not to the skirmishes of power. He was indeed the one coming in the name of the Lord – in the name of a God of reconciliation and of peace, and to achieve that would be costly.

When Jesus came to Jerusalem his entry turned heads, but when he failed to live up to expectations, they turned away again.

John Cox

Acclamation – a Sketch

Palm Sunday is the bridge between Lent and Holy Week. Until now the unthinkable reality of the Messiah's arrest, trial and death has been etched only in the mind of Jesus; his followers are still in denial, even though the raising of Lazarus has proved beyond doubt that, when their Master is involved, there is indeed life after death. The decision to go up to Jerusalem for the Passover turns the unthinkable into the probable. Once through the city gate, the lives of this little group of followers spiral inexorably downward into suspicion, betrayal, confusion and flight.

Bible source:
Matthew 21:1-11

Performance time:
Five minutes with reading

Characters:
Reader
Nathan – a merchant
Reuben – a chandler

Scene setter:
A street in Bethphage. Nathan is off Right, Reuben off Left.
The Reader enters and takes centre stage.

Reader

Jesus enters Jerusalem.

As they approached Jerusalem and came to Bethphage (Beth- fa-geh) on the Mount of Olives, Jesus sent two disciples, saying to them, 'Go to the village ahead of you, and at once you will find a donkey tied there, with her colt by her. Untie them and bring them to me. If anyone says anything to you, tell him that the Lord needs them, and he will send them right away.'

This took place to fulfil what was spoken through the prophet:
'Say to the Daughter of Zion,
"See, your king comes to you,
gentle and riding on a donkey,
on a colt, the foal of a donkey."'

The disciples went and did as Jesus had instructed them. They brought the donkey and the colt, placed their cloaks on them, and Jesus sat on them. A very large crowd spread their cloaks on the road, while others cut branches from the trees and spread them on the road. The crowds that went ahead of him and those that followed shouted,
'Hosanna to the Son of David!'
'Blessed is he who comes in the name of the Lord!'
'Hosanna in the highest!'
When Jesus entered Jerusalem, the whole city was stirred and asked, 'Who is this?'
The crowds answered, 'This is Jesus, the prophet from Nazareth in Galilee.'

The Reader exits. Reuben enters Left, slightly before Nathan enters Right.

Reuben   Nathan!

Nathan   Reuben! *(they embrace)*

Reuben   I see the beasts are back.

Nathan   The beasts?

Reuben   Yes, the donkey and the foal. *(gestures over his shoulder)*

Nathan   Oh, those beasts. *(laughs)* Yes, they're back. One of his followers came over with them this morning. A good deal of thanks but *(he laughs)* no payment! *(shrugs his shoulders)* Why should I worry? I was happy to loan them. More than happy, seeing it was him. But I'm still puzzled why he did it.

Reuben   You saw him start off?

Nathan   Yes. I followed them down the Jerusalem road for a while. I was curious to see what he wanted them for. And then they put their cloaks over the animals and he sat on the foal, his feet dangling, almost scraping the ground. At first I laughed out loud. It seemed ridiculous for him to ride that animal into Zion. Some of his followers thought so too; I could see that. But they went along with it; laying their cloaks on the ground in front of him like some royal carpet and throwing down palm fronds. Some shouted 'Hosanna' and a good many other things. As I say, I laughed at first – and so did your wife, she was there along with some other women. But then he turned his head and I saw his face and my laughter died. He was . . . different; older, sterner than I'd seen him before. Looking back up towards the olive trees as though he was seeing them for the last time.

Reuben   Yes, he had just that look when he entered the city.

Nathan   You saw him in the city?

Reuben   Yes, I had to take a batch of candles to the temple. These festivals bring a good trade for some of us. Anyhow, I had a job to get through the crowd. Pilgrims mostly but some Pharisees and the usual hangers-on, all going out of the city to meet him.

Nathan   Sightseers no doubt. Heard about that business with Lazarus of Bethany.

Reuben   Possibly. Possibly. Whatever the reason, they were making a real din. Singing. Shouting. 'Welcome to David's son' some of them were saying. They seemed to think he's the Messiah.

Nathan   Of course! Why didn't I think of that before! It's the Zechariah prophecy, isn't it? Now how does that go? Ah. *(he thinks)* Something about the king will come in peace – riding on an ass! Yes, that's it. Riding on the foal of an ass. That's why he wanted them.

Reuben   Well, whatever the reason, it was as much as I could do to get past into the city. And when the two groups met up – pandemonium!

Nathan   I can't believe the Pharisees would have been pleased at that!

Reuben   You're not wrong, Nathan, you're not wrong! Long faces! *(they laugh)* And they might have a point. On my way back I heard that he'd been causing trouble in the temple. Attacking the traders apparently, for defiling his father's house. His father's house? It's beyond me.

Nathan   But if he is the Messiah he'd be attacking the Romans, surely? Not his own people. *(silence)* No, there's something not right about all this. Did he seem like a conqueror to you? A military leader? *(Reuben shakes his head)* You know, I can't help thinking about when Pilate came down that same road. No donkey for him. A great white horse and half the Roman army clanking along behind. And d'you know, he had that same look. Tight-lipped, stern. But not looking back. No, Reuben. No looking back for that one.

They both turn and look Left for a moment.

Reuben   Come on Nathan. Business is good. I'll buy you a drink.

Both exit Right, talking.

Peter Jackson

Three Cheers for Jesus

(For up to five readers)

Three cheers for Jesus!
He comes to be our king.
He'll overthrow the tyrants,
and wealth and freedom bring.

He'll outlaw every evil –
all pain and fear and greed.
He'll take over the government
and meet our every need.

Two cheers for Jesus.
He claims to be our king,
but he's striding through the Temple
and upsetting everything.

He's scattering our profits
and the businesses we've made;
is he really fit to rule us
if he spoils our holy trade?

One cheer for Jesus.
He came to be our king,
but now he stands on trial,
red with the whip's sharp sting.

With crown of thorns they mock him,
scorned by official power.
He's helpless with authority;
this cannot be his hour.

No cheers for Jesus.
He's surely not our king.
They've nailed him to a wooden cross
while people laugh and sing.

The one we thought would save us
they curse and wound and kill.
Our hopes and expectations
die with him on that hill.

Now heaven cheers for Jesus.
The world has had its say;
and God has raised him from the dead –
there dawns another day.

Disciples stand bewildered
beside an empty grave,
but soon they will be cheering too
for the Christ who came to save.

Peter Dainty

A Royal Welcome

Read

After they had brought the colt to Jesus and spread their cloaks over it, he sat on it. Many among the crowd spread their cloaks out on the road, while others cut down branches from the fields and spread those likewise. Those in the vanguard of the procession and those bringing up the rear cried out, 'Hosanna! Blessed is the one who comes in the Lord's name! Blessed is the coming kingdom of our forefather David! Hosanna in the highest heaven!'

Mark 11:7-10

Ponder

Coming in with a bang, going out with a whimper – in the eyes of many that could be said to describe the last days of the life of Jesus leading up to the cross. One moment he was accorded a positively rapturous welcome as he rode into Jerusalem, and the next they were baying for his blood, declaring that they had no other king than Caesar. It's a truly breathtaking turnaround in his fortunes, and a reader coming to the story for the first time could be forgiven for thinking that those who greeted Jesus as their king on Palm Sunday were sadly mistaken – misguided if not deluded. To a point they'd be right, for any hopes they may have had that Jesus was intending to stage some kind of political coup in order to establish an earthly kingdom were to be thoroughly quashed in the week ahead. But it was precisely through all that followed – the mocking and flogging, the crown of thorns, the agony of the cross – that he took up his throne, opening the way to a kingdom beyond this world.

The betrayal, arrest and crucifixion of Christ were not some unfortunate error that was somehow rectified at Easter but the fulfilment of God's purpose: Jesus established his rule through surrendering his all. That is the Lord we worship – the one who came to serve rather than conquer, to bring life through enduring death. That is the Saviour we seek to honour. If we see him as sovereign yet not as servant, as raised high without also being brought low, then we, too, like so many who welcomed him on that first Palm Sunday, will have altogether missed the point.

Ask yourself

What does it mean to honour Christ as king? Does the analogy with an earthly monarch help or hinder a proper understanding of his kingdom and reign? What form does Christ's rule take?

Pray

Lord Jesus Christ, save me from confusing the values of this world with your own, from seeing your heavenly rule as one that forces itself on people – demanding, coercing, imposing. Teach me that, instead, yours is the way of love; it invites a response – surrender, sacrifice, service. Help me, then, to deny myself in order to discover who I really am; to be last so as to be first; to lose my life in order to find it – to walk the royal way of the cross.

Remember

Exult with all your heart, my daughter Zion! Cry loudly, daughter Jerusalem! Behold, your king is coming; glorious and triumphant yet humble, seated on a donkey – on a colt, a donkey's foal.

Zechariah 9:9

Close

Teach me, Lord, that if I would honour you as King of kings and Lord of lords, I must recognise you first as the suffering messiah and servant of all, and walk your way in turn.

Nick Fawcett

Holy Week

In the final week of Lent – Holy Week – the Revised Common Lectionary uses the first three days to recall some of the events from Jesus' last week on earth. Holy Week then continues with Maundy Thursday and Good Friday, ending with Holy Saturday. The four Gospels all relate differing events for that last week between Jesus' triumphal entry into Jerusalem and his crucifixion. The lectionary highlights three of these events as Gospel readings for the first three days, and they appear to show Jesus preparing his disciples for his coming death.

On the Monday of Holy Week, the lectionary recalls Jesus being anointed by Lazarus' sister Mary at Bethany. Judas questions the use of expensive perfume and we see the beginnings of his road to betrayal. Jesus tells his disciples that Mary was, in effect, anointing his body for burial. John's Gospel tells us that this took place six days before the Passover and the day before the triumphal entry into Jerusalem (John 12:1-11).

The reading for the Tuesday of Holy Week continues on from the triumphal entry and shows Jesus in the Temple telling all his listeners of his forthcoming death. His relationship with the Father is confirmed by God speaking directly to the crowd (John 12:28). Here Jesus is openly talking about what is going to happen to him.

The appointed reading for Wednesday is part of what are called 'the farewell discourses': Jesus and the disciples are eating a final meal together, and Jesus is preparing them for what is to happen and for their future ministry. In this reading, we hear Jesus telling his disciples that he will be betrayed. He doesn't name the betrayer to his friends but indicates to Judas that he is aware of his actions (John 13:21-32).

David Schofield

MAUNDY THURSDAY

PRAYERS

The Bread of Sacrifice

During supper he took bread, and having said the blessing he broke it and gave it to them, with the words: 'Take this: this is my body.'

Mark 14:22

So this is the reason
for the secrecy, Lord:
not only for a new command,
but for new sign and symbol, and new meaning.

The Passover bread of sacrifice
is now sign of your sacrifice.

Whether they had roast lamb that night or not,
you yourself are the Lamb,
the Lamb slain from the foundation of the world.
This now is sign and symbol of your self-offering,
laid wide open,
exposed,
vulnerable.

And not only sign and symbol, it is sacrament:
our oath of allegiance to you
and means of your grace to us.

Lord, as you opened the bread
and opened yourself to us,
help me to open myself to you,
open my hands,
open my heart.

Ken Taylor

The New Covenant

Then he took a cup, and having offered thanks to God he gave it to them; and they all drank from it. And he said to them, 'This is my blood, the blood of the covenant, shed for many. 'Truly I tell you: never again shall I drink from the fruit of the vine until that day when I drink it new in the kingdom of God.'

Mark 14:23-25

I wonder,
in that upper room,
and as tradition bids . . .

did you pour a cup for Elijah, Lord,
when he is come already,
and the way prepared already,
and the kingdom at hand?

You give your own new meaning to the last cup, too:
the traditional cup of covenant
is now sign and symbol and sacrament of your new Covenant.

Long looked for
and always needed,
the ancient hope becomes reality:
and we hold in our hands
what Jeremiah dreamed of.

Now by your dying and self-giving love
is your new law written on our hearts and within them.

Lord,
as we pour out our wonder and our love to you,
pour your love in our hearts;
write your new law of love upon our hearts;
and as you come to live in us,
so may we live in you.

Ken Taylor

A Night to Remember

Lord Jesus Christ,
you broke bread with your disciples
you shared wine,
and you told them to go on doing likewise
in memory of you.
For countless years,
across countless generations,
your people have done just that.
And so now we come,
to share in your supper,
and to remember.
This night of all nights
reminds us of the great truths of
the gospel –
of who you were,
what you did,
why you came,
and when you shall come again.

Help us, as we recall everything
you went through in Gethsemane,
and all that went after,
to remember you did it for us as much as any.
To you be all praise and glory,
now and for evermore.   *Nick Fawcett*

Broken Bread, Shared Wine

Lord Jesus Christ,
you broke bread, you shared wine –
with the one you knew would betray you,
with the one you knew would deny you,
with those you knew would soon abandon you to your fate.
Despite everything you stayed true,
freely offering your life.
Lord Jesus Christ,
you invite us to break bread and share wine,
even though we too betray you,
we too deny you,
we too abandon you time after time.
Despite everything, you stay true:
your body broken, your blood shed, for us!
Lord Jesus Christ,
we praise you and thank you with all our hearts.   *Nick Fawcett*

As we share this cup, Lord,
we remember your words:
'My blood, poured out for you and for many,
for the forgiveness of sins.'
A cup not of pleasure but of pain,
drunk not for you but for all,
representing the greatest of gifts,
precious beyond words.
Whenever we drink, Lord,
remind us of the true vine,
and the new wine you offer through it.   *Nick Fawcett*

Lord Jesus Christ,
we have broken bread, we have shared wine –
and we have done it,
together with your people across the centuries,
in remembrance of you.
You promise that the time will come
when we share with you in your Father's kingdom,
a time when your will shall be done
and all things shall be made new.

Until then, may the memory of all you have done
shape our lives
and guide our footsteps,
to the glory of your name.

Nick Fawcett

Years A, B and C

Lord, we pray that in our service to others
we can show the humility and the loving service
that your Son demonstrated to the disciples
in the act of washing their feet.
We give thanks that he has also shared
the bread and the wine of the last supper in remembrance of him.
Your Son taught us a new commandment
to love one another as he loved us.
May our service to each other be modelled on our service to you
and may our hope be in him who has saved us
from our selfishness and pride.
Lord, hear us.
Lord, graciously hear us.

We rejoice that our Teacher and Lord has stooped
to wash the feet of those he led and served.
Let our church leaders follow his example
in the humble ministry and exemplary leadership
they show in carrying out their duties.
Let prayer and worship
underpin all that bishops and priests do in your name.
Create in churches across the world a focus and a priority
on an event which makes all things new.
Lord, hear us.
Lord, graciously hear us.

Let us remember that water is often scarce
and servanthood in short supply,
where oppressor and oppressed
are locked in unequal struggle
and where Christian love
needs to break through barriers of hate.
May the example of your Son, our Saviour,
break the shackles of sin and death,
through the love of others leading to the self-giving love of the cross.
Lord, hear us.
Lord, graciously hear us.

In our own community we pray for . . .
Lord, hear us.
Lord, graciously hear us.

Grant to the sick the touch of your healing hands
and the comfort of your loving arms,
as we pray for those in urgent need at this time, especially . . .
Support the carers and strengthen the patience
of family and friends.
Lord, hear us.
Lord, graciously hear us.

Let all who have died, Lord, rest in peace
in the fulfilment of the hope we all desire.
Comfort the mourners and wipe away their tears
as fond memories take over from grief.
Merciful Father,
accept these prayers
for the sake of your Son, our Saviour Jesus Christ.

Rupert Bristow

In Remembrance

Lord Jesus Christ,
we praise you and thank you with all our hearts.
Lord Jesus Christ,
we are here at your invitation –
here to share,
as so many have shared before us,
in your supper,
this simple act which you commanded us to do
in remembrance of you.
We come, then, to remember –
to remind ourselves of all you suffered to set us free,
to recall the extent of your love
and the enormity of your sacrifice.
But we come also to celebrate –
to rejoice in all you have done for us
through your death,
and to thank you for all you go on doing for us
through what you achieved there on the cross.

Nick Fawcett

Your Body Here

Lord Jesus Christ,
you broke bread,
you poured wine,
your body broken,
your blood shed for us.
Help us, as we eat and drink together,
to receive you more completely into our hearts,
to welcome you more fully into our lives,
and so to represent you more truly

as your body here on earth,
until that day when we are wholly one with you,
and you are all in all.

Nick Fawcett

Reaching Gethsemane

When they reached a place called Gethsemane, he said to his disciples, 'Sit here while I pray.'
And he took Peter and James and John with him. Horror and anguish overwhelmed him, and
he said to them, 'My heart is ready to break with grief; stop here and stay awake.' Then he
went on a little farther, threw himself on the ground, and prayed that if it were possible this
hour might pass him by. 'Abba, Father.' he said, 'all things are possible to you; take this cup
from me. Yet not my will but yours.'

Mark 14:32-36

You just wanted their company
didn't you, Lord?
Not only for their sakes
but for *your* sake . . .
in the darkness and the wrestling.

There are times for all of us when we simply need
the company of our friends.

Thank you for the people who "company" us:
for those closest to us,
for those who share with us,
especially when we're in trouble.

As we remember them now,
and name them
in the stillness of our hearts,
and bless you for them,
bless each of them
according to their need.

Ken Taylor

Gethsemane

'If it is possible, take this cup from me.'
Lord Jesus,
we remember that desperate cry of yours
in the darkness of Gethsemane;
that cry of anguish as you faced up to the horror of the cross.
We remember that, knowing full well what the future held,
you were still able to say, 'Not my will, O God, but yours',
and you did so, not because you are different
but because you are fully one with us,
sharing our humanity,

ready, out of love, to offer your all
so that we might taste life in all its fullness.
Lord,
help us to recall everything you went through for our sakes,
and to appreciate the magnitude of what you did.
Teach us how much you loved us,
and so may we offer our love in return,
to you and to all,
for your name's sake.

Nick Fawcett

Lord Jesus Christ,
you spoke about loving our enemies,
praying for those who persecute us,
turning the other cheek,
and there in Gethsemane
you showed that you meant those words,
no matter what the cost.
Lord,
we are good at saying the right things,
but all too often it is merely talk,
found wanting when the real test comes.
Help us,
like you, to practise what we preach.

Nick Fawcett

Dearest Christ,
you have given love, given it exquisitely.
In your tiredness you washed your friends' tired feet.
In your generosity you gave bread to your betrayer.
In your all-seeing provision you bequeathed
a sacrament of bread and wine
that makes you constantly present to us.
In your anguish in the garden
you fought with demons and with doubt.
In your prayers you ever place your people
in the divine heart.
You call us to watch and pray.
Out of love for you we will watch and we will pray.

Ray Simpson

We Remember

Lord Jesus Christ,
we remember today the hours of testing
you endured in Gethsemane:
the heartbreak you felt,
the fear you experienced,
the questions you wrestled with
and the uncertainty you faced.

117

We remember that, despite it all, you stood firm,
refusing to be swayed from your calling.
We remember how you went on to endure
the agony of the cross
and the darkness of death.
So now we come,
able to look forward in faith,
anticipating that time when we will share with you
in your Father's kingdom;
a time when there will be an end to sorrow and suffering,
sin and death.
Save us from ever losing sight of that destiny.
We look back,
we look forward,
and thus we commit ourselves in confidence
to your service here and now,
knowing that you are the same Lord,
yesterday, today and tomorrow –
the one in whom we can safely put our trust.   *Nick Fawcett*

Come to Us

Lord Jesus Christ,
you invited all who love you,
all who sincerely desire to be your disciples,
to share together in this Supper.
So now we come around this table,
in fellowship with you,
with one another,
and with all your people in every place and time.
Lord Jesus, as we come to you,
so come to us.

We come to remember your sharing bread and wine
with your disciples in the upper room;
a simple expression of fellowship
with one who would soon betray you,
one who would deny you,
and others who would abandon you.
Lord Jesus, as we come to you,
so come to us.

We come to remember your anguish in Gethsemane
as you faced the awful,
awesome cost of your calling,
alone.
Lord Jesus, as we come to you,
so come to us.

We come to remember your arrest and brutal interrogation,
your sorrow and humiliation,

your suffering and death.
Lord Jesus, as we come to you,
so come to us.

We come to remember your quiet acceptance
of human evil and hatred directed against you,
you who had done no evil and knew no hate.
Lord Jesus, as we come to you,
so come to us.

Lord Jesus Christ,
we remember your great love,
and we marvel at how much you were willing to bear
for our sakes!
So now we praise, thank and worship you,
with all our hearts and minds and souls.
Lord Jesus, as we come to you,
so come to us,
for your name's sake.   *Nick Fawcett*

Denial

Lord, forgive us,
that, like Peter,
we can swear we do not know you
even louder than we swore
when we said we'd never leave you.
Lord, forgive us:
Lord, forgive us.

Lord, forgive us
when our courage
is a thing of bluff and bluster,
which, when someone calls our bluff,
soon dissolves in tears and fluster.
Lord, forgive us:
Lord, forgive us.

Lord, forgive us
when we praise you
with our lips, but not our action;
may the cock crow wake us up
from our blind self-satisfaction.
Lord, forgive us:
Lord, forgive us.

Lord, redeem us
when we fail you
not just three times, but more often;

119

may our conscience not grow hard,
lest it grow too hard to soften.
Lord, redeem us:
Lord, redeem us.

When hosannas
turn to catcalls
and we're tempted to deny you,
give us faith that will not fade
and the courage to stand by you.
Keep us faithful:
Keep us faithful.

Peter Dainty

Praise – Broken for Us

Lord Jesus Christ,
we celebrate today the astonishing truth
that lies at the heart of this week –
the fact that you endured the humiliation of Gethsemane,
the agony of the cross
and the darkness of the tomb,
not because you had to
but because you chose to.
You gave your life so that we might live.
You were broken so that we might be made whole.
Receive our praise.

We marvel that, from the beginning of your ministry,
you knew the fate it would lead to,
the cost involved,
and yet you continued undeterred,
despite ridicule, threats and outright hostility,
your concern always for others rather than yourself.
You gave your life so that we might live.
You were broken so that we might be made whole.
Receive our praise.

We celebrate your awesome commitment,
your refusal to be deflected from your chosen path.
You could have courted public acclaim,
seized earthly power
or secured personal gain,
but instead you chose the way of humility,
service and self-sacrifice,
the lonely path of the cross.
You gave your life so that we might live.
You were broken so that we might be made whole.
Receive our praise.

We thank you for your faithfulness to the last,
conscious of how tempting it must have been
to save yourself instead of us.
You could have taken a road
other than towards Jerusalem,
walked away from Gethsemane,
stepped down from the cross,
but you didn't,
preferring to put your will
second to the will of the Father,
your immediate future second to our eternal destiny.
You gave your life so that we might live.
You were broken so that we might be made whole.
Receive our praise.

Lord Jesus Christ,
however often we hear it,
we never fail to be amazed
by the magnitude of your love
and the awesomeness of your sacrifice.
We deserve so little, yet you gave so much.
We serve you so poorly, yet your grace is so rich.
So we come in thanksgiving and celebration
to offer you our heartfelt worship,
and to commit ourselves again to your service.
You gave your life so that we might live.
You were broken so that we might be made whole.
Receive our praise.

For your name's sake.   *Nick Fawcett*

Facing Trials

Lord Jesus Christ,
we will never know just what you felt
in that week leading up to the cross,
but what we do know
is that you were human just as we are,
experiencing the same emotions that we feel,
wrestling with the same pressures and temptations.
And we have little doubt how we would have acted
had we been in your shoes,
facing the awful prospect of suffering and death –
our love of life so great,
our fear of death so strong.
Yet though you were tempted like us,
and though you longed for the cup of suffering to be taken from you,
you stayed true to your calling,
faithful to the last.
When we face trials in turn,
Lord, deliver us from evil.

We marvel at the constancy of your love,
at the fact that though, from the beginning of your ministry,
you knew what it would cost you,
still you continued on your chosen path,
refusing to be deflected from your purpose.
You could have used your powers for your own ends,
succumbed to the attraction of popular acclaim and worldly glory,
and had it been us in your place,
we would probably have done precisely that,
our yearning for acceptance so great,
our fear of rejection so strong.
Yet though you were tempted like us,
and though you longed to see your kingdom
established here on earth,
you stayed true to your calling,
faithful to the last.
When we face trials in turn,
Lord, deliver us from evil.

We rejoice that you refused
to compromise your mission in any way,
your thoughts all for others rather than yourself.
While we would have toned down our message,
avoided controversy,
taken the course of least resistance,
you refused even to countenance such an option,
knowing that to do so
would have been to deprive people of your love,
and to dilute the good news you had come to bring.
You healed the sick even on the Sabbath,
you proclaimed forgiveness of sins,
you dined with those deemed the dregs of society,
condemning hypocrisy and corruption,
and overturning the tables of the money-changers in the temple.
We know we would have taken an easier path,
avoiding confrontation wherever possible,
our instinct for self-preservation so great,
our fear of suffering so strong.
Yet though you were tempted like us,
and though you longed for the cup of suffering to be taken from you,
you stayed true to your calling,
faithful to the last.
When we face trials in turn,
Lord, deliver us from evil.

Lord Jesus Christ,
we rejoice today at the wonder of your love,
and we pray for strength to walk in your footsteps,
firm in our faith and true to our calling.
Hear our prayer,
for your name's sake.

Nick Fawcett

SERVICES

Maundy Thursday

Introduction

'This is my body, broken for you . . . my blood, shed for you . . . Do this in remembrance of me' – words of Jesus to his disciples that have been repeated across the centuries in countless observances of the Lord's Supper. And Maundy Thursday, of all days, reminds us just what it is we remember and celebrate, focused as it is on that last meal Jesus shared with his intimate circle before going out to face his death. It reminds us of how, betrayed, denied, abandoned, still he stayed true to his path; of how he wrestled with fear and doubt in Gethsemane; of how he knelt to wash his disciples feet – Lord, yet servant of all; of how he faced the darkness of death to bring light to the world. And we rejoice in his promise that one day we will break bread and share wine again, with him and all his people, in his Father's kingdom. In this service, then, let us once more remember, and give thanks.

Opening prayer

Gracious God,
nothing we can do,
nothing we can say,
can ever thank you enough for what you have done in Christ –
for your great love made flesh through him.
As we remember once more his anguish in Gethsemane,
his sacrifice for those who would fail him,
his faithfulness to the last,
we marvel,
awed and humbled by his selfless devotion,
his offering himself for us all.
Help us, today and every day,
whenever we share this meal,
to do so not as a matter of routine,
the observance of a traditional ritual,
but with a sense of wonder and privilege,
recognising what you endured.
what you achieved
and what you promise,
through him.

Hymn

From heaven you came

Reading

John 6:51-58

Meditation of one of the crowd listening to Jesus

This has gone from bad to worse! It's not just weird,
but gross,
grotesque,
for he's talking of giving us his flesh,
of his body being living bread that all must eat.
What does he think we are?
Cannibals!
He's got us not just puzzled but angry,
arguing bitterly over his words.
And can you blame us?
Oh, I've tried to make sense of them,
to see them in a different light,
but what else can he mean?
It seems more than plain.
Even his supporters are struggling with the idea,
some siding openly with his enemies,
and it's no surprise,
for what sane person wouldn't draw the line
at such strange teaching?
It's caused confusion and offence as nothing before.
He's got to be careful, Jesus,
if he doesn't want to meet a sticky end,
for the mood's turning ugly,
many who once followed him starting to feel enough's enough.
And though the Pharisees have backed off so far,
afraid of sparking riots,
if the crowds abandon him, he'll be sunk.
Mark my words,
there'll be no mercy.
Blood will be spilt,
his body broken,
his flesh pierced and torn.
Doesn't he know that?
He must do,
for whatever else, he's no fool,
yet he carries on regardless.
Well, let him talk of giving life to the world if he wants to;
it will end with him giving up his life . . .
and what will he achieve by that?

Silence

Prayer

Lord Jesus Christ,
thank you for willingly being broken to make us whole,
for enduring death to bring us life.
Thank you for seeing our emptiness

and offering food for the soul,
for understanding our hunger deep within
and providing eternal nourishment,
sufficient for all our needs.
Teach us to recognise all you gave,
all you so readily sacrificed,
and to marvel afresh at the extent of your love.
In faith, may we eat of your living bread,
and be truly satisfied.

Hymn

Bread of heaven, on thee we feed

Reading

John 13:21-32

Meditation of the Apostle John

We didn't have a clue,
not the first idea what was going on,
so we looked around in utter confusion.
What could he mean: one of us would betray him?
We were his friends,
devoted and loyal to a man,
or so at least we'd thought,
but it was scary how quickly that assumption changed.
Suddenly we doubted each other,
our expressions a mixture of guilt and accusation,
eyes studiously averted from too long a gaze.
I could tell that some even wondered about me,
and why not,
for clearly our assessment of character
was not as good as we'd liked to think.
Even after Judas got up and went out,
having taken that piece of bread,
we still didn't get it,
assuming instead he'd business to attend to.
But Jesus knew what he was up to,
as he'd no doubt known all along.
What, then, of you and me?
Does he know what we're thinking too,
what's going on deep inside?
I rather think he may do,
and that's disconcerting, to put it mildly,
for there's so much I'd rather keep hidden,
firmly under wraps.
Would he still have time for me if he knew the worst?
Would he still welcome me as a follower
if he saw who I really am?

I'd think twice in his shoes, that's for sure.
But I tell you what,
when Jesus dipped that bread into the dish and gave it to Judas,
there was no anger in his eyes,
no disgust or rejection.
Quite the opposite.
It was as though he cared for him as much as ever,
as though he valued him still as a friend.
Could that be true?
Could Jesus have died not only because of Judas,
but *for* him, as well?

Silence

Prayer

Almighty God,
thank you for the love you have shown in Christ –
a love that sees us as we are,
with all our weaknesses and faults,
and goes on caring;
that knows the worst about us,
coming up against rejection, denial and betrayal,
yet goes on accepting us,
faithful to the last.
Thank you that your grace
is not dependent on anything we might do,
but rests solely with you,
your nature being always to have mercy –
to forgive and restore.
With grateful hearts, we give you our praise.

Hymn

Overwhelmed by love

Reading

John 13:1-17, 31b-35

Meditation of Simon Peter

I nearly refused, you know,
the idea of Jesus washing *my* feet
instead of *me, his*
seeming all wrong,
but when he looked me in the eye,
insisting it be done,
I soon changed my tune.
He was the boss after all,

and if that's what he wanted,
that's what he'd get.
In fact I went further,
suggesting he wash my hands and head as well,
for I yearned to walk his way,
and share in his kingdom –
to be made truly clean.
He laughed then,
saying there was no need.
But would he have said the same later,
after I fled from his side
and denied even knowing him?
Nothing after that, I felt, could wash away the dirt and shame,
but I was wrong,
for through his death on the cross he did exactly that,
bearing the guilt that was mine.
He made me clean –
my feet,
my hands,
my head,
my all –
and if that can be true for such as me,
it's surely so for you.

Silence

Prayer

Lord Jesus Christ,
make us clean, we pray;
wash and make us new.
We are unworthy of your love,
so much in our lives being contrary to what you seek.
We are weak and foolish,
our thoughts impure,
our deeds self-centred.
Forgetful of you, we disobey your commandments,
flout your will
and ignore your guidance.
Have mercy upon us, and, by your grace,
cleanse, redeem, restore.

Hymn

Jesu, Jesu, fill us with your love

Reading

John 12:20-36

Meditation of James

He was in anguish,
wrestling with himself in a way I'd never imagined possible.
Gone was the inner calm we knew so well,
the tranquillity of spirit that we'd come to take as read.
He was trembling,
hurting,
struggling.
We assumed, at first, he was simply scared –
after all, *we* were,
for his enemies were out to get him,
the net closing in.
But there was more to it than that.
He *was* scared, of course,
the thought of what he must go through filling him with dread,
and if there had been an alternative,
some way of avoiding the agony
of body, mind and spirit that lay ahead,
naturally he'd have taken it.
Yet that only made his torment worse,
for he knew also that to be true to himself
and to God
he had to face the future in all its awfulness.
It was his destiny,
the reason he'd come into the world –
to die that we might live –
and what troubled him most was the possibility of failing in that call.
He *could* have done, you know.
He could have walked away,
saved his own skin,
and no one would have blamed him,
least of all me.
But he didn't;
he trusted instead that God would see him through.
The way ahead was hard,
too dreadful to contemplate,
yet he took it,
in fear and trembling accepting the way of the cross.
Never underestimate what it cost him.

Silence

Prayer

Lord Jesus Christ,
too easily we forget what you went through,
what you suffered for our sake.
We focus on your victory over darkness and death,
and overlook the immense price you paid to secure it.

Remind us that your fear was as real as any we experience,
your pain as intense,
your sorrow as overwhelming,
your torment as acute.
Help us always to remember that, for you,
the cross was no charade,
no play-acting with a guaranteed happy ending;
that, rather, it was an awesome act of faith,
the most powerful demonstration of love and courage
that anyone could ever show.
For that great truth,
thank you.

The Eucharist Hymn

An upper room did our Lord prepare

Closing prayer

Lord Jesus Christ,
bruised and broken,
make us whole.
Gracious Christ,
poured out for many,
fill our hearts.
Vulnerable Christ,
trembling in Gethsemane,
strengthen us in time of need.
Crucified Christ,
hanging in agony,
support those who suffer.
Redeemer Christ,
bearing our sins on the cross,
have mercy upon us.
Saviour Christ,
dying to bring us life,
gladly we receive and rejoice.

Nick Fawcett

The Exodus Meal

In this service the various elements in the accounts of the Last Supper are not only read but 'enacted'. If possible the altar/table to be used is set at one side, unadorned. The cloth, the vessels, the lights and the linen are ready to be brought on. As far as possible the area at the front of the church is bare, waiting for the preparations to be made.

A large pottery jug containing warm water, a bowl and a towel should be set to one side.

Ideally there should be a washing of feet, but in some churches it may be felt only possible to enact this part of the evening by washing people's hands. Three to five people will be needed for this, depending on the numbers attending. As well as the president/celebrant someone will be needed to carry the bowl and the jug.

A loaf, not wafers, should be used – ideally it should be unleavened bread. Wine is still in its bottle ready to be 'poured out'. If possible a pottery plate and goblet should be used.

Different people may be used for the readings and the prayers of intercession. The president/celebrant may be the person who also gives the Reflections, or this may be a different person.

All who are to be particularly involved should be well briefed beforehand and given a full explanation of what they are expected to do. All liturgy is drama, but on this occasion the dramatic element is especially obvious and should therefore be properly directed so that it runs smoothly and does not detract from but rather enhances the act of worship.

The following 'Foreword' might be printed at the beginning of the order of service:

The Liturgy of Maundy Thursday brings us close to the events of the night before our Lord's death. It is the night of fellowship and betrayal, a night of humility and humbling, a night of agonising conflict and courageous obedience, a night of brave words and a traitorous kiss. It is a night of such contrasts and such richness that we can only glimpse its meaning, only approach the edges of its tragic darkness and radiant glory.

This service recalls that night of the institution of the Last Supper, and in doing so it seeks more explicitly than is usual at a regular Eucharist to recall that night of Passover. We shall share in preparation and offering. The Christ will serve us and we shall receive his service. We shall join in the meal and in the hymn of departure. We shall spend a short while watching with him and we shall leave with him.

Welcome and opening prayer

Lord, you welcome us to share this meal of celebration with you.
We will come, Lord Jesus.
Lord, you call us to prepare this place and the place in our hearts.
We will obey, Lord Jesus.
Lord, you reveal to us the way of humble service.
We will serve, Lord Jesus.
Lord, you share with us the broken bread and the wine poured out.
We will eat and drink, Lord Jesus.
Lord, you are on your way to crucifixion.
We will follow, Lord Jesus.

Hymn

Let all mortal flesh keep silence

Preparation and Passover

Reading

Luke 22:7-16

Reflection 1 – The table is prepared

We don't have to have an excuse to have a meal together, of course, but it's quite common for a meal to be the way we mark an event – just think of regimental dinners, works dinners or wedding receptions. To understand what is really happening you need to know more than just what is on the menu.

So it is with this meal – this Lord's Supper, this Eucharist, this Mass, and especially on this occasion when we recall the last supper that our Lord had with his friends.

Jesus' friends thought they knew what the meal was all about. They had been brought up to know about it and to look forward to celebrating it on a visit to Jerusalem at the time of the feast. They may well have heard the youngest son ask the head of the house why it was they were sharing this meal, what it all meant. No Jewish family would have been in doubt about the meaning of the meal that Jesus is said to have shared with his friends.

For generations, Jewish people celebrated Passover as a way of recalling their origins as a people of slavery and a people whom God had rescued. At the meal the family would recall the story of how their ancestors had gone to Egypt during a time of famine, how they had become enslaved by the powerful pharaohs and been driven into forced labour to satisfy the desire for grand palaces and mighty tombs. And they would hear of Moses, the boy rescued by Pharaoh's daughter and brought up at the court, and how he had become a spokesman of the Hebrew people in their plight. Through Moses and his brother Aaron God brought plagues upon the Egyptians and then made arrangements for the Israelites to leave Egypt in a great act of rescue – an Exodus.

The Passover meal each year was a time not only for recounting the story of God's wonderful act of rescue but also for showing through the very meal itself something of the meaning of the story. They would break bread to remind them of the crusts that were all an enslaved people had to eat. The bread was unleavened, made without yeast because it was made in a hurry on the night of escape. The sauce that they dipped their crusts into was like the clay from which the bricks were made. And, most important of all, there was the whole lamb whose sprinkled blood had been spread on the lintels of the doors to show that this was a Hebrew home when the angel of death swept through the land of Egypt. Prayers were said and psalms were sung as the people's history and the events of the Exodus were recalled.

This was the meal Jesus and his friends were sharing that evening. They knew that this was the reason for coming together. What Jesus was to show them was a different meaning, one they didn't really grasp at the time – that this was the final Exodus and a new Passover. This was the night of a rescue even greater than that of the Hebrew people from Egypt. Jesus had called them together for the ultimate Exodus meal.

As the table is prepared we also prepare our hearts and minds to discover anew the meaning of this meal – the Lord's Supper, the Last Supper, the Exodus meal.

Psalm

(part of Psalm 103)

(all stand)

During the saying of this psalm the altar/table is brought on and prepared with cloth, lights, etc.

Bless the Lord, O my soul, and all that is within me, bless his holy name.
Bless the Lord, O my soul, and all that is within me, bless his holy name.

The Lord works vindication and justice for all who are oppressed.
He made known his ways to Moses, his acts to the people of Israel.
Bless the Lord, O my soul, and all that is within me, bless his holy name.

The Lord is merciful and gracious, slow to anger and abounding in steadfast love.
He does not deal with us according to our sins,
nor repay us according to our iniquities.
Bless the Lord, O my soul, and all that is within me, bless his holy name.

Let us admit to God the sin which always confronts us.
Lord God, we have sinned against you;
we have done evil in your sight.
We are sorry and repent.
Have mercy on us according to your love.
Wash away our wrongdoing and cleanse us from our sin.
Renew a right spirit within us
and restore to us the joy of your salvation,
through Jesus Christ our Lord.

Almighty God, who forgives all who truly repent,
have mercy upon you.
Through the love of Christ and his life given for you,
may he pardon and renew you,
that strong as goodness you may walk the path of holiness,
now and for ever.

The meal begins

(all sit)

Reading

John 13:1-17

Reflection 2 – The washing

Water in the Exodus story was involved in warning, in rescue and in judgement. Pharaoh, we are told, did not easily give in to Moses' request to let the Hebrews go. They were, after all, a significant workforce, part of the pharaonic economy not only financially but also part of what kept the power and memory of the pharaohs before the people. They were part of the workforce that built the great palaces. Big buildings are statements of wealth, power and status. They always have been. These days it's not individuals so much as corporate businesses that create the biggest, the tallest, the grandest buildings to show how important they are.

Moses had warned Pharaoh that there would be trouble. Pharaoh did not heed the warnings and Egypt suffered a whole series of plagues – flies, locusts, frogs, boils, hail. And to set it all off Moses had struck the water of the Nile with his staff and it had turned to blood. It stank. Pharaoh paid no attention to the warnings.

The water of the Red Sea was a boundary between the fertile delta of Egypt and the desert to the north. Rivers are so often territorial boundaries – between countries, between counties, between villages. There are plenty of examples around Kent; which side of the Medway you are born on, for example, determines whether you are a Kentish man or a Man of Kent. So it was significant for the Hebrew people to get across this stretch of water – it was not only a boundary but also an obstacle. The story of the parting of the water was yet further evidence for the Hebrew people that their exit from Egypt was no mere running away but was rescue by the hand of God.

The parting of the water that had made the Israelites' escape possible was now reversed and the sea became water of judgement upon the Egyptian armies. The Exodus was an act of God's power – rescuing his people from the pagan people. And in time he would lead them to a promised land.

Jesus' act of washing the disciples' feet was more than a piece of domestic hygiene. It was a deeply symbolic act. It was, of course, a sign of humble service. Washing feet was the job of the lowliest servant in the house and, as *Upstairs, Downstairs* on TV decades ago taught us, the hierarchy of servants is every bit as detailed and rigid as the hierarchy of masters and mistresses. Jesus was setting an example to his disciples of the true nature of his kind of leadership – the servant leader, rather than the status leader.

But his words to Peter make it clear that there is something more to this than getting the dust of the day off your feet. Washing is both a judgement upon dirt and uncleanness and a cleansing and renewal of the one washed. The washing Jesus gave is a sign of the forgiveness that he offers. It was a sacramental act –in John's terms, a kind of baptism. The Israelites passed through the waters from the slavery of sin to the freedom of the promised land, the freedom of the kingdom. What we have here is a sign by Jesus that he was the one through whom the promises to Israel were finally being fulfilled – a promise of Exodus, of forgiveness.

It was an Exodus act in an Exodus meal.

During the washing Psalm 51:1-10 will be said together.

Have mercy on me, O God, according to your steadfast love;
according to your abundant mercy blot out my transgressions.
Wash me thoroughly from my iniquity, and cleanse me from my sin.
For I know my transgressions, and my sin is ever before me.

Against you, you alone, have I sinned, and done what is evil in your sight,
so that you are justified in your sentence
and blameless when you pass judgement.

Indeed, I was born guilty,
a sinner when my mother conceived me.
You desire truth in the inward being;
therefore teach me wisdom in my secret heart.

Purge me with hyssop, and I shall be clean;
wash me, and I shall be whiter than snow.
Let me hear joy and gladness;
let the bones that you have crushed rejoice.

Hide your face from my sins,
and blot out all my iniquities.
Create in me a clean heart, O God,
and put a new and right spirit within me.

Glory to the Father, and to the Son, and to the Holy Spirit,
as it was in the beginning, is now, and ever shall be,
world without end.

If necessary music may be played until the washing is completed.

Hymn

Brother, sister, let me serve you

The bread and wine are brought to the table.

Reading

1 Corinthians 11:23, 24

Reflection 3 – The bread

Bread and wine were part of the highly symbolic Passover meal.

The Israelites ate unleavened bread because on the night of the Exodus there was no time to wait for the dough to rise. It was a matter of urgency. This was fast food Hebrew-style because there was no time to be leisurely about it. Crusts of bread were broken as a sign of the small broken pieces of bread that the slaves of Egypt were given – never a whole loaf for oneself. One is reminded of images on television of scraps shared by desperate refugees, of little fistfuls of bread or meal crammed into the hungry mouths of children in the camps of the desperate.

The bread on the table at the Last Supper would have been unleavened, and Jesus would have broken it as was done at every Passover. But in breaking this bread, at this time, in his way and with his words, Jesus did more than repeat the Passover story – he was creating his own new Passover story. For what this broken bread was now to symbolise was not the broken bread of slavery but the broken body of release, of exodus. Although the disciples could not take it in, he was showing them that he would be broken. 'This is my body that is for you.' He would not be broken as a failed victim but as the one through whom God would achieve the final act of exodus for his people – to bring them out of all the slavery of their past wrongs, their times of idolatry and disobedience. In and through Jesus, God would bring about his final act of rescue for Israel and for all.

Prayers of thanksgiving

Father, we give you thanks for this night of fellowship, for the presence of our Lord amongst us and with us. He is the host, the head at our table and he invites us to join him.
Let us bless the Lord. **Thanks be to God.**

Father, we give you thanks for our world, for all its resources and for its beauty. We thank you for bread – for all that sustains us. We thank you for wine – for all that delights us. We remember with sadness the hungry and the unhappy.
Let us bless the Lord. **Thanks be to God.**

Father, we give you thanks for all who serve you in the church and in the community. For those who do the lowly jobs no one else wants to do. For those who are busy when we are at rest.
Let us bless the Lord. **Thanks be to God.**

Father, we give you thanks for freedom, for peace, for good health, and we remember all prisoners, all who suffer because of violence, all who are sick, at home and in hospital.
Let us bless the Lord. **Thanks be to God.**

Hymn

Broken for me
or My God, and is thy table spread

Reading

1 Corinthians 11:25, 26

Reflection 4 – The wine

Four cups of wine were offered and drunk at the Passover. It was the third one, when the meal was over, that Jesus took and reminded the disciples of the promises God had made to the Hebrew slaves that he would rescue them. It was called the cup of blessing, and with it thanks were offered to God for all his blessings. Jesus offered thanks not just for the blessings of the past but for those to be achieved through him on the cross. It was the wine of thanksgiving, Eucharist.

Just as his body would be broken for them, so his blood would be poured out for them. It is the language of sacrifice. The blood of the lamb sprinkled on the doorposts meant life for the Hebrew people when the angel of judgement swept across Egypt. My blood, Jesus told his friends, is God's way through which life will be offered, new life, life that leads us out of the past and into the final promised land of God's kingdom. Jesus shared the cup and told them all to drink of it. It was a cup of fellowship. In sharing it with Christ they would share in the benefits of his death. But they would also share in his life of service and obedience and, if necessary, share his cup of suffering.

Here, as we eat and drink in the context of this account of Christ's self-offering, we share in the new life that his broken body and poured-out blood make possible. We join in fellowship with him and with one another, and we join in a commitment to follow him, whatever the cost.

Prayers of intercession

Father, on this night of meeting with his disciples Jesus was betrayed. We pray for all whose loyalty is being tested and who will tonight be tempted to betray friends, loved ones or themselves. Grant them your strength, and grant us grace when we are tempted to deny you.
Lord, in your mercy, **hear our prayer**.

Father, on this night Jesus prayed that his disciples might be one. We pray for your Church throughout the world and we pray for its unity. We pray for all church leaders, that they may be guided by your Spirit, be true to your teaching and serve your people with wisdom and humility.
Lord, in your mercy, **hear our prayer**.

Father, on this night your Son commanded his disciples to love but suffered rejection himself. We pray for all who feel themselves rejected and unloved and for those who feel that their lives are useless and who are in despair. We pray for those we know who are unwell and who grieve at this time. May we be bearers of love and hope to those around us who look to us for care and support.
Lord, in your mercy, **hear our prayer**.

Father, on this night they came with soldiers bearing arms to arrest your Son. We pray for all victims of injustice, persecution and war. We pray for members of the armed forces who fight on our behalf to maintain peace and justice. We pray for the injured and the maimed, for the terrified and the grieving, for all who work for reconciliation and peace.
Lord, in your mercy, **hear our prayer**.

Lord Jesus, on this night before your crucifixion, we pray for all who will die this night. For those whose lives will end in violence or accident, and for those who will slip peacefully into their final sleep. We pray for those who watch and wait and grieve.
Lord, in your mercy, **hear our prayer**.

**Merciful Father, accept these prayers for the sake of your
Son, our Saviour, Jesus Christ.**

Collect

God our Father, you have invited us to share in the supper which your Son gave to his Church to proclaim his death until he comes again; may he nourish us by his presence and unite us in his love. For his sake we ask this.

The Peace

(all stand)
On the night he was betrayed and arrested Jesus said to his friends:
Peace I leave with you; my peace I give to you.
The peace of the Lord be always with you.
And also with you.

Hymn

Lord Jesus Christ
or A new commandment

A prayer of blessing for the gifts of bread and wine may be said.

Blessed art thou, O Lord of all creation; you bring forth wheat from the earth.
Blessed art thou, O Lord of all creation; you bring forth vines from the earth.
Blessed art thou, O Lord of all creation, for the bread and the wine we share together.

The Eucharistic Prayer

(If desired, an authorised denomination Eucharistic Prayer may be used here.)

The Lord is here.
He is present among us.
He calls us to his table.
We come in his name.

Holy God, Father of us all,
you gave us your Son
and sent him to live among us.
He came in humility,
born of the Virgin.
He taught of your kingdom
and healed the sick.

He lived with integrity
and in obedience died on the cross,
revealing your forgiving love.
We praise his holy name.

On the night before he died
he had supper with his friends.
He took the towel of the servant
and washed their feet.
During the meal he took the bread,
he gave thanks and broke it.
He gave it to the disciples, saying:
Take, eat, this is my body which is given for you;
do this in remembrance of me.
We remember him:
he is the true bread,
the bread of life.

At the end of the meal
he took the cup of wine.
He gave thanks and shared it with his disciples, saying:
Drink this, all of you;
this is my blood of the new covenant,
which is shed for you for the forgiveness of sins;
do this in remembrance of me.
We remember him:
he is the true vine,
the wine of salvation.

We proclaim his death
and we celebrate his rising.
In the power of the Holy Spirit
may this bread and this wine
be for us his body and his blood.
Fill us with your grace,
empower us by the Spirit
and draw us into the glory of your kingdom.
Praise to our God,
the Holy One,
for all that he has done
through the Son
in the power of the Spirit.

Our Father . . .

Jesus is the Lamb of God
who takes away the sins of the world.
Blessed are those who are called to his supper.
Lord, I am not worthy to receive you,
but only say the word and I shall be healed.

All gather round the table/altar to receive the bread and wine or a blessing. After receiving, the people remain standing close to the table/altar.

Prayer

Lord, you are with us in the sacred meal;
you share fellowship with us and call us to follow you.
Nourish us through the gifts of your body and your blood;
they speak of your self-giving love and your death for us.
Grant us the courage and the faith that we may follow you in the way,
taking up our cross and looking for the coming of your kingdom.
In your name we ask this.

The table is cleared. As the hymn is sung the people move back to their seats.

Hymn

Thy way not mine, O Lord
or Go to dark Gethsemane

When they had sung the hymn, they went out to the Mount of Olives.

If there is no vigil the people leave quietly at this point.
*A vigil may follow. Its length will depend on local wishes. The vigil that is set out here is quite brief
but may be extended as appropriate.*
The lights are dimmed. The scene changes from the Upper Room to the Garden of Gethsemane.

The vigil

Reading

Mark 14:32-40
Watch and pray.
The Lord is in distress of soul, torn between his own desires and the will of the Father;
torn between escape and the demands of his own integrity.
We watch and pray.

Silent prayer and reflection.

Reading

Mark 14:41-50

Watch and pray.
The Lord is betrayed with a kiss. With swords and with cudgels they make the arrest. He has
not hidden from them and he does not resist. He is to fulfil his destiny and the work of God's
saving plan foretold in Scripture.
We watch and are afraid.

Silent prayer and reflection.

All of them deserted him and fled.

In silence everyone leaves.

John Cox

The Servant

Hymn

I am the Bread of Life

Introduction

In order for there to be good beginnings there have to be good departings. On his last full day on earth Jesus gives love. He gives it exquisitely. In his tiredness he washes the tired feet of faithful friends. In his generosity he gives bread to his betrayer. In prophetic provision he bequeaths, through shared bread and wine, a sacrament that keeps him always alive to us. In his prayers he places the universal Church in the divine heart. In his anguish in the garden he fights with demons and with doubt, is led away captive to be mocked and tried. He will not sleep tonight. He calls us to watch and pray.
Lord, we will watch with you and pray with you.

Reading

Luke 22:7-13

Reflection

Whoever is faithful in little things will be faithful in large ones, said Jesus (Luke 16:10). He prepared the details of his last supper with care. Simple actions done with thought, without fuss, hit the mark.
Lord, teach us to honour you by doing little things well.

A typical Jewish family would gather once a year for a meal during which the head of the household retold the story of how their forebears had been rescued from oppression as slave workers in Egypt. They passed over a sea inlet that their military pursuers could not pass over, due to a movement of nature that they ascribed to God.

For some, the Passover, and its successor Christian form, is about looking back and remembering. For others it is also an opportunity to celebrate those who are being freed from oppression today. For Jesus, this Passover meal was his opportunity to reset the Jews' one-time deliverance from slavery into the much vaster frame of humanity's all-time deliverance from godlessness. In a stroke of inspired genius he turned the annual Jewish Passover meal into a memorial – his masterpiece – to make him for ever immortal in the hearts of his people.

Hymn

Once, only once, and once for all

Reading

Luke 22:14-20

Reader

Places a loaf of bread and a glass or chalice of wine or red grape juice on a table or altar.

Jesus transformed the Passover meal. He told them that the bread was his body (that is, himself) and the wine was his blood (that is, his life), to be poured out for the forgiveness of many.
You are the Bread of Life in whom our deepest hungers are satisfied.

Among early Christians this became a love feast – an agape meal – a sharing of the love of Christ. It is a commemoration: Jesus' last gestures are re-enacted and remembered. It is a Thanksgiving, a Eucharist. Jesus thanked God for the food and wine. At different stages in the meal the president says: Blessed are you, Lord our God, King of the Universe, who brings bread out of the ground. Blessed are you, King of the Universe, Creator of the fruit of the vine.

Blessed are you, Lord our God, King of the Universe, who brings bread out of the ground. Blessed are you, King of the Universe, Creator of the fruit of the vine.

The Apostle Paul wrote: 'Because there is one loaf of bread, we who are many are one body, for we all partake of the one bread' (1 Corinthians 10:17). The food we receive is the communication of Jesus' very own self to us.

John provides a helpful image: that of Jesus as the vine and us as the branches that grow out of him (John 15:1-11). The same sap, the same life, circulates between Jesus and us. This is what we mean by the words 'Holy Communion'.

Hymn

I am the vine, you are the branches

Banner bearing

Two people walk to the centre carrying appropriate banners or flags.

First banner bearer

'Every time you eat this bread and drink this cup you show forth (proclaim) the Lord's death until he comes' (1 Corinthians 11:26). Many Christians believe that when they gather around the Lord's Table, they are not just having fellowship, or remembering, or thanking; they are also showing forth and proclaiming Christ to the unseen spirit powers and to those present. The Church receives the benefits of Christ's passion, and pleads these benefits on behalf of others.

Second banner bearer

Jesus said, 'I will never eat this meal with you again until it is given its full meaning in the kingdom of God' (Luke 22:16). The kingdom of God stands for justice; love, peace, and solidarity with all people. The Eucharist opens up the vision of the divine rule which has been promised as the final renewal of creation, and is a foretaste of it. In it the Church thanks God for signs of this kingdom such as works of justice, and joyfully anticipates the coming of Christ's kingdom. The Eucharist also points to the full and final completion of the kingdom of God for which our hearts yearn, which Jesus described as a banquet. The scholar Pierre Benoit described Jesus' promise to one of the two criminals crucified alongside him (Luke 23:43) as 'an appointment in paradise'.

Prayer

'This is my body' (Matthew 26:26b). 'If a person does not discern the Lord's body when he eats the bread and drinks the cup, he eats and drinks damnation to himself' (1 Corinthians 11:29). This is the Real Presence of Christ.

Thank you that in this sacrament we touch the Tree of the Cross that pours out immortality on the world like a new river from Paradise. By it all things are made alive. O God of compassion, receive us this day as guests at your supper.

Hymn

Here we sing our great thanksgiving

Sharing Christ's Peace

Reconciled in the Eucharist, the members of Christ's Body are called to be servants of reconciliation among people. As Jesus went out to publicans and sinners and had table fellowship with them, so Christians are called in the Eucharist to be in solidarity with the outcast and to become signs of the love of Christ who lived and sacrificed himself for all, and now gives himself in the Eucharist.

Reading

The reader places a bowl of water and a towel in the centre, kneels and reads the following:
John 13:1-15

Chant

Come to me, come my people *(Gerard Markland)*

Intercessions

Five intercessors kneel beside the reader, one by one, and pray their words:

Intercessor 1: May I wash up for someone as you washed your disciples' feet.

Intercessor 2: May I clean my town as God cleans my heart.

Intercessor 3: May I give you gave bread to Judas.

Intercessor 4: When busyness makes me forget what you have done for me, may I come again to your unforgettable feast.

Intercessor 5: When I forget that you have other sheep, in other lands, whom you call to be one flock around one table, may I pray with you 'May they be one'.
May we be one.

Reading

Mark 14:24-51

Taizé chant

Stay with me, remain here with me

During the singing someone breaks the loaf into small pieces. While still singing, each who wishes takes a piece of broken bread and after the blessing takes it out into the world.

Departing blessing

Broken Bread,
Christ broken for us.
Let us hold on to you
through the darkness of this night.
We make the sign of the cross of Christ.
All make the sign.

Our Christ our Saviour in light, in dark,
in life, in death,
our dear One,
our Eternal Home.

Ray Simpson

SERMON IDEAS

Giving Blood

Then he said, 'This is my blood, the blood of the covenant, shed for many. I tell you the truth, I will not drink of the fruit of the vine again until that day when I drink it new with you in the kingdom of God.' (Mark 14:24, 25)

Do you regularly give blood? Some can't for medical reasons, but if all that's stopping you is a squeamishness about needles, or simply laziness, maybe it's time to think again. I resumed giving some years back, having chickened out of doing so for a considerable time previously, and though I can't say I enjoyed the experience I was keenly aware of the importance of donations. Any possibility of my forgetting to donate was countered by regular bulletins that are sent out to donors, each full of facts, figures and heart-warming stories detailing how blood transfusions can change people's lives – indeed, often meaning the difference between life and death itself. But for my unexpected illness, I would still be donating now.

At the heart of the gospel is the giving of blood in a different sense – the blood shed by Jesus on the cross. It wasn't just a bagful, gently extracted and followed by a refreshing cup of tea; it was his lifeblood, freely offered for the life of the world; a sacrifice involving physical, emotional and spiritual cost. Yet it was gladly surrendered to transform human lives, making the difference not just between life and death but between life and life eternal. Rejoice then, today, in what God, through Christ, has so wonderfully given, for you, for me and for all.

Nick Fawcett

Look Both Ways

During supper, he took bread, and having given thanks he broke it and gave it to them, saying, 'Take this; it is my body.' Then he took a cup, and, giving thanks to God, he handed it to them; and they all drank from it. Then he said, 'This is my blood, the blood of the covenant, shed for many. I tell you the truth, I will not drink of the fruit of the vine again until that day when I drink it new with you in the kingdom of God.' (Mark 14:22-25)

There's a piece of advice we will all have received many times as children: 'Look both ways.' I refer, of course, to learning to cross the road, and to the advice of the Green Cross Code: 'Look right, look left, look right again.'

In a sense, Maundy Thursday invites us to do something very similar, only this time we are called to look not left and right but to the past and the future, and to the difference those make to the present. As Paul reminds us in his letter to the Corinthians, our sharing in the Lord's Supper is to serve as a constant reminder to Christians, calling to mind his suffering and death. Yet it was not all solemnity, for there was also a message of hope; a hint of joy to come in his words, 'I will not drink of the fruit of the vine again until that day when I drink it new with you in the kingdom of God.' Here, then, is a call to look backwards and forwards, to remember and to anticipate. It is a message not just for Maundy Thursday, nor simply for each time we break bread and share wine, but for each day and every moment. We are called to live, here and now, in the light of what God has done and what he promises to do.

Nick Fawcett

ALL–AGE SERVICES

To Love and Serve

Theme
Loving and serving each other

Scripture
John 13:1-17, 31b-35

Resources
- Equipment for foot/hand-washing:
  - two jugs of warm water, one soapy and one clean
  - a large bowl
  - a supply of small hand towels or paper towels
- Music and words
- Two wipe-clean tables for bread-making
- Ingredients for making unleavened bread *(see note)*
  - plain flour
  - water
  - measuring cups
  - mixing bowls
  - baking trays lined with greaseproof paper
  - rolling pins
  - some forks
- A cooker. If your church doesn't have a kitchen, you could use a tabletop mini oven cooker.
- Plates
- A plain cup (such as an earthenware cup or goblet)
- Unleavened bread (some you made earlier)
- The Communion cup
- Communion bread or wafers (unconsecrated)

Leaders
Minimum: 1
- Leader

Optimum: 7
- Leader *(Introduction and Conclusion)*
- Storyteller

- Music Leader
- Explorer
- Activity Leaders x 2
- Prayer Leader

Suggestions for additional music

- Let there be love
- The world is full of smelly feet

Welcome/Activity 1

Anyone involved in leading the service should be ready with water and towels. As people arrive, invite them to have their feet or hands washed. Hold each foot or hand over a large bowl and carefully pour warm soapy water over it, then rinse with clean water and pat dry.

Introduction

Today is Maundy Thursday. 'Maundy' comes from the Latin word for 'commandment' and today we remember when Jesus gave us a new commandment. Many of the original Ten Commandments tell us what not to do, such as do not steal, do not kill and do not tell lies. Jesus' new commandment gave his disciples, and us, something positive to do: love each other. Jesus said, 'Just as I have loved you, you also should love one another. By this everyone will know that you are my disciples, if you have love for one another.'

Jesus practised what he preached by rolling up his sleeves, taking off his disciples' sandals and washing their dusty, smelly feet. This was usually a servant's job, so Jesus' disciples were shocked to see him getting down on his hands and knees, but Jesus explained that he was setting them an example. Loving other people means helping them, serving them, putting yourself out for them.

This morning we've followed Jesus' example: we have washed each other's feet and hands as one small way of loving each other as he loved us. Whenever we remember today's service and recall what it was like to wash someone else's feet, or have our own feet washed, let's think what else we might do to love and serve each other.

Music

Great God, your love has called us here

Storytelling/Activity 2

Invite everyone to gather round the bread-making tables and show them how to mix the dough and press it out onto a baking sheet, then prick it all over. Encourage everyone to make their own small loaves of unleavened bread as you tell the story.

Imagine that you're making this bread in a big hurry. You're living in the slave camp in Egypt and all your relatives are Pharaoh's slaves. Terrible things have happened in Egypt, and last night was the most terrible of all. God's spokesperson, Moses, gave you special instructions about killing and eating a perfect lamb, marking your doorposts with its blood and getting packed and ready for a long journey. During the night, God's angel of death killed all the eldest children in Egypt, but the children in your families were saved. God passed over your houses that were marked with the lamb's blood, so last night was called 'Passover'.

Now Pharaoh has finally agreed to give you your freedom. You've got to go straight away, before he changes his mind. You're going to escape into the desert, and after that, who knows? You've packed up everything you can carry and now you've just got to make some food for the journey. You've got a long way to walk, and who can say when your next meal will be? So you're making this bread without yeast – there's no time for it to rise. Just mix it, flatten it, bake it and go. It's time to escape – time to be free!

Quickly finish making the bread and then have volunteers ready to bake it during the rest of the service. It should only take a few minutes, so more than one batch can be cooked.

Exploring

When Jesus washed his friends' feet, they were about to celebrate Passover together. This was the special meal that reminded them of their ancestors' escape from slavery in Egypt. They ate lamb and unleavened bread, just like the flat loaves we have made today, and there were cups of wine on the table.

Hold up the unleavened bread and the plain cup.

Because it was the last meal Jesus shared with his friends before he died, we call it the Last Supper. It is special because Jesus took the Passover bread and wine and gave them a new meaning. This is what happened:

> The Lord Jesus on the night when he was betrayed took a loaf of bread, and when he had given thanks, he broke it and said, 'This is my body that is for you. Do this in remembrance of me.' In the same way he took the cup also, after supper, saying, 'This cup is the new covenant in my blood. Do this, as often as you drink it, in remembrance of me.'

Jesus knew he was going to die and he used the bread and wine to show what his death would mean for us. His body would be broken and his blood would be spilled on the cross so that we would receive a new promise, or covenant, from God: the promise of forgiveness for all our wrongdoing and the gift of eternal life.

At the Passover meal, the Jews remembered the night God gave them their freedom, when they killed a perfect lamb and were saved by its blood on their doorposts. Jesus used the Passover bread and wine as a sign that he was like the perfect lamb – he was going to die so that God's people might live. God freed his people from slavery in Egypt; Jesus freed us all from sin and death.

Hold up the Communion cup and bread.

Whenever Christians share bread and wine together, we remember the sacrifice Jesus made for our sake.

Music

One whose heart is hard as steel

During the hymn, take the bread out of the oven and put it on plates on the altar, ready for sharing during the prayer.

Prayer action

For our prayers today, we will share this unleavened Passover bread. May it remind us of the love of Christ and the new life he gave us through his death and resurrection.

Pass round the fresh bread and invite everyone to eat a piece.

Living Lord,
may this bread remind us that your body was broken for us,
and your blood was shed for us,
so that we might be freed from sin and death.
We thank you for life and liberty.

Conclusion

Lord Jesus,
you loved your own who were in the world and you loved them to the end.
Help us to follow your example
and love one other in your name.

Note

Ingredients for making unleavened bread (Matzah)

This bread is easy and very quick to make: in fact, according to Jewish tradition, kosher Matzah must take no longer than 18 minutes from the moment the ingredients are mixed to the end of baking. First, preheat your oven to its highest temperature, then:

1. Mix one part water to three parts flour and form a small ball of dough.
2. Roll out the dough very thinly.
3. Put it on a lined baking sheet and prick it all over with a fork.
4. Bake for 2–3 minutes.

Claire Benton-Evans

A Passover Celebration

Blessed are you, Lord God of all creation . . .

The familiar signs and symbols of the Eucharist take on new depths of meaning when we share the uplifting experience of a Maundy Thursday Passover celebration. That Last Supper Jesus ate with his disciples is suddenly seen in the context of God's saving love stretching from creation over the whole course of human history. As Christians we share common roots with our Jewish brothers and sisters, and the festival of Passover is part of our shared faith heritage. So to celebrate the meal like this together is a wonderful opportunity to discover a fresh way of telling the story of God's love, and finding it to be our own story.

The traditional order, or Seder, of this special evening takes place in the home, by candlelight, with family and friends around the table. It tells the profound story of the people's slavery in Egypt and their God rescuing them. The story is told through tastes and textures, prayers, readings and songs, the drinking of four cups of wine or grape juice, the breaking of bread, the eating of specially prepared food, and, through questions asked by the children, about what the meal means. The occasion is full of thanksgiving and praise as we remember God's love and care, but also full of empathy with the suffering of all who are oppressed and in great need. Rather than being simply a festive meal built on memories, the experience brings those saving events right into the present, binding the community together as children of God, reliving their escape in the presence of their Creator and Redeemer.

So both Jews and Christians meet with God in the simple act of sharing a cup of wine and a piece of bread together, full of thankfulness and praise for the One who made us, provides for us, and rescues us. And of course it was during a Seder meal that Jesus spoke of his own life being broken and poured out to save us from the slavery of sin. The bittersweet tastes of the Passover are there too in our Eucharist, as we thank God for saving us, yet know it to be through Jesus' costly suffering. We rejoice in the way we have been set free, yet at the same time hunger for the whole world to know that freedom.

Preparations for Passover

Have a good clearout of the church hall before the meal, paying particular attention to anything which has been sitting there for ages without being used. Traditionally this is the perfect time to distribute things we are no longer using to those who can make use of them!

Set the tables beautifully, with cloths and, if possible, real cutlery, glasses and dishes, rather than disposable ones. Each place setting will also need a finger bowl with water in it. Involve the children in preparing the place names and place mats and arrange the table so that everyone can see the leader's section, which should feel central, rather than separate.

The buffet meal and all the special dishes are arranged in clusters on each stretch of table, so that everyone has access to the same kind of food. Wine and grape juice are placed at regular intervals around the table and one place is left empty.

For each group of six people you will need the following:
- candles and flowers
- a glass of salty water
  sprigs of parsley or another springtime herb
  dish of maror ('bitter herb' of slavery, such as horseradish sauce)
- dish of haroseth ('sweetness of freedom', a mixture of chopped or grated apples, raisins, finely chopped nuts and cinnamon, made into little balls with grape juice or wine and coated with chopped nuts; or you can use dates)
- a basket of matzo (unleavened bread)

At the leader's table you will need the following:
- a candlestick for at least two candles, and some matches
- a glass of salty water
- a beautiful plate containing the springtime herbs, the bitter herb (maror), the sweet stuff (haroseth), a lamb or chicken bone and a hard-boiled egg
- three squares of matzo (unleavened bread) under a napkin

The rest of the food for the buffet can be anything delicious, and it is served with the matzo, the haroseth and vegetables.

The Order of Service

1. The candle lighting

The leader welcomes everyone to the Passover, which is a celebration of the way God rescues his people from slavery. Everyone is asked to keep silence as they get ready to receive God's blessing at this Passover meal.

A short time of silence

The leader lights the candles, saying:

Blessed are you, Lord God of all creation.
Of your goodness we have the gift of light to lighten our darkness.

The light is passed all around the tables until every candle in the room is lit. 'The Lord is my light' (Taizé) may be sung quietly. As this is happening the leader prays:

May the brightness of these small lights
remind us of the great light of your love
which brings us joy and hope.
Blessed be God for ever!

2. We say Grace

We fill our glasses and raise them as we pray:

Blessed are you, Lord God of all creation.
Through your goodness we have this wine to drink,
fruit of the vine and work of human hands.
Blessed be God for ever!

Everyone drinks their wine or grape juice and fills the glass again

3. We wash our hands

As we wash our fingers in the bowl of water we pray:

Blessed are you, Lord God of all creation.
You alone can make us clean.
You alone can make us holy.
Blessed be God for ever!

(At the Last Supper it was not just hands that were washed, but feet as well.)

4. Eating a springtime herb

The leader dips some of the parsley into the salty water, saying:

Blessed are you, Lord God of all creation.
Each springtime, through your goodness,
the earth brings forth plants and fruit,
to renew the world we inhabit.
Blessed be God for ever!

Everyone dips some parsley in salty water and eats it.

5. The bread-sharing

The leader picks up the three pieces of matzo, and puts aside half a piece for unexpected guests, saying:

Blessed are you, Lord God of all creation.
Through your goodness we have this bread to eat
which earth has given and human hands have made.
Let us always share our bread with the hungry.
We remember now all those who are persecuted or poor.
Next year may we and they be free.
Our Passover cannot be complete until all God's people are free.
Blessed be God for ever!

This is the bread of pain and affliction
which our ancestors ate in Egypt,
when they were slaves,
and which our oppressed brothers and sisters eat now.
Take this, all of you, and eat it.

The leader shares the bread with those around, and everyone else shares the bread near them with one another, dipping it in the salty water of tears, remembering the poor and oppressed. The piece of bread put aside is now hidden, for the children to find later on.

Leader Let one of the children open our door to show that we welcome all who are hungry, in body and in spirit.

One of the children opens the door wide.

All Let all who hunger for bread and for freedom, for truth, and for inner peace, come and share the bread which our God provides for us.

6. The story

The children   Why is this night different from all other nights?

Leader   Thank you for asking that question, children. It is always good to ask questions, and find out the answers. That way you will learn the story we share and understand the traditions we value.

                    Tonight is different from all other nights because we are celebrating something amazing. Once our ancestors were slaves of Pharaoh in Egypt, and God rescued our people, bringing us out of slavery into the promise of freedom and redemption. Our terrible suffering was turned into a time of happiness and blessing.

Child   Why do we eat only flat bread without yeast tonight?

Leader   When Pharaoh let the people go they had to escape in a great hurry. They had no time to wait for their bread to rise, so they baked it flat, like the bread we are eating tonight.

Child   Why do we eat bitter herbs tonight?

Leader   The bitter herbs remind us that life was bitter and sad for the people when they were oppressed as slaves in the land of Egypt. When we taste the bitter herbs we taste the bitterness of every person who is sad and oppressed, and longs to be free.

Child   Why do we have the sweet stuff to eat?

Leader   The sweet stuff reminds us of the sweetness of freedom when God brought us out of slavery. It reminds us of the sweetness of God's goodness and love which always triumphs over evil.

Child   Why do we eat parsley?

Leader   We have parsley because it reminds us of all the fresh green plants of springtime which bring fresh new life to the world each year. Our God loves us and looks after us, and that makes us happy.

Child   Why do we dip our parsley and bread in salt water?

Leader   The salt water reminds us of tears which people cry when they are very sad. As we taste the salty water we remember the tears of the people when they were slaves, and the tears of everyone who is not free or at peace with God.

Child   Why is there a lamb bone?

Leader   Because the people ate a lamb that last night in Egypt, just before they were rescued. They put its blood on their doorposts and so they were protected from the plague of death that night. This was the tenth and last plague before Pharaoh agreed to let Moses and the people go. Let us express our compassion for the Egyptians who suffered those plagues. They were our enemies, but still they were children of God and fellow human beings, and we feel sorry for all who suffer – whether they are friends or enemies.

As each plague is mentioned, everyone dips a finger in their wine and drips it on their plate to remember the suffering:

Blood . . . Frogs . . . Vermin . . . Flies . . . Locusts . . . Cattle disease . . . Boils . . . Hailstones . . . Darkness . . . Death of every firstborn.

Child	Why are we taking so much trouble over this meal tonight – with clean cloths and candles and flowers and party food?
Leader	Because thanks to God's loving rescue, we have all been set free from slavery and sin! In spite of all the tears and sadness in our world there is lots and lots to thank God for, and we want to enjoy thanking him as well as we can for all he has done in our lives.

Blessed be God for ever!

Everyone drinks their wine or grape juice, and refills the glass.

Leader	Now we are ready to enjoy the Passover meal!
All	We'll taste the bitterness of pain and oppression and the sweetness of hope and freedom. We'll eat thankfully of all God's gifts and rejoice that we can share this time and this food together in God's company.

7. The meal

The meal is eaten.

8. Hide and seek

After the meal the children can search for the afikomen (the hidden piece of matzo) and the one who finds it is given a reward. This piece of bread is broken and shared out among everyone. The bread is held as the leader says:

This bread is broken and shared to remind us of the Passover lambs which were sacrificed and shared, to give the people strength for their journey ahead and protection from the plague of death.

Everyone eats the fragment of bread.

A song is sung, such as 'Our God is so great, so strong and so mighty', 'You shall go out with joy', 'Give me joy in my heart' or 'Jubilate everybody'.

9. Grace after the meal

Leader   The Bible tells us that when you have eaten and are satisfied you shall thank the Lord our God for the good land which he has given you. We have eaten and are satisfied, so let us thank God now.

Everyone raises their glasses as they pray:

All   O Lord our God, we praise you
and thank you for feeding us all in body and spirit.

Women and girls   We thank you for the good earth and its fruitfulness.

Men and boys: We thank you for the friendship we have shared tonight
and for the loving kindness you shower on us each day.

All   We thank you for freeing us from slavery and sin
through the gift of your forgiveness.
We pray that all God's children may be freed
from hatred and hunger, oppression and guilt,
free to live contentedly in your love.

Everyone drinks their wine or grape juice.

Leader   Let us go in God's peace.
Peace for us and peace for all people in the world.
No more war. No more oppression.
Justice and peace for everyone.
Let it be so. Amen. Let it be so.

Everyone sings 'Shalom, my friends'

For an 8-page downloadable version of the Order of Service and illustrations that accompany the Service, please see the CD-Rom.

Susan Sayers

The Lord's Supper

Equipment:
pack of playing cards
bread and wine/juice
music and lyrics

Select sufficient cards for each member of the group to have one card. Make sure you include either the Queen of Clubs or the Queen of Spades, but not both. Shuffle the cards and distribute one card to each member of the group. The group must not show their card to any other member of the group. The game is simple. The holder of the black queen has to eliminate the other members of the group by winking at them once. The person winked at counts to ten, then places their card in front of them and say 'I'm out'.

They must not identify the person who winked at them. If a member of the group thinks they know who's 'winking' then they are allowed to accuse them. If they are wrong, the accuser is out of the game. The game continues until everyone is 'out' or the eliminator is discovered.

(Allow 10 minutes for this activity)

It's infuriating trying to sort out the innocent and the guilty.

Take a look at 'We do not presume' by Andy Piercy.
or
'Here is bread' by Graham Kendrick.

(Allow approximately 5 minutes for this)

Another meal but this time the mood is sombre.

Read
Luke 22:14-23

The Passover meal was a celebration of the release of the Israelites from slavery in Egypt (see Exodus 12–13). Jesus brought his disciples together to share in his last Passover meal, which the disciples understood was a special meal because everyone in Jerusalem, and many visitors to the city, celebrated the Passover. For Jesus, this meal held more significance than the disciples appreciated.

The relationship between Jesus and the religious authorities had become tense. He had challenged their traditions and thinking and they were worried he was becoming too popular. The disciples were also aware of the tension but they seemed confident that Jesus had everything under control. Jesus did have everything under control, but not in the way the disciples thought.

On the night of the original 'Passover' the angel of death killed every first-born son but passed over the homes where the lintels of the doors had been smeared with the blood of a lamb. Jesus had already been referred to as the 'Lamb of God' (see John 1:29).

During his meal with the disciples, Jesus took the unleavened bread (made without yeast as a reminder of how the Israelites had to escape from Egypt as quickly as possible – there hadn't been any time to wait for the dough to rise). The bread was a symbol, recalling a significant event. Jesus took the bread, broke it and told his disciples that the bread represented his body, to be broken as a sacrifice. Next, Jesus took the wine, another symbol, and drank it. The wine was to act as a reminder of Jesus' blood, which again represented a sacrifice.

The death and sacrifice of Jesus was the only way in which a relationship with God could be restored. The symbols of the bread and the wine are constant reminders that we have continuous access to God because of the sacrifice of Jesus.

Place the bread and the wine/juice on a table in front of the group.

Can the group think of other symbols that remind us of events or special occasions? For example cross, dove, fish. Discuss the importance of symbols.

- Why do we need symbols?
- Would we forget without symbols to remind us?

  (Allow 5 minutes)

Leave the bread and the wine/juice on the table and ask the group to be quiet while you read the following:

Shout praises to the Lord!
He is good to us, and his love never fails.
Everyone the Lord has rescued from trouble
should praise him.
Everyone he has brought from the east and the west,
the north and the south.
Some of you were lost in the scorching desert,
far from a town.
You were hungry and thirsty and about to give up.
You were in serious trouble,
but you prayed to the Lord,
and he rescued you.
Straight away he brought you to a town.
You should praise the Lord for his love
and for the wonderful things he does for all of us.
To everyone who is thirsty, he gives something to drink;
to everyone who is hungry he gives good things to eat.

Psalm 107:1-9

Pete Townsend

The Last Supper

Focus of the service:
The Last Supper. The Passover with new meaning of Bread and Wine. Servanthood and foot-washing. The command to love one another as Jesus loves us.

Mood:
Solemn and important for the whole community. Reflective and thankful. Mystical.

Possibilities for worship:
- Consider a Eucharist in the context of a Passover celebration.
- White and gold cloth, streamers and flags.
- Projected images of foot-washing, bread and wine, wheat and grapes.
- Bread and wine with wheat and grapes in a focal display.
- Foot-washing – with several bowls and towels so everyone can wash one another's feet.
- Set up a 'Garden of Gethsemane' with plants, rocks and water, and hold a prayer vigil through the night.

Susan Sayers

Foot-washing

Resources

- One or two large bowls
- Jugs full of water
- Lots of small towels.

Leader

In Jesus' time, it was a servant's job to wash guests' feet before a meal. Those feet would have been dusty, sweaty and smelly. Jesus amazed his friends by getting down on his knees and washing their feet himself. He did this to show that rather than lord it over each other, we should help and serve other people, as he did. Today we will pray an active prayer that we might learn to serve each other. We will take it in turns to wash each other's feet or hands. As you do so, and as your own feet or hands are washed, pray that God might speak to you through this simple action.

Prayer action

The leader holds the first person's foot or hand over the bowl and pours a little water over it, then dries it. Then the first person washes the second person's foot or hand, and so on. If you have a large congregation, you may need more than one foot-washing station.

Closing words

Foot-washing Lord,
you knelt with wet hands and rolled-up sleeves.
May our washing of feet and hands
be for us a reminder that we should love and serve one another,
in your name.

Claire Benton-Evans

Maundy Thursday

Maundy Thursday is not usually considered as all-age worship territory. There are practical reasons for this, but the rapidly increasing trend towards children being prepared to receive Communion long before they're confirmed has also given rise to the need for ongoing teaching about the sacraments and their significance. Maundy Thursday's worship is centred around thanksgiving for Holy Communion and if children are not able to receive the bread and wine in your church it will be necessary for some other arrangement to be made, or at least an explanation given, so that they don't feel excluded. (Please note that children who are allowed to receive the elements in their own church may receive them anywhere.)

Restrictions invite children to ask 'Why?' and barriers to their understanding will be erected if the reasons given don't satisfy them. Children have many questions about the Eucharist and it's more important to tackle these than dwell on the 'qualifications' for receiving the sacrament. What's the relevance of these events 2000 years ago; why bread and wine; why can only a priest consecrate them; why does he wear vestments (where that's the tradition)? Different traditions will give slightly varying answers to these, but all Christians share the same belief about the significance of the sacraments, which only makes more scandalous the barriers born of past disputes about this.

The material offered here aims to help in the process of increasing awareness and could be used on other occasions when the church is offering thanks and praise for this central part of its worshipping life. Some churches follow the traditions of the foot-washing, the stripping of the altar and the Maundy Watch, all of which are highly visual and can involve children actively – they have a profound effect on most adults, too.

There's also the possibility of preceding this service with a passover meal, or a fellowship supper, to emphasise its context. Although these normally take place in the evening, which would limit the number of young children present, if there's a sufficiently wide age-range the opportunities engendered fully justify adopting an all-age worship approach.

Hymns
Traditional

- And now, O Father, mindful of the love
- An upper room
- At the Lamb's high feast
- My God, and is thy table spread
- Thou, who at thy Eucharist
- We hail thy presence glorious

Contemporary

- A new commandment
- Among us and before us
- Broken for me, broken for you
- Gifts of bread and wine
- Here is bread
- Jesus took a piece of bread

Chant

- Eat this bread

Children's song

- In the upper room

Readings
Years A, B and C :
Exodus 12:1-4 (5-10), 11-14
1 Corinthians 11:23-26
John 13:1-17, 31b-35

Confession
God our Father,
your Son Jesus Christ came,

not to be served but to serve,
and to give his life as a ransom for many.
We are sorry for acting out of self-interest,
and failing to walk his way of sacrifice
and service.
Forgive our selfish attitudes,
and deliver us from narrow prejudice,
that we may follow the example of our Saviour,
and live to your praise and glory.

Absolution

Almighty God,
whose love is everlasting,
have mercy on you,
pardon and deliver you
from your sins and failings,
and give you the humility and strength
to follow the way of the Servant King,
through Christ our Lord.

Prayer

We bring to God our sacrifice
of praise and thanksgiving
and offer our requests to him, saying,
Lord, accept our praise,
and receive our prayers.

We thank you for the gift of creation,
reflecting your nature,
and for making us stewards of its resources.
In gratitude may we treat it wisely
and with care.
Especially we pray . . .
Lord, accept our praise,
and receive our prayers.

We thank you for the gift of your Son Jesus,
who lived as one of us
and gave his life for our sake.
In gratitude may we share his love
with all whom we meet.
Especially we pray . . .
Lord, accept our praise,
and receive our prayers.

We thank you for the gift of forgiveness,
freely available through Jesus' death
on the cross.

In gratitude may we live as those
whose guilt has been taken away
and extend your saving love
to those around us.
Especially we pray . . .
Lord, accept our praise,
and receive our prayers.

We thank you for the gift of new life,
ours because Jesus was raised from death,
victorious over all the forces of evil.
In gratitude may we witness
to the hope of eternal life you set before us.
Especially we pray . . .
Lord, accept our praise,
and receive our prayers.

We thank you for the gift of bread and wine,
the symbols of your complete salvation
and unending love for us.
In gratitude may we remember
your death and resurrection until you return in glory,
and be strengthened to follow and serve you.
Lord, accept our praise,
and receive our prayers,
for the sake of the one whose death
opens the gates of eternal life,
Jesus Christ our Saviour.

All-age address

Begin by asking the congregation what events they would mark by having a special meal. You may find it helpful to write these up on an OHP or flip-chart. Birthdays and Christmas will probably head your list, followed closely by anniversaries, christenings, housewarmings, reunions or notable achievements. Usually we celebrate something that's happened already which we want to remember. Most people enjoy a good party or celebration, but it would be considered very odd if we wanted to make merry on our own! We invite special friends for the occasion, and prepare the sort of food we wouldn't normally eat. If you can find a couple of volunteers (this may be best organised in advance!) they can illustrate the point by sitting at a table, on which you place Christmas crackers, then a wrapped present, followed in turn by a bottle of champagne, an old photograph, party hats and finally a cake (if you don't want to use a real cake, a local bakery may let you borrow a 'dummy' used for sales purposes).

Explain that the Jews always remembered the Passover in a special meal as God had commanded them. It was shared by the whole family, and acted out as a way of making sure no one forgot the most important event in Israel's history. In a way, we do the same – a couple celebrating their anniversary are reliving the day they got married, for example, or when they first met, and entering into the emotions and excitement they felt then.

The evening before his death Jesus celebrated the Passover with his friends, the disciples, and during the meal he drew some obvious parallels between that event and what was about to happen to him. He instructed them to carry on with this way of remembering him after his death, resurrection and ascension, so Christians have done this ever since.

Conclude by saying that Jesus invites all of us to this special meal to celebrate what he's done for us, and because he wants us to experience the reality of it ourselves. As we take the bread and wine, just as Jesus and the disciples did to remember God's great act of releasing them from slavery in Egypt, so we enter into the events of his death and resurrection and they become real to us. We know the bread and wine are symbols of his body and blood, but as we take and eat them we too can experience the presence of Christ, and share more deeply in his risen life.

Stuart Thomas

Sign of Christ's Presence

Aim

To show that Holy Communion is a special meal which speaks powerfully of everything God has done for us in Christ.

Preparation

Print the following on separate strips of card:

Shrove Tuesday	Pancake
Christmas	Christmas pudding
Cream tea	Scone, jam and cream
Good Friday	Hot cross bun
Wedding reception	Wedding cake
Picnic	Cakes and biscuits
Barbecue	Hot dog
Breakfast	Cornflakes
Passover Festival	Bitter herbs
Garden party	Tea and cucumber sandwiches
Birthday party	Jelly and blancmange
McDonald's	Hamburger
Burns' Night	Haggis
Harvest supper	Fruit and vegetables/Bread and wine

Arrange those in the first column down the left-hand side of a display board. With a piece of sticky tack stick the items in the second column around the front of the church where they are visible to all. (If you're feeling adventurous, you might consider offering samples of the items in the right-hand column for volunteers to taste.)

Talk

Explain that around the church you have scattered the names of different types of food, all of which might be eaten in different places and at different kinds of meals. Invite volunteers to come forward and match the foods to the occasions on the board (as above).

These occasions are all different meals in which we might share at different times. Some are for celebrating; some are about remembering the past; some are simply a way of sharing socially. But how about the two things left over, bread and wine – when might we use these? The answer, of course, is the occasion we call Holy Communion, or Eucharist, or the Lord's

Supper. A simple but special meal which is not only a way of sharing together but also a way of remembering and celebrating. And in this week, of all weeks, we remember how that meal started, as Jesus shared his last supper with his disciples.

They had gathered together to share in the traditional Jewish celebration of Passover: a meal and a festival at the heart of the Jewish faith.

This day shall be a day of remembrance for you ... When your children ask you, 'What do you mean by this observance?' you shall say, 'It is the Passover sacrifice to the Lord, for he passed over the houses of the Israelites in Egypt, when he struck down the Egyptians but spared our houses' (Exodus 12:14).

For the Jews this was, and is still, a way of remembering and celebrating all God had done for them, most particularly in delivering them from slavery in Egypt centuries before. It is a meal which unites them as individual families and as a nation, in a common faith.

But there, in a simple upstairs room, and an even simpler meal, Jesus gave this festival a new meaning to his followers. Suddenly it spoke not of what God had done centuries before, but of what he was doing there and then among them. And across the centuries since, this meal of bread and wine has spoken to countless people of what God has done and is still doing in Jesus Christ. It reminds us first that Jesus died for our sakes on the cross:

While they were eating, Jesus took a loaf of bread, and after blessing it he broke it, gave it to his disciples and said, 'Take, eat, this is my body' (Matthew 26:26).

It reminds us also that he rose again and is with us now:

Then they told what had happened, and how Jesus had been made known to them in the breaking of the bread (Luke 24:35).

And it reminds us finally that Jesus will come again to establish his kingdom and rule the earth:

I tell you, I will never again drink of this fruit of the vine until that day when I drink it new with you in my Father's kingdom (Matthew 26:27).

A meal can simply be a time for enjoying food, or for sharing; a time for remembering the past, or for celebrating a special occasion. But this meal, though simpler probably than any, says more than all, for it is a testimony to God's love and a sign of Christ's presence.

Nick Fawcett

Judas

Background

People who betray others are often accused of being a 'Judas', and indeed Judas Iscariot deserves to be remembered as one who betrayed his best friend. But before we all decide that Judas was a bad man through and through we've got to remember that he was also one of those chosen by Jesus to work with him and to be one of the special friends, the disciples. Judas was with Jesus when he healed the sick, and when he spoke words of peace and hope. But for him this was not enough. Perhaps he wanted Jesus to be a warrior, or perhaps he wanted him to be a political leader. Whatever Judas wanted, he wasn't happy with Jesus, and he decided to help the chief priests to find Jesus and have him arrested.

Bible

Then one of the Twelve – the one called Judas Iscariot – went to the chief priests and asked, 'What are you willing to give me if I hand him over to you?' So they counted out for him thirty silver coins. From then on Judas watched for an opportunity to hand him over.

Matthew 26:14-16

The opportunity soon came, and after Jesus had been praying and the disciples resting in a quiet place after their last meal together, Judas brought the soldiers to Jesus and he was arrested. As soon as he had done this Judas realised he had gone badly wrong, and he tried to return the silver coins.

When Judas, who had betrayed him, saw that Jesus was condemned, he was seized with remorse and returned the thirty silver coins to the chief priests and the elders.

Matthew 27:3

But it was too late, and Judas soon realised that he could no longer live with his guilt and betrayal.

Actions and Activities

- Find out a little more about how much the silver coins would have been worth. Judas could have enjoyed a little luxury with the money, but he couldn't buy forgiveness.

- Betrayal is always based on selfishness. Think about how it feels to be betrayed by someone, and how it feels to betray someone else in order to look after yourself.

- Why do you think Judas led the soldiers to Jesus in the quiet of night with no crowds around? Do you think Judas was ashamed of what he was doing? Do you think it was easier for the soldiers to do it in the dark?

- *Guilty Secrets*
  Judas could not live with the guilt of having betrayed Jesus, especially after he realised that Jesus would be put to death. Guilt is a bad thing to carry. Take a piece of paper and write down all the things you feel guilty about and sorry for.

- *What Cost?*
  Ask each person to talk about how much they would have to be paid to betray someone. Sometimes it is hard to fight our natural feelings to protect ourselves!

- See what else you can find out about Judas Iscariot, and what he wanted Jesus to do and be like. What do you think made him change from being a loyal friend to being an enemy?

Pausing and Praying

- Think of all the times when you have been driven by selfishness and greed, as Judas was. Picture in your mind Judas trying to return the coins, and ask God to help you think of others and not yourself.

- Sit quietly and think about how much pain and hurt was caused by Judas' betrayal of Jesus. Think about the other disciples and the crowds who followed Jesus. Remember that acts like that of Judas often have very painful results.

- *Thank you, God, for giving us all we need. Thank you, God, for working your plan out. Thank you, God, for choosing us.*

- Spend some time in prayer, thinking about your wish for money, and whether this Lent you could use it differently, or give some away to do good things and to serve God.

Nick Harding

Jesus on the Edge

(Before you begin, make sure the point is driven home that this story, although sad and rather threatening, worked out wonderfully well in the end. But the children won't actually get to it on this occasion.)

Narrator Jesus was very unhappy. He'd just had his last supper with his disciples, and he knew that he was soon going to die. People who hated him were plotting to get rid of him. He trusted his Father God to work things out, but he knew it was going to be very scary and very painful along the way. His disciples followed as he got up from the table and led them to the Garden of Gethsemane. Thomas was worried.

Thomas Jesus seems very thoughtful tonight, James. I get the feeling something really dreadful's going to happen.

James Oh, I wouldn't worry, Thomas. God'll keep us safe – he's good like that – he won't let any harm come to Jesus.

Thomas Well, I don't know. I trust God of course, but I don't think it's quite as simple as that.

Narrator By now, they'd arrived in the garden. They'd never seen Jesus look so upset – and it was Peter's turn to be worried.

Peter If I didn't know better, I'd say he was frightened.

Jesus Peter, James and John, you come with me. The rest of you, sit here while I go and pray.

Narrator Jesus led his three closest friends a little further on.

Jesus This is a very difficult time for me. Will you watch with me?

Narrator Then Jesus went a little further on his own and lay down on the ground to pray.

Jesus Father, this is awful – isn't there some way I can avoid what's going to happen? Isn't there another way? But it's your will that matters, so I'll go through it if I have to.

Narrator He got up and walked back to his three friends, who had fallen fast asleep.

Jesus Oh, Peter, couldn't you manage to stay awake for just one hour, to pray with me? Come on, stay awake – pray that you don't have to go through what I'm going to. I know you mean well, but you're just not strong enough to hack it.

Narrator As he went way, the disciples looked at one another in bewilderment.

James What was that all about?

John I dunno, but I wish we could just go home – it's scary here.

Narrator   He was right. It was very dark, with the moonlight casting sinister shadows among the trees – but that was nothing compared with the fear that Jesus was feeling as he lay down again to pray to his Father.

Jesus   It's not that I don't trust you, Father, but this is such a terrible thing I'm going to have to bear, and I really wish there was another way. Surely, we can avoid it somehow? Still, it's your will that matters, not mine.

Narrator   When Jesus went back to his friends, they were completely out of it – fast asleep and dead to the world. This time, he didn't wake them but went and prayed again – saying just the same as before. The silence was terrible. Although he prayed harder than ever he had prayed in his life, there seemed to be no answer. Just that awesome silence – not even the rustling of the usual wildlife or the movement of the breeze. Nothing. It was as if all creation was holding its breath to see what Jesus would do. Jesus knew what he had to do. But knowing didn't make it easy. For what seemed like hours he lay there on the ground, praying, but all his words seemed just to vanish into the still, horrible silence of the night. Eventually, he got up and went back to his sleeping friends.

Jesus   Time to wake up. This is it – I've got to do what God sent me to do. Look, they've come to get me.

Narrator   Suddenly, the garden was full of people with swords and sticks, all looking for Jesus. Jesus faced up to them calmly.

Jesus   I'm the one you want. Let my friends go.

Narrator   Peter wanted to make a fight of it, and pulled out a sword; but Jesus stopped him.

Jesus   I've preached love and non-violence all my ministry, and I'm not going to throw all that away just to save my own skin.

Narrator   So Jesus was captured and led away, and his friends turned and ran. Jesus had made his choice. He stayed true to God, and true to his own faith. Even as they nailed him to the cross, he prayed for them and kept on trusting God. When he died, some people thought it was all over – but it wasn't. He'd won the battle – he'd kept faith with God even when everything seemed hopeless. And now, God was going to keep faith with him – soon he would be raised to wonderful new life.

Michael Forster

164

RESOURCES

Introduction to Maundy Thursday

The Gospel accounts of the Last Supper are closely related to the liturgical practice of the early Church in its understanding and celebration of the Lord's Supper. This is true even of John's Gospel where the account of the feeding of the 5000 (John 6:1-14, 25-35) is his equivalent to an inauguration of the Lord's Supper, as can be seen from the language used in verse 11 and in Jesus' description of himself as the true bread that has come down from heaven.

In broadest terms, the Lord's Supper celebrates the redemptive, sacrificial death and resurrection of Jesus; the sacramental nature of the meal whereby the community of the Church is linked in fellowship with its Lord, and the understanding that in some way this meal symbolises and foreshadows the banquet in the kingdom of God. In its language and its symbolism it recalls the Jewish experience of the Exodus and looks forward to the time of fulfilment in the new age of God. It is the new Passover for the new Israel realised through the death of the Lamb of God, making all future paschal sacrifices obsolete. This remains true even though the actual meal is never explicitly said to be the Passover.

Passover is a key theme in helping to convey the evangelists' theological understanding of both the significance of the Last Supper and the meaning of the Passion. It is this rather than precise dates and times that are uppermost in the Gospel writers' minds. Remembering this can help cut through the difficult and frequently debated question of when the Last Supper took place and therefore when Christ was crucified.

Here are just a few of the issues:

- The Synoptic Gospels indicate that the Last Supper was a Passover meal, the paschal lambs having been sacrificed in the Temple earlier that afternoon. John, by contrast, indicates that the meal was the night before the sacrifice of the paschal lambs, which occurred the next day at the time when the true Lamb of God himself was being 'sacrificed' (cf. 1 Corinthians 5:7).

- Mark, followed by Matthew and Luke, causes some confusion by identifying the first day of Unleavened Bread with the time of the sacrifice of the Passover Lamb – i.e. 14th Nissan – when actually it should have been the day after – i.e. 15th Nissan (see Numbers 28:1-17). John says that the supper took place 'before the festival of the Passover'.

- Some of the legal and customary requirements of the Passover provide conflicting evidence. The Passover meal could only be eaten in Jerusalem and at night. It meant that pilgrims wishing to celebrate the Passover with the meal had to go to Jerusalem and make arrangements for a place in which to hold the meal. They then had to stay that night in Jerusalem, which meant that many camped out in bivouacs. For this purpose the boundaries of the city were deemed to extend to the Mount of Olives. As a sign of the freedom that the Passover achieved at the Exodus, the meal was eaten 'reclining' rather than either standing or sitting. Wine, rather than water, was drunk at four different points in the meal. The Hallel Psalms (Psalms 112–118) were sung, and the person presiding at the meal gave a descriptive commentary in which the various elements of the meal – e.g. the bitter herbs, the broken bread, the Passover lamb itself – were explained in terms of the Exodus event.

- Some of these elements can be clearly seen in the Synoptic accounts, supporting the Passover date, while others are missing. There is, for example, no reference to the bitter herbs or the Passover lamb, nor any direct recounting of the Exodus story. That Jesus should have been brought before the Sanhedrin and Pilate, and scourged and crucified on a festival day (the first day of the festival of Unleavened Bread) is considered by many scholars to be extraordinary and can only be accounted for if a series of exceptions was made to various regulations.

Such matters continue to fuel the discussion and, while they remain interesting, there is no clear way of resolving the exact timing. It is more profitable to concentrate on the meaning of the events rather than their precise chronology.

Mark's account of the preparations that were made for the meal recall the way in which the arrangements were made at the start of the week for obtaining the donkey on which Jesus rode into Jerusalem. As on that occasion, Mark says that two disciples were sent to get things ready. Luke identifies them as Peter and John while Matthew simply refers to 'the disciples'. The identification of the man carrying the water jar (rather than the more usual water skin) and the availability of the room have been variously explained in terms either of Jesus' supernatural knowledge or, more mundanely, of his having made prior arrangements. What the Gospels convey is, as has already been noted in the section on Betrayal, that what was happening was not taking Jesus by surprise. He was in control of events, not their hapless victim.

Central to the Synoptic accounts of the Last Supper are Jesus' words as he took, blessed and shared the bread and the wine. He did this not as a prelude to the meal but during it, which might suggest the Passover meal with its various 'courses'. He gave an explanation of what the two elements mean – just as the person presiding at the Passover would do. Two important themes are brought together here:

- With the bread is the notion of a continuing fellowship in which the disciples are given authority to continue the mission of Jesus.

- With the wine is conveyed the sacrificial 'outpouring' in death through which God and humankind are reconciled and the new covenant established. Jesus identified the bread with his body. By his distributing it and the disciples sharing it he promised that he would be with them and that they were 'incorporated into him' – they were 'in Christ', members of his Body. He was not only providing them with a sacramental means by which he would be in 'communion' with them but also thereby giving them the authority to continue his mission to the world during that period between his departure and the coming of the kingdom. Jesus was sharing this meal with the inner group, those who would be the future leaders of the Church. (Luke emphasises this by calling them 'apostles' in Luke 22:14.) The broken nature of the bread, which in the Passover has the symbolic meaning of the bread of slavery, is here the broken bread of freedom and forgiveness achieved through the body of Christ broken on the cross.

  Forgiveness is more strongly associated with the wine where the words 'poured out' focus attention on the notion of sacrifice. So the blood of Christ would be poured out in sacrifice 'for the forgiveness of sins' (Matthew 26:28). As blood inaugurated the Exodus covenant, so blood would inaugurate the new covenant – the new relationship with God made possible through the coming death of Christ. This covenant, this new relationship, that began with the disciples, would spread to the new Israel and ultimately to all people. The fact that the cup was shared strengthens the sense of fellowship among those present and of all who in the future would share the cup.

The combined symbolism of sharing and authorising, of sacrifice and forgiveness, of a new relationship and a new covenant, finds its future fulfilment in the banquet of the kingdom. The scope of association goes back to the Exodus, points to the events of Good Friday and proclaims the future of God's kingdom that the Messiah's death would bring in.

John makes no mention of the bread and wine as part of his account of the Last Supper. But he uniquely includes the account of Jesus' washing of the disciples' feet. For John this is not a Passover meal but the start of the Passion, and he still understands the Passion as a fulfilment of the Exodus Passover. For John, Jesus is most clearly the true Paschal Lamb.

Jesus knew his hour had come and that betrayal and evil were abroad. Just as his coming from the Father was an act of humility (incarnation), so his returning to the Father would be achieved through an act of humility (crucifixion), and to give this symbolic meaning he broke off the meal, disrobed, took a towel and washed his disciples' feet. He did it as an act of service and a demonstration of the nature of the love God shows and the love the disciples were to show. Roles were reversed: the lord was the servant, glory came through service, victory through humility. Jesus laid aside his clothes (his life) and took up the symbol of service (the resurrection). Through this God's glory would shine and he would find glory. Crucifixion for John is not a humiliating and shameful ignominy from which Jesus' true glory would be restored through resurrection. The cross itself is the place of glory.

As happens so often, the disciples (through their spokesman Peter) did not understand what was happening. Peter's outburst here and the response it called forth from Jesus recall the conversation at Caesarea Philippi (Mark 8:27-33). It was through being 'washed' that the disciples would receive forgiveness, be in fellowship with Christ (part of his Body) and share in the glory that comes through humility. There are clear references to baptism here. The way of humility is to be the way of their mission – but it was something that they had to learn, as can be seen by their disputes about who would have the places of eminence (Luke 22:24-7 and Mark 10:35-45).

In this account of the washing of the disciples' feet, John conveys his understanding of the Passion as the sacrificial cost of forgiveness, as the means of incorporation into the Body of Christ, as a demonstration of the way of humility that the disciples (and therefore the Church) must tread in its mission and as the revelation of God's glory and victory.

John Cox

Maundy Thursday

The Thursday of Holy Week takes its name from the Latin opening of Jesus' new commandment, *Mandate novum*: 'I give you a new commandment, that you love one another. Just as I have loved you, you also should love one another' (John 13:34). This commandment was given as Jesus and his disciples celebrated the Passover. This was to be their last meal together and is known as the Last Supper, upon which the Eucharist of the Church is based.

During their Passover meal, Jesus took the Jewish traditions of the cup of wine and the breaking of bread and instilled them with a new meaning. All three Synoptic Gospels record the event:

While they were eating, he took a loaf of bread, and after blessing it he broke it, gave it to them, and said, 'Take; this is my body.' Then he took a cup, and after giving thanks he gave it to them, and all of them drank from it. He said to them, 'This is my blood of the covenant, which is poured out for many (Mark 14:22-4). (See also Matthew 26:26-8 and Luke 22:19-20.)

167

Traditionally, the service on Maundy Thursday begins the three-day period of the Easter Triduum – the Last Supper, the crucifixion and burial, the vigil and the resurrection – ending on Easter evening. The Anglican *Common Worship* book has no blessing at the end of the Thursday evening Eucharist as it sees the worship of these three days as one continuum. The blessing comes at the end of the first Eucharist of Easter.

Often this Eucharist will include a ceremonial foot-washing and stripping of the altars prior to a vigil being kept. Sometimes the vigil is just a short one, and in some churches it goes through until Good Friday morning. Where there is an all-night vigil, often the Blessed Sacrament is reserved on a side altar where the watch is kept until the sacrament is used for Communion the following morning. The vigil commemorates Jesus' agony in the garden of Gethsemane.

David Schofield

Imagine

What must it have been like to have sat with Jesus in the upper room as he broke bread and shared wine, as he prophesied that one of those sitting there would betray him, and as he spoke of his coming death? What must it have been like to see him wrestling with his inner torment in the garden of Gethsemane, betrayed with a kiss and finally taken off before the Sandhedrin?

We know the stories so well that we can read them with barely a flicker of emotion, but if we put ourselves into the shoes of those who lived through these events, we can begin to glimpse something of the pain, the shock and the disbelief they must have faced as the events of that astonishing night unfolded. As we break bread and share wine together this evening, imagine yourself there in that upper room, there in the garden watching with his disciples, there fleeing in haste as the soldiers march him away, and marvel afresh at the selfless love, the astonishing sacrifice, which lies at the centre of it all.

Nick Fawcett

Humility – A Sketch

It seems entirely appropriate that on the day before we remember the death of Jesus, we commemorate his command (in French *mande*) to his disciples to wash each other's feet, following his example. This washing, as they sat in the upper room beginning the Passover meal, was one of those extraordinary moments in Jesus' ministry when he completely overturned accepted custom; dining with tax collectors, talking to a Samaritan woman, touching lepers. Although this foot washing is still repeated in some parts of the Christian world as a symbolic act, we need to find a deeper level of understanding in the picture of the Son of God with a towel round his waist, bending over the dirty feet of his followers.

It was a picture he intended them to fix in their minds to motivate their behaviour long after he had died, risen and ascended. The Last Supper was a remarkable meal and it would seem quite feasible that when it was over the two disciples who had prepared it would be the last to leave.

Bible source:
John 13:1-15

Performance time:

Five minutes with reading

Characters

Reader
Peter
John

Scene setter

The playing area is in darkness while the Reader, spotlit, is on stage. Peter and John are both off Right.

The Reader enters and takes centre stage.

Reader

Jesus washes his disciples' feet.

It was just before the Passover Feast. Jesus knew that the time had come for him to leave this world and go to the Father. Having loved his own who were in the world, he now showed them the full extent of his love.

The evening meal was being served, and the devil had already prompted Judas Iscariot, son of Simon, to betray Jesus. Jesus knew that the Father had put all things under his power, and that he had come from God and was returning to God; so he got up from the meal, took off his outer clothing, and wrapped a towel round his waist. After that, he poured water into a basin and began to wash his disciples' feet, drying them with the towel that was wrapped round him.

He came to Simon Peter, who said to him, 'Lord, are you going to wash my feet?'

Jesus replied, 'You do not realise now what I am doing, but later you will understand.'

'No,' said Peter, 'you shall never wash my feet.' Jesus answered, 'Unless I wash you, you have no part with me.'

'Then, Lord,' Simon Peter replied, 'not just my feet but my hands and my head as well!'

Jesus answered, 'A person who has had a bath needs only to wash his feet; his whole body is clean. And you are clean, though not every one of you.' For he knew who was going to betray him, and that was why he said not every one was clean.

When he had finished washing their feet, he put on his clothes and returned to his place. 'Do you understand what I have done for you?' he asked them. 'You call me "Teacher" and "Lord", and rightly so, for that is what I am. Now that I, your Lord and Teacher, have washed your feet, you also should wash one another's feet. I have set you an example that you should do as I have done for you.' *(John 13:1-15)*

The Reader exits.

The scene lights up. Peter walks on from Right, looking back and waving a hand. John follows him.

Peter   Goodnight.

John   Goodnight – and thank you again.

Peter What an evening! I tell you John, my head is spinning!

John Yes, mine too! So much to take in.

They pause centre stage.

Peter The things he said. The bread – his body, the wine – his blood. I couldn't get my head round that. And all that about his going away and sending someone else to take his place. And saying one of us would betray him. Us, who would go to hell and back for him!

John And what about when he washed our feet, Peter? Extraordinary! A servant's job.

Peter Nothing but a servant's job. That's why I told him he wasn't to wash my feet.

John But he did. He washed the feet of everyone of us. *(ticks off the names on his fingers)* Me, you, James, Andrew, Matthew, Philip, James, Thomas, Bartholomew, Simon, Judas and Judas Iscariot.

Peter *(a thought strikes him)* And do you know what? Not one of us offered to wash his feet. I should have thought of that.

John No, Peter. I don't think he would have wanted that. Do you remember what he said? Something like, 'This is an example for you. Just as I have washed your feet so you should wash one another's.'

Peter *(puzzled)* But that would be a bit complicated, wouldn't it? All of us going round washing each other's feet?

John No, I don't think he meant we should actually wash each other's feet. It's more like one his parables. It has another meaning. He wants us to defer to each other, serve each other, show the humility to others that he showed to us this evening. *(pause; he looks up at the sky)* Time's getting on. We'd better hurry after the others.

Peter *(catches his arm)* Wait just a moment, John. You're the closest to him of all of us. What's going to happen now? What has he said?

John I wish I knew. After those shouts of Hallelujah when he entered the city I thought he would – reveal himself somehow as the chosen one, Messiah. But all this talk of suffering and death – and going away. Is that really going to happen? Or does he mean something else by it?

Peter How can we tell? Remember how furious he was when I suggested such things were not to happen to him?

John Yes. It's as though his future is planned out for him and he won't turn aside from it, no matter what happens.

Peter It's a strange business and no mistake. Here am I, a Galilee fisherman, walking round Jerusalem in the middle of the night, with an old sword (he slaps his left side with his right hand) like some mountain bandit and knowing nothing of what's to come.

(slight pause) Except that Jesus of Nazareth is the Christ, the Son of the living God. And that I intend to stick with him through thick and thin.

John   And so do we all, Peter. Although – I have my doubts about Iscariot.

Peter   Yes, why did he go off that like that, in the middle of the meal?

John   I don't know, but there was something – not quite right about it. I was lying next to Jesus as you know and when he passed Judas the soaked bread it was as though he was committing himself to something from which there was no going back. And when he told him to go – 'do what you have to do', I think he said – there was such a strange look in Judas' eyes; almost of fear, but fear mixed with shame. But whether that was to do with the master or himself or was about something entirely different, I couldn't say.

Peter   Well they were both acting strangely, if you ask me. Perhaps we'll find out more when we see them again. Well, we'd better be going. They'll be at the garden by now. At least we'll be able to have a good rest when we get there. *(begins to move off Left)*

John   *(following him)* Yes, that's something to look forward to. Mind what you're doing with that sword. You could give someone a nasty injury.

They laugh as they exit.

Peter Jackson

Would You Have Washed My Feet? – Simon Peter

He came to Simon Peter, who said to him, 'Lord, are you going to wash my feet?' Jesus answered, 'You do not know now what I am doing, but later you will understand.' Peter said to him, 'You will never wash my feet.' Jesus answered, 'Unless I wash you, you have no share with me.' Simon Peter said to him, 'Lord, not my feet only but also my hands and my head!'

John 13:6-9

Meditation
Would *you* have washed my feet?
I wouldn't have done, in his place,
for they were dirty,
sweaty,
smelly,
so when Jesus came round to me with that bowl and towel,
well, there's no other word for it,
I was mortified!
He was the teacher,
I the pupil;
he the Lord,
me a mere disciple,
so what was he thinking of,

171

demeaning himself like that,
as though I were the master
and he the slave?!
He was right in one thing though:
I *did* understand later, just as he'd said I would.
After they'd whipped him,
struck him,
abused him,
killed him,
everything became clear.
Finally, *finally*, it got through to me:
that the last will be first and the least greatest;
that those who lose their life will find it;
that the humble will be lifted up and the proud brought low.
I needed to learn those values of his kingdom,
so different,
so contrary to our own,
and that night,
as he stooped before me,
was another lesson in love.
He humbled himself,
in life and in death.
a servant to us all.
Will you serve him in turn?

Prayer

In a self-serving world, Lord,
where greed rules,
profit is everything
and looking after number one is the all-consuming creed, teach us your way:
the way of humility, sacrifice and service. Give us the love and courage we need not just to learn of it
but to put it into practice;
to take up our cross and follow you.

Nick Fawcett

Meditation – Peter 1

It was ready for us, just as he'd said it would be,
everything arranged,
everything in its place,
down to the very last detail,
as if our arrival there had been planned long before;
yet – can you believe it? –
still the penny didn't drop!
It was only later –
after we'd shared supper together,

after his enemies had come for him in the garden,
after they'd beaten him, broken him,
nailed him to the cross –
it was only then that the awesome truth suddenly hit us:
he *had* planned it! –
every move, every step, meticulously prepared,
weeks, months, even years beforehand –
and our minds reeled at the enormity of it all.
When we'd walked by his side,
blissfully unaware of anything untoward,
he'd known that death was waiting for him,
lurking greedily around the corner.
When we watched as he healed the sick
and comforted the distressed,
his thoughts all for others rather than himself,
he was aware, nonetheless, of the awful fate in store for him,
the horror, the hurt, the humiliation.
When we'd accompanied him proudly
as he entered Jerusalem,
basking in his reflected glory,
revelling in the adulation,
he'd had one eye already fixed on the days ahead –
on this last meal we would share together,
on the darkness to come in Gethsemane,
on the torture of crucifixion.
Suddenly it all made sense –
how that stranger had been waiting to meet us inside the city,
how we'd only to say 'The teacher asks . . .'
and it was done,
how we were shown upstairs to that little room
without any need for explanation.
He'd realised, all along,
probably from the very beginning,
that this moment would come,
that the path he had chosen
would lead to suffering and death,
yet still he carried on,
undeterred,
undaunted.
And as that truth dawned on me,
a lump came to my throat,
for he'd done it, willingly,
for people like me.
He'd known I would deny him,
that we'd all fail him in our own way,
yet it didn't matter,
still he cared enough to die for us.
He saw us at our worst,
recognising our deepest weaknesses,
yet still he walked the way of the cross,
faithful to the last.

I can't believe it, even now –
that anyone could love us that much –
but it's true,
I saw the proof for myself.
We deserved nothing, as he well knew,
yet he went to the cross
and gave everything.

Nick Fawcett

Meditation – Peter 2

He warned me it would happen,
told me exactly how it would be,
but I just didn't believe him.
If he'd said anyone else I'd have thought otherwise –
I mean you can't trust anyone finally can you,
not even your friends?
And, to be honest, I expected a few of them to cave in
when the pressure was on.
But me, I felt I was different.
It was me after all whom he called to be his first disciple,
me who realised he was the Messiah
when the rest were still groping in the dark,
me he called 'The Rock'.
And I thought I was just that:
unshakeable,
firm,
dependable.
I'm not saying I was better than anyone else,
just that my faith always seemed stronger.
So I told him,
confidently,
proudly,
'Though all else fail you I will not. Lord, I am ready to die for you.'
God, how those words haunt me now,
how stupid they make me feel.
If only I'd kept my mouth shut,
if only I hadn't been so full of myself,
if only I'd had more courage.
We all failed him, all of us in our own way.
They look at me and say, 'He denied him.'
They talk of Judas and say, 'He betrayed him.'
They point at the others and say, 'They abandoned him.'
Well, let them judge if they want to.
Let them imagine they're a cut above the rest;
I've learnt the hard way that I'm not.

Nick Fawcett

Meditation – Judas Iscariot

'Do what you have to do,' he told me.
And I realised then, as he looked at me,
from the expression in his eyes,
that he knew full well what I'd been up to,
and understood precisely what I had planned
for later that evening.
Call me a fool, but I thought until then I'd covered my tracks,
played the part of doting disciple to a tee.
And I was right to a point,
for my fellow apostles fell for it hook, line and sinker.
You should have seen their faces
when Jesus suddenly turned during supper
and solemnly announced that one of us would betray him.
'Who is it, Lord?' they gasped.
'Surely not I?'
But they actually believed it might be –
as much one of them as me.
Not Jesus though –
I realised the moment he looked at me
that there was no pulling the wool over his eyes.
He saw through the charade,
behind the lamb to the wolf,
beneath the dove to the serpent,
and suddenly I was ashamed,
sickened by what I was doing,
disgusted at what I'd become.
I should have stopped it there and then,
confessed everything before them all
and begged for mercy.
But I didn't.
I was too proud,
afraid of losing face,
terrified of what Caiaphas might do to me
if I failed to deliver the goods.
So I slithered out of the room,
leaving the rest of them wide-eyed in disbelief.
It still wasn't too late, even then –
I could have called a halt to the whole business,
and I only wish I had.
But I didn't –
I led the soldiers into the garden,
and greeted Jesus with a kiss –
the last revolting act of a repulsive evening.
It was bad enough betraying a friend,
but what made it worse
was that we'd eaten together such a short time before.
He'd washed my feet,
shared bread and wine,

kept faith with me to the very last,
despite everything.
If he'd cursed me,
accused me,
rebuked me,
it would have made it easier.
If he'd only shown some sign of resentment,
maybe then I could have lived with myself,
knowing he wasn't so perfect after all.
But there was none of that.
A hint of sorrow, perhaps,
but apart from that, only love,
compassion, forgiveness.
He knew what was happening,
yet it made no difference.
He knew I was leading him to his death,
and he carried on regardless.
Why?
You tell me!
I only hope he had more idea what he was doing than I had.

Nick Fawcett

Meditation – One Who Arrested Jesus

To be perfectly honest,
I thought he'd run for it the moment he saw us,
make himself scarce before it was too late.
He must have seen us coming,
heard us at any rate,
what with the noise we made marching into the garden.
He must have known the game was up,
the writing on the wall,
long before that so-called friend of his singled him out.
But he just stood there,
watching,
waiting,
almost as though he wanted it to happen,
as though he was relieved to see us.
Yet it wasn't that simple – not that simple at all.
In fact, even now, years later,
it's still a mystery,
a puzzle I'm constantly trying to unravel.
You see, in some ways he was just a man, that Jesus,
like you or me,
with all the emotions you'd expect to see –
fear,
despair,
hurt.

Yet there was more;
feelings I hadn't expected to see,
emotions that made no sense –
peace,
assurance,
expectation.
He looked at that snake Judas,
and there wasn't hate in his eyes such as I would have felt –
there was love!
He looked at us,
and there wasn't that usual mixture of resentment and contempt –
there was understanding,
forgiveness,
even pity.
And when one of his followers tried to make a fight of it,
whipping out his sword and hacking off one of my men's ears,
he didn't laugh or gloat –
he reached out and healed the fellow,
right before our very eyes.
I wish we could have more like him, I can tell you,
a welcome change from the usual rabble we have to deal with.
To be honest I couldn't make out why we were arresting him;
he seemed harmless enough,
likeable, in fact,
not at all the villain they made him out to be.
But orders are orders –
I was just doing my job, that's all.
And I suppose he must have done something to deserve his fate.
So we marched him away –
off to Caiaphas, off to Herod, off to Pilate,
off to the cross.
He could have run for it, I'm sure of that,
and when I saw what they did to him,
I almost wished he had.
Yet he didn't run,
and I don't think he ever would have,
for looking back it still seems to me,
strange though it may seem,
that it wasn't us in the garden coming for him,
but he who was waiting for us.

Nick Fawcett

The Choice

Bread of God
broken for us,
wine of God
crushed for us;

Grain ground down
to give us food,
grapes destroyed
to give us drink,

each dying
to become
something greater.

Lord, you gave us
the pattern of life
in this bread
and this wine,
the ancient message
that is quickly
forgotten by
every generation;
the law of love
that was laid down
before the foundation
of the world,

that there is
no gaining
without losing,
no joy
without pain,
no singing
without sadness,
no light
without darkness,
no living
without dying.

For without breaking
the bread will be locked
in the grain,
without crushing
the wine will
stay in the grapes,
each of us
must die to
something greater.
Bread of God broken for us,
wine of God crushed for us
you gave us
the
pattern,
you came to show us the way
– but the choice is ours.

Mary Hathaway

Agony in the Garden

Luke 22:29-36; 29:42-43

As you kneel there in the garden
in the coldness of the night,
and you contemplate the terror
of the quenching of the light,

do you think back to that garden –
and I speak now like a child –
to that perfect heaven,
which was your home,
that Paradise undefiled,

and remember how you trembled
with your love for this poor earth,
as you emptied all your self
into that lowly stable birth:

the first step of a journey
through this world of sin and power,
on the path of loving service
which has brought you to this hour?

Do you remember how you left behind
that glorious world of light,
as you kneel there in the garden,
in the coldness of the night?

As you fall in prayer upon the grass
of dark Gethsemane,
are you thinking of that story
of the serpent and the tree?

Just a story known from childhood,
now rewritten in your life –
through the agony of temptation
and the sweat of inner strife.

As you ask if God is willing
to remove the cup of pain,
does the memory of Eden
steel your heart to think again,

and to bow before your calling
as the Father's loving Son,
and to say in calm acceptance:
'Not my will, but yours, be done?'

Lord, we thank you for your courage
and we thank you for your love;
we have failed in our own Eden,
we're not fit for heaven above;

but we dare to claim the mercy
promised to the dying thief
as he cried out, 'Lord, remember me!'
in penitence and grief;

and you answered in your pity,
'Come with me to Paradise';
then submitted to the Father,
as you paid the sinner's price.

Peter Dainty

GOOD FRIDAY

PRAYERS

Before Pilate

O Jesus, Son of God,
who was silent before Pilate,
do not let us wag our tongues
without thinking of what we are to say
and how to say it.   *Nick Fawcett*

Mark 15:21-39

Lord Jesus Christ,
we come today to remember,
to marvel,
to give thanks
and to worship.
We come to recall the agony you endured,
the sorrow, humiliation and despair,
and to celebrate the fact that you bore all this for people like us –
weak, foolish, faithless –
people who repeatedly fail you and betray your awesome love.
Help us to glimpse today, through all we share,
more of what you have done for us,
to appreciate all that it cost you
and to respond with thankful, joyful hearts,
and lives consecrated to your service.
In your name we pray.   *Nick Fawcett*

Intercession

Lord Jesus Christ,
we are reminded today that you were broken for us,
that you gladly endured sorrow, suffering and death
for our sakes.
You identified yourself with humanity,
standing alongside the broken-hearted,
accepting the limitations of life and death.
So now we pray for all who are broken in body, mind or spirit.
Lord, in your mercy,
hear our prayer.

We pray for those who are in pain,
racked by illness and disease,
physically disabled,
maimed or injured through war, terrorism, disaster or accident.
Lord, in your mercy,
hear our prayer.

We pray for those who mourn loved ones
or who face death themselves,
those tormented by fear or anxiety,
the mentally ill or handicapped,
and all who are confused or overwhelmed
by the complexities of daily life.
Lord, in your mercy,
hear our prayer.

We pray for those whose spirit
has been broken in the storms of life –
overwhelmed by sorrow,
overcome by disappointment, crushed by tragedy.
Lord, in your mercy,
hear our prayer.

We pray for those whose faith has been battered
by the harsh realities of this world –
their confidence shaken,
their trust destroyed,
their love grown cold.
Lord, in your mercy,
hear our prayer.

Lord Jesus Christ,
who endured such turmoil of mind in Gethsemane,
whose body was broken on the cross,
who surrendered your spirit to the Father,
reach out now in love and compassion
to all in any such need,
bringing the assurance of your presence,
the comfort of your peace,
and the joy of your love.
Lord, in your mercy,
hear our prayer,
for we ask it in your name.   *Nick Fawcett*

Barriers

Lord Jesus Christ,
your body was broken for us.
You endured the agony of the cross to reconcile us to God,

to break down the barriers that divide us,
to make us one.
Forgive us that we have erected new barriers in place of old,
that divide us from one another,
that separate church from church
and Christian from Christian.
Help us to recognise
that you died not just for some
but for all.
And help us to understand
that nothing which keeps us apart
can be more important
than the truth which binds us together.   *Nick Fawcett*

Matthew 26:36-56

Lord Jesus Christ,
we remember today how you were
betrayed,
abandoned,
denied,
your disciples' commitment evaporating
as the heat was turned on.
We come,
conscious that our faith is likewise flawed and frail,
strong enough when little is asked of us
but vulnerable if put to the test.
Remind us, however, that you went to the cross
knowing our weakness,
ready to die for us despite our faults.
In that knowledge we come now –
humble,
thankful,
joyful.
Receive our praise.   *Nick Fawcett*

To Golgotha

When they had finished their mockery, they stripped off the purple cloak and dressed him in his own clothes. Then they led him out to crucify him.

Mark 15:20

And [he] went out, carrying the cross himself, to the place called The Skull (in Hebrew, 'Golgotha').

John 19:17

I'm glad that they allowed
you to be yourself, Lord,
in the clothes that you chose,
for the path that you chose.
Not someone else's picture of you,
or their idea of what a king should look like,
or their idea of what glory is,
or their narrow idea of love even.

Now we can see you yourself
as you really are.

Paul was right:
we can see the glory of God
in your face ...
tired and worn, bruised and bleeding,
we can see true glory.

And now
as your passion unfolds before us
we can see what is truth:
the truth about God,
the truth about ourselves,
the truth about sin,
and the truth about Love,
your forgiving, healing, redeeming Love.

Blessed Lord,
help us to see and understand.

Ken Taylor

Crucifixion

Coming to a place called Golgotha (which means 'Place of a Skull'), they offered him a drink of wine mixed with gall; but after tasting it he would not drink.

Matthew 27:33-34

When the soldiers had crucified Jesus they took his clothes and, leaving aside the tunic, divided them into four parts, one for each soldier. The tunic was seamless, woven in one piece throughout; so they said to one another, 'We must not tear this; let us toss for it.' Thus the text of scripture came true: 'They shared my garments among them, and casts lots for my clothing.' That is what the soldiers did.

John 19:23-24

Two bandits were crucified with him, one on his right and the other on his left.

Matthew 27:38

Redeeming Lord,
the Cross now dominates our sky.
Such brutality and cruelty are offensive to our eyes,
but we dare not turn away from this
as you come to your throne.

Many can hardly believe what they are seeing;
but the barracking priests are here,
harrowing you till you are dead;
and soldiers, too familiar with this distasteful duty,
are dicing for their 'perks';
and the women who attend so many crucifixions
have brought their sour wine:
but you, my Lord, have none of it
you want a clear head to handle what is coming . . .
and show us how you deal with suffering.

Crucified Lord, you are not high and exalted,
for this low Cross is coarse and crude,
but you are 'lifted up,'
and you are still where we will always find you:
. . . with the outcasts,
. . . in the midst of those who are suffering,
. . . alongside the dying.

At the foot of your Cross
. . . we pray for all who are outcast,
. . . all who are suffering today,
. . . all who are dying now.

And for ourselves at the foot of your Cross we pray.
Help us to hear what you are saying to us.

Ken Taylor

Confession – Broken by Us

Lord Jesus Christ,
we are happy to remember that you were broken for us,
less willing to acknowledge that you were broken by us;
yet that is the inescapable truth.
You took on *our* punishment,
suffered for *our* sin,
paid the price for *our* mistakes,
so that we might receive mercy and discover new life.
For all the ways we continue to break your body,
gracious Saviour, forgive us.

You call us to break bread and share wine
in remembrance of you,
but, though outwardly we obey,
inwardly it is a different story,
our lack of love,
timid witness,
stunted vision
and half-hearted commitment,
each revealing our forgetfulness of your love.
For all the ways we continue to break your body,
gracious Saviour, forgive us.

You call us to live as your people,
a family testifying to your grace
through the love we show for one another
and the unity we share,
but all too often we demonstrate
division,
mistrust,
intolerance,
even hatred.
For all the ways we continue to break your body,
gracious Saviour, forgive us.

You call us to minister in your name,
to express your care for all through word and deed,
but day after day we let you down.
Through the compassion we fail to show,
the love we fail to express
and the justice we fail to fight for;
through the hungry we fail to feed,
the sick we fail to visit
and the needy we fail to clothe;
through the truths we distort,
the hurt we cause
and the selfishness we indulge in,
we inflict more pain upon you,
driving the nails once more through your hands and feet,
hanging you once again upon your cross.
For all the ways we continue to break your body,
gracious Saviour, forgive us.

Lord Jesus Christ, broken for us,
broken by us,
you owe us nothing,
we owe you everything,
for you gave your all to set us free,
and yet still we fail you,
time after time,
day after day.
For all the ways we continue to break your body,
gracious Saviour, forgive us.
Cleanse us, renew us
and restore us
for your name's sake.

Nick Fawcett

Intercession – Broken for All

Lord Jesus Christ,
we remember today that you were broken not only for us,
or even for many,
but for all.

We rejoice that your love isn't for the select few but for everyone –
young and old,
rich and poor,
male and female,
black and white.
So then we pray for our world in all its need.
May your grace bring hope;
may your love bring healing.

We pray for all who feel broken today –
shattered by disappointment, tragedy and bereavement;
overwhelmed by poverty and hunger, disease and deprivation,
crushed by injustice, oppression, imprisonment and violence –
all those who have been broken in body, mind and spirit,
battered by the circumstances and events of life.
May your grace bring hope;
may your love bring healing.

We pray for those who long for wholeness –
delivery from physical pain, sickness and disease,
freedom from fear, anxiety and depression,
an answer to inner emptiness and spiritual longing,
the opportunity to be at peace with you,
their neighbour and themselves.
May your grace bring hope;
may your love bring healing.

Lord Jesus Christ, broken for all,
reach out now to our broken world
and teach us to reach out in turn.
Show us where you would have us serve,
teach us what you would have us do,
and use us to fulfil your purposes.
May your grace bring hope;
may your love bring healing.
To the glory of your name.

Nick Fawcett

Based on a Prayer by St Bridget

O Jesus!
I remember the multitude of wounds
which afflicted you from head to foot,
torn and reddened by the spilling of your precious
blood.

O great and universal pain which you suffered in your
flesh for love of us!
What is there you could have done for us which you
have not done?

May the fruit of your sufferings be renewed in my soul
by the faithful remembrance of your passion
and may your love increase in my heart each day
until I see you in eternity,
you who are the treasury of every real good and joy,
which I beg you to grant me in heaven.

Nick Fawcett

Based on a Prayer by St Catherine of Siena

Precious Blood,
ocean of divine mercy:
flow upon us!
Precious Blood,
most pure offering:
procure us every grace!
Precious Blood,
hope and refuge of sinners:
atone for us!
Precious Blood,
delight of holy souls: draw us!

Nick Fawcett

Immense Love

Help us today, Lord,
to recognise the awfulness of your death,
the awesomeness of your sacrifice;
to remember how nails pierced your hands and feet,
crushing flesh and bone,
the pain too dreadful to contemplate,
never mind the agony afterwards.
For the immense love that could endure all this,
willingly,
gladly,
for such as us,
receive our heartfelt praise.

Nick Fawcett

Matthew 27:32-54

Lord Jesus Christ,
like those who stood at the foot of the cross,
watching as you writhed in agony,
cried out in despair
and breathed your last,
help us today to glimpse the astonishing extent of your love,
the immensity of your sacrifice
and the awful reality of what you suffered.

Help us through that to understand
how much you love us
and how much you were ready to bear
to overcome everything that keeps us from you,
and may that knowledge feed our faith,
deepen our discipleship
and reinforce our resolve to follow you, by your grace,
and in your strength.

Nick Fawcett

Death for Him – Life for Us

Lord Jesus Christ,
forgive us that, living as we do in the light of Easter,
we lose sight sometimes of the darkness of Good Friday.
Remind us today that for those who saw the life slip
from you
as you hung on the cross,
there could be no mistaking the truth,
no escaping the awfulness of the moment.
You endured the pain of betrayal,
the hurt of denial,
the humiliation of mockery
and, finally, the awful isolation of separation from your Father
as you took our sins on your shoulders –
and you did it for such as us.
Lord Jesus,
we marvel at your love;
at the fact that you were willing to go not just part of the way
but the whole way
to redeem the world.
We marvel that you,
in whom is life eternal,
were willing to experience death
so that we might taste that life.
Teach us today to appreciate the wonder of that sacrifice
and to recognise all that it continues to mean in so
many ways.

Nick Fawcett

Faithful to the Last

Lord Jesus Christ,
we marvel again today at your astonishing love:
the way you endured the humiliation of Gethsemane,
the agony of the cross
and the darkness of the tomb,
not because you had to
but because you chose to.

191

We praise you that,
despite the jeers and ridicule you faced,
your concern was always for others rather than yourself,
and thus you freely chose the way of humility,
service
and self-sacrifice:
the lonely path of the cross.
Above all,
we praise you for your faithfulness to the last –
that though you could so easily have stepped down from the cross,
you didn't;
and though you could have saved yourself,
you preferred instead to save the world.
Lord Jesus Christ,
however often we hear it,
still we are amazed by the magnitude of your love
and the awesomeness of your sacrifice.
Receive our praise and accept our worship,
for your name's sake.

Nick Fawcett

The Thief's Words

Lord Jesus Christ, whoever we are,
whatever we have done,
we know it is never too late to respond to your love,
for you are always ready to forgive and forget,
always waiting to pick up the pieces of our lives
and help us start again.
We praise you that this is why you came –
to offer a clean break to everyone who recognises their need;
a new beginning in this life and the life to come –
and, in that assurance,
we come now seeking your help and mercy,
for our sin and weakness is ever before us.
Lord Jesus Christ,
as the thief asked on the cross, so we ask too:
'When you come into your kingdom, remember me.'

Nick Fawcett

The Cross

Speak afresh, Lord, to us and your world,
of the cross of Christ and all it continues to mean;
of how he staggered under its weight
and hung on it finally in agony.
However familiar it may be,
save us from taking it for granted
and forgetting the awesome love of which it speaks.

Nick Fawcett

Remind us, Lord,
that your cross speaks not just of a single day,
but of every day,
changing every moment and everything.
Help us more fully to understand
and celebrate your grace,
so that it may shape our lives,
now, and always.

Nick Fawcett

Lord Jesus Christ,
you suffered so much for our sakes –
pain of mind as well as body:
the pain of waiting for the end,
of mockery and rejection,
of betrayal, denial and misunderstanding,
of flogging and physical blows,
of thorns pressed on to your head
and nails driven into your hands and feet,
of hanging in agony on that cross.
Lord Jesus Christ,
as we celebrate all you have given us,
help us never to forget what it cost you.

Nick Fawcett

Lord Jesus Christ, broken for us,
remind us that the cross was not the end:
that from death came life,
from despair, hope
and from sorrow, joy –
your love bringing new beginnings.
And remind us, above all,
that this same love is still at work, here and now today,
able to take broken people, broken lives,
and make them whole.

Nick Fawcett

Father,
if we as the Church
are truly to be the body of Christ,
then let us stand at the foot of the cross
and learn what it means to love and keep on loving;
to serve and keep on serving.

Nick Fawcett

Terrible Yet Wonderful

Living God,
in so many ways this is the blackest of days
recalling the darkest of moments:
a day on which hearts were broken

and faith tested to the limit,
a day of appalling suffering
and agonising death,
a day when all hell was let loose
and love seemed overwhelmed.
Yet we can call this day 'Good Friday',
for in all of that horror you were there.
In the despair,
pain,
humiliation
and sorrow,
you were supremely at work,
demonstrating the immensity of your love.
Living God,
as we recall those terrible yet wonderful events,
give us new insight into what you did that day,
for us and for all,
through Jesus Christ our Lord.

Nick Fawcett

Hope

If the world is ever to see real hope,
then purify and transform our lives
and stretch out our arms in loving forgiveness,
with no exceptions and no small print,
so that we shine as lights in the darkness.

Nick Fawcett

Eternal Joy

Father,
through the life-giving death of Jesus,
may we turn to you
and know your merciful love;
may we be comforted,
and may we all one day share
with those who have died
the eternal joy of your heaven.

Susan Sayers

Costly Love

As we face up to the costly loving shown by you, our God,
we approach you in humility
and pray to you now
to make us strong
to do your will in all things.
O God, in all the heartaches and joys of human relationships,
may we be governed by selfless love,
and forgiving like you, without limit.

Susan Sayers

True Unity

Lord Jesus,
you taught that your chosen people
can only fulfil their calling
if they become like a seed that dies,
buried in the earth,
in order that many new ones may grow.
We pray that our brothers and sisters in Christ,
Palestinians and people of every race,
may know that they are now at the heart of your purposes
on Earth and in heaven.
Lord Jesus, as you are lifted up on a tree placed in the earth,
the rulers and empires of this world are exposed
for what they are – cheap and short-lived substitutes
for true government.
You become the way for true unity in the human family;
all who are buried, humbled and earthed
become your common ground. So may it be.   *Ray Simpson*

Your Cross

May we carry your cross
in our hearts through this day.
Your cross be in our eyes and in our looking.
Your cross be in our mouths and in our speaking.
Your cross be in our hands and in our working.
Your cross be in our minds and in our thinking.
Lift each of us on to your shoulders
like a shepherd who does not neglect one lost sheep.
Lift us from Earth to heaven.   *Ray Simpson*

Crucified Christ

Crucified Christ,
Son of the Father,
conceived by the Holy Spirit,
born of the Virgin Mary,
we adore you.

Crucified Christ,
bearing contempt,
forgiving your enemies,
remaining always true,
we adore you.

Crucified Christ,
treasure house of wisdom,

champion of justice,
fount of love,
we adore you.

Crucified Christ,
faithful to the end,
gatekeeper of paradise,
eternal friend,
we adore you.

Ray Simpson

The Way of the Cross

Father,
look upon your family,
for whom our Lord Jesus Christ
was willing to undergo betrayal and torture.
Forgive our unfaithfulness.
Cure us of our sins.
Restore our unity.
Strengthen us to walk the way of the cross.
Bring us to the place of resurrection.

Ray Simpson

Lord Jesus Christ,
there are many who suffer,
many who have endured untold agony of body, mind and spirit,
but there are few who do so willingly,
fewer still who would choose that course
as their vocation in life.
Yet you came and walked the way of the cross
with single-minded determination,
and you gave your life freely,
so that one day there will be an end
to all suffering and sorrow,
a time when all will rejoice
in the wonder of your love
and experience the joy of your kingdom.
Until then, Lord, reach out
into our world of darkness,
into every place of need,
and bring the comfort, the strength,
the peace and the hope which you alone can bring.
In your name we ask it.

Nick Fawcett

A Man of Sorrows

Lord Jesus Christ,
you know what it is to feel sorrow,
for you endured some of the deepest hurt
anyone could ever face.

You were betrayed by one of your chosen followers,
denied by another who you counted as the closest of friends,
abandoned by those who had followed you
throughout your ministry,
and yet still you were willing to give everything for them,
even life itself.
For all the ways we add to your sorrow,
Lord, have mercy.

Forgive us that we prolong your grief each day,
betraying our convictions,
denying our faith through the way we live,
abandoning your way and rejecting your love.
We are weak and faithless,
proud, greedy, selfish,
careless in discipleship
and poor in our commitment.
For all the ways we add to your sorrow,
Lord, have mercy.

You brought life to the world,
hope, love and light,
but you endured the heartbreak of seeing it all rejected,
the world turning its back on your grace
and spurning your goodness.
Forgive us that sometimes we do the same,
keeping you at arm's length,
resisting your guidance,
even while we believe we are serving you.
For all the ways we add to your sorrow,
Lord, have mercy.

Lord Jesus Christ,
you endured pain and humiliation,
an inner turmoil beyond words,
and you faced that for *us* as much as anyone.
You were wounded for *our* transgressions,
crushed for *our* iniquities.
You bore the punishment which made us whole,
and by *your* bruises we are healed.
We thank you for the awesomeness of your grace,
and we acknowledge with shame the poverty of our response.
Forgive us our failure to honour you as you deserve,
our inability to love as you have loved us.
For all the ways we add to your sorrow,
Lord, have mercy.

Hear us,
cleanse us
and renew us,
for in your name we pray.   *Nick Fawcett*

The Pain of Christ

Lord Jesus Christ,
on this day we marvel again at the extent of your love,
and especially the pain you were ready to face
so that we might receive life in all its fullness;
a pain that goes far beyond anything
we can ever imagine or understand.
Gracious Lord, for all you willingly endured,
we thank you.

We remember the pain of body
as thorns were twisted into your head,
as the lash tore into your body,
as you staggered under the weight of the cross,
as nails were hammered into your hands and feet,
as you writhed in agony,
waiting for the blissful release of death.
Gracious Lord, for all you willingly endured,
we thank you.

We remember the pain of mind
as you came to terms with the betrayal of Judas,
the denial of Peter,
the faithlessness of your followers,
and the shouts of 'Crucify!'
from those who just days before
had welcomed you as their king.
Gracious Lord, for all you willingly endured,
we thank you.

We remember the pain of spirit
as you bore the sins of the world on your shoulders,
as you experienced that dreadful sense of isolation from God,
as you felt yourself to be abandoned,
left there to face the awfulness of your fate, alone.
Gracious Lord, for all you willingly endured,
we thank you.

Lord Jesus Christ,
we can never begin to grasp what you went through,
nor ever fully appreciate
the scale of the suffering you endured.
But we know that yours was a love greater
than any we can ever show,
and a sacrifice more costly than any we can ever offer.
Gracious Lord, for all you willingly endured,
we thank you.

Open our eyes to the wonder of this day,
and help us to respond in the only way we can –

with heartfelt gratitude,
with joyful praise,
and with loving service,
offered in your name and for your glory.
Gracious Lord, for all you willingly endured,
we thank you.

Nick Fawcett

Make Them Whole

Lord Jesus Christ, broken on the cross,
tortured there in body, mind and soul,
you know what it means to suffer.
So now we pray today for the broken people of our world,
all those who have experienced something of your pain.
Reach out in love, and make them whole.

We pray for the broken in body –
those injured in accidents, those maimed in war,
those disabled by disease.
Reach out in love, and make them whole.

We pray for the broken in mind –
those tormented by fears,
those wrestling with depression,
those who have suffered a mental breakdown.
Reach out in love, and make them whole.

We pray for the broken in spirit –
those whose dreams have been destroyed,
those whose love has been betrayed,
those whose faith has been crushed.
Reach out in love, and make them whole.

Lord Jesus Christ,
you came to make us all whole,
to mend broken lives,
to restore broken people.
Reach out in love, and make them whole,
for in your name we ask it.

Nick Fawcett

Victorious in Defeat

Gracious God,
when you seemed furthest away
you were nearer than you had ever been,
when you seemed at your most weak
you were at your most strong,
when you seemed overwhelmed by hatred

199

you were enfolding all in love,
when you seemed defeated
you were victorious.

Nick Fawcett

No One Is Beyond Your Love

Gracious God,
we come to you on this day
which seemed so full of evil,
yet which we can call 'Good Friday',
and we thank you for the proof it brings us
that no person, no place and no experience
is outside your love or beyond your purpose.
Receive our praise,
accept our thanks;
through Jesus Christ our Lord.

Nick Fawcett

Years A, B and C

All we, like sheep, have gone astray.
We have been rescued, Lord, by the lamb sacrificed for us.
On this day of terrible mystery and darkness,
we look for signs of hope.
We marvel at the pity of your Son for his mother and brother,
at the acceptance of his destiny and the fulfilment of his mission.
We are deeply grateful, Father God, that you enabled Jesus
to go through his ordeal without your intervention
and shared the grief of those around him.
Lord, in your mercy
hear our prayer.

This is a time of challenge for your Church, loving God.
We give thanks that you have graciously steered it through to this day,
despite the twin challenges of the world outside
and quarrels within.
Bring us together at the foot of the cross in common purpose,
so that we may share in the fruits of the salvation
of the resurrection.
Lord, in your mercy
hear our prayer.

Create in the world a yearning for the liberation
that comes out of the suffering of your Son on the cross, redeeming God.
We ask that in hills and valleys, islands and continents,
there can be a true appreciation of the diversity of your creation.
May neighbours seek to know each other
rather than distrust one another.
And may the bonds of peace hold sway over the seeds of conflict.

We ask especially for reconciliation in . . .
Lord, in your mercy
hear our prayer.

In our own community we pray for . . .
Lord, in your mercy
hear our prayer.

Release the sick and suffering from the burden of pain,
we ask, Lord, and bring them hope of recovery.
Give to those who care for them
a touch of the love your Son showed on the cross
and help them in their compassion.
We pray especially for . . .
Lord, in your mercy
hear our prayer.

May those who have died in the hope of Christ
rest in the peace of your presence.
Give to mourners the love of friends
and the support of your Church.
Merciful Father,
accept these prayers
for the sake of your Son,
our Saviour Jesus Christ.

Rupert Bristow

Act of Witness beneath the Cross of Jesus

Loving God,
we gather around this cross in the name of Christ,
thanking you again for its astonishing message,
its power to speak and challenge in so many ways.

We rejoice in the love it represents,
the sacrifice so freely offered on our behalf,
so that we might experience life in all its fullness.

We celebrate the forgiveness it proclaims,
an end to all that has gone before
and a new beginning, the slate wiped clean.

We praise you for the freedom it brings,
liberation from everything that destroys love,
devalues life and denies the future.

May it be a sign of the faith we share,
a simple witness to Christ reaching out into this community,
and a challenge to all to consider his call
and respond to his love.

Loving God,
give us courage to take up our cross in turn,
and to walk the way of Christ.
May our lives speak of him,
even as this cross speaks so clearly of you.
In his name we pray.

Nick Fawcett

Praise – a Man Like Us

Gracious God,
we praise you for the astonishing love we recall today,
the love you showed to all humankind
through your coming, living and dying among us in Christ.
We thank you for being willing to endure so much for our sakes –
to face the mental agony,
the physical torture
and the spiritual torment involved in the cross.
But, above all, we praise you that you did that
through a person as human as we are,
experiencing the same temptations,
torn by the same fears,
sharing the same joys and sorrows,
suffering the same pain.
You became one with us:
may we become one with you.

We thank you for the assurance this brings –
the knowledge that you understand
the trials and tribulations we go through;
the worries, concerns, doubts and problems which confront us each day.
We thank you for the inspiration this brings –
the example in Christ of humanity at its most selfless,
courageous,
compassionate
and loving.
We thank you for the challenge this brings –
the call to follow in his footsteps,
to take up our cross,
to deny ourselves
and to offer our service.
You became one with us:
may we become one with you.

You could have disassociated yourself from our sinfulness,
yet you identified with us fully.
You could have demanded we pay the price for our folly,
but you chose rather to pay it yourself.
You could have lectured us about the importance of love,
but instead you demonstrated what love really means.

You experienced humanity at its worst and revealed it at its best,
opening up a new dimension of life for all who will receive you.
You became one with us:
may we become one with you.

Gracious God,
you became human,
flesh and blood like us.
Accept our praise
and receive our thanksgiving,
through Jesus Christ our Lord.   *Nick Fawcett*

Thanksgiving – a Man Apart

Lord Jesus Christ,
we thank you again today for the wonder of your grace
and the awesomeness of your sacrifice.
Though you were human just as we are,
experiencing the same feelings and sensations as we do,
you were unlike anyone has been before or since,
unparalleled in the extent of your love,
matchless in your selflessness –
truly, a man apart.
For your willingness to give and go on giving,
Lord, we thank you.

You could have served yourself,
secured wealth, influence, personal glory,
anything you cared to name.
You could have saved yourself,
avoided the heartache of Gethsemane,
the agony of the cross,
no power able to hold you.
But you didn't,
resolved instead to stay true to your calling –
truly, a man apart.
For your willingness to give and go on giving,
Lord, we thank you.

You chose to suffer and die
so that we might be set free
from everything that holds us captive.
You freely surrendered all
so that we might inherit life
and enter into the joy of your kingdom.
You made yourself as nothing
so that we might receive everything –
truly, you are a man apart.
For your willingness to give and go on giving,
Lord, we thank you.

203

Lord Jesus Christ,
there is no one like you,
no one to whom you can be compared,
your greatness beyond measure,
your love beyond words.
In you we see human life as it has never been seen elsewhere,
yet we glimpse also what life could and should be for all.
Inspire us through your example,
renew us through your grace,
and refashion us through your Spirit,
so that we may reflect a little of your goodness
and live to your glory.
Come to us now and help us to be a little more like you –
truly, a man apart.
For your willingness to give and go on giving,
Lord, we thank you.

Nick Fawcett

Intercession – a Man for Others

Lord Jesus Christ,
we remember today
how your concern throughout your ministry
was not for yourself but for others –
the vulnerable,
the distressed,
the sick,
the despised;
all those who were marginalised in society –
downtrodden,
oppressed,
rejected.
You came as the man for others:
come again to our world today.

We remember how you had a special place in your heart for the poor,
and so we pray for the millions suffering still
under the yoke of poverty
with all the attendant misery that involves –
victims of failed harvests,
natural disasters and civil wars,
crying to us for help,
begging for food to stave their hunger,
homes to house their children,
resources to build a better future,
an opportunity to start again
free from the shackles of debt.
You came as the man for others:
come again to our world today.

We remember how you suffered at the hands of others,
and so we pray for all who endure violence and cruelty,
all who are wounded in body, mind and spirit
by acts of inhumanity.
We pray for victims of racism and discrimination,
of verbal and physical bullying,
of assault and abuse,
intimidation and torture,
terrorism and war.
You came as the man for others:
come again to our world today.

Lord Jesus Christ,
you lived for others,
you died for others
and you rose for all.
Help us to live in turn as your people,
seeking to serve rather than be served,
to give rather than to receive.
Teach us to reach out in love
and so to make real your compassion
and represent your body here on earth.
You came as the man for others:
come again to our world today.
We ask it in your name.

Nick Fawcett

It Is Accomplished

A jar stood there full of sour wine; so they soaked a sponge with the wine, fixed it on hyssop, and held it up to his lips. Having received the wine, he said, 'It is accomplished!'

John 19:29-30

Love is so vulnerable and precarious
that it was always possible that Love would fail;
but you, dear Lord, have not stopped loving . . .
and your great city of victory echoes against the darkened sky.

Your work is done.
It is accomplished!

O Saviour of the world,
what you have done for us is wonderful and true.

You have achieved

victory,
and Love is proved supreme;

a perfect sacrifice,
the self-offering of the Suffering Servant;

true revelation,
and the only Son has made plain
the Father's heart of love;

atonement,
for the Temple veil is sundered
and we have clear access to the Father;

reconciliation,
and we may now be reconciled to God;

and a new covenant,
so that now God can work in our lives.

You have accomplished more than we can understand!
Liberating Lord, this is breathtaking.
We stand in awe and wonder – and adore you.

Ken Taylor

true revelation,
and the only Son has made plain
the Father's heart of love;

SERVICES

Good Friday

Introduction

From 'Hosanna!' to 'Crucify!' From 'the King of Israel!' to 'We have no king but Caesar!' There, in miniature, is not just the backdrop to Good Friday but the rationale behind the cross, the reason Jesus had to suffer and die. For in that stark about-turn, that abrupt shift from welcome to rejection, we see the human condition writ large. The shouts of praise as Jesus entered Jerusalem had been real enough, but they had rested on a misunderstanding of who Jesus was and what he came to do. Even the disciples, when the moment came, were found wanting, failing to grasp the truth. 'He was in the world, and the world came into being through him; yet the world did not know him. He came to what was his own, and his own people did not accept him. But to all who received him, who believed in his name, he gave power to become children of God, who were born, not of blood or of the will of the flesh or of the will of man, but of God' (John 1:10-13). That's why Jesus went to the cross: to do what we could never do alone, to make possible what we could never deserve. Today, as we reflect again on the immensity of his love and extent of his sacrifice, let us marvel afresh at the debt we owe and the gift we have received through him.

Opening prayer

Loving God,
we come to worship,
to rejoice,
to give thanks –
to remember that,
in Christ,
you endured the darkness of sorrow,
suffering and death in order to bring us light.
We come seeking pardon and new beginnings,
not because we have any claim on your blessing,
but trusting solely in your grace,
in your love which,
while we were yet sinners,
freely gave all.
Weak,
foolish,
unworthy though we may be, take what we are
and direct what we shall become,
through Jesus Christ our Lord.

Hymn

Who can sound the depths of sorrow

Reading
John 18:33-37

Meditation of Pontius Pilate

He was putting words into my mouth, and must have known it,
for I'd offered a question,
not a statement.
It was *him* claiming to be a king, or so his enemies said,
and, much as I wanted to,
I couldn't just ignore it,
for any talk like that,
from the Jews especially,
spelt trouble.
They'd rebelled before, remember,
and felt the full weight of our displeasure as a result,
so the last thing any of us wanted
was some misguided pretender
stirring up a hornets' nest once more.
Yet the strange thing is, he wasn't pretending,
of that I'm sure.
He knew, quite clearly, both who he was and what he was doing,
there being an unnerving assurance about him,
an inner integrity,
that nothing could shake.
Believe me, I tried to break him,
but it couldn't be done,
for he bore whatever we threw at him with quiet dignity,
even that crown of thorns pressed on to his head –
almost as if he were *glad* to wear it,
as if such suffering said it all.
I was baffled by the man,
troubled,
for though I held his fate in my hands,
he seemed to think otherwise –
seriously imagining that, beaten and broken,
he could yet be Lord of all.
I should have discounted the idea, I know that,
but I couldn't,
for such was his extraordinary demeanour
that part of me feared he was right.
He'd got under my skin,
so I vainly attempted to offer him life,
but he chose death instead,
as though somehow that could offer more.
Ridiculous, isn't it,
for what kind of king takes his throne through a cross?
Yet strangely,
disturbingly,
though *I* put the question,
I couldn't help feeling it was *he* who asked it.

Silence

Prayer

Lord Jesus Christ,
teach us the way of your kingdom,
so that we may understand what it means to honour you.
Teach us that you reign on high,
not because you seized a crown,
but because you endured a cross;
not because you considered
equality with God something to be grasped,
but because you emptied yourself,
taking the form of a servant,
and humbling yourself to the point of death.
Help us to recognise that your kingship
runs contrary to the way of the world,
turning so many of our values and expectations upside down,
your rule being through consent rather than coercion,
lovingly offered rather than forced upon us.
Saviour Christ,
King of kings and Lord of lords, we address you as such –
help us to mean it.

Hymn

O dearest Lord, thy sacred head

Reading

John 18:1–19:42

Meditation of Pontius Pilate

I tried to save him, give me that.
Okay, so I caved in eventually,
but wouldn't you have done the same in my shoes?
I'm answerable to Caesar, remember,
and if he thought, even for a moment, that I'd let him down,
sanctioned what might be construed as treason,
then it would have been me facing death,
never mind Jesus.
Not that he was guilty –
any fool could see through that –
but for some reason his accusers despised him,
refusing to back down until he was sealed in a tomb.
I did everything I could to change their minds –
offered to release him,
tried to compromise,

gave chance after chance for them to think again –
but they wouldn't listen,
and neither would *he*!
In all honesty, what could I do?
Yet, despite my efforts, I still feel bad,
not just because he was so clearly innocent,
but because there was something about him
that shook my confidence,
leaving *me*, the most powerful man in Jerusalem,
feeling powerless,
as though I – the one hearing his case – was being tried.
I should have made a stand,
set him free and faced the consequences,
for in failing to be *for* him,
I was *against*.
I realise now that you can't wash your hands of some decisions,
however much you try.
You must choose between good and evil,
right and wrong –
for taking no decision is a decision in itself.
He offered forgiveness, so they tell me, as he hung from his cross.
Can you believe that!
Well I hope he includes me in that pardon,
for though I pretend otherwise,
I've no excuse for what I did,
and for what I failed to do.
Jesus, if it's not too late,
believe me, I'm sorry.

Silence

Lord Jesus Christ,
we mean to stay true to you,
to stand up for what we believe,
but time and again, when put to the test,
we sit on the fence,
reluctant to commit ourselves,
afraid of the consequences.
We come up with excuses to justify our actions,
with reasons for what we do and fail to do,
but the reality is we put self first and you second,
our own interests before those of your kingdom.
Forgive us,
and give us deeper faith,
greater courage,
truer commitment.
Have mercy,
for we are truly sorry.

Hymn

O sacred head, surrounded

Reading

Luke 2:33-35; John 19:25-27

Meditation of Mary, the mother of Jesus

We'd done our best for him,
packing straw into the manger
to make it as soft and safe as possible.
But if I thought I could protect Jesus from danger,
such confidence was swiftly to be questioned,
those words of Simeon's about a sword piercing my soul
sending a chill up my spine.
And, as if to reinforce the threat,
soon afterwards we had to rush off to Egypt,
in fear for our lives from Herod.
Afterwards though, I dared to dream again,
for we enjoyed years of happiness together in Nazareth,
just another family quietly going about our business.
I still worried of course –
mums always do, don't they? –
but it was only after he began preaching and teaching,
healing the sick,
restoring the broken,
proclaiming the kingdom of God,
that my fears resurfaced.
Many followed him,
loving Jesus just as I did,
but inevitably he ruffled feathers,
plenty not liking what they heard.
He challenged so much they held dear,
not just questioning the status quo
but threatening to sweep it away altogether.
No surprise, then,
that the scribes and Pharisees resolved to silence him,
and eventually seized their chance.
I watched bereft as they nailed him to that cross;
blood seeping from his head, his hands and his feet.
And as he hung there,
convulsed by the pain,
I shared his agony,
my heart broken as only a mother's can be.
I wanted to reach out to hold, protect and comfort.
And when he finally spoke,
entrusting me into the care of his most trusted friend,
I realised he wanted to do precisely the same for me.
I held a special place in his heart,

understandably,
but I'm not the only one.
You do, too,
every one of you.
In the awfulness of his suffering, his concern was still to love –
to bring healing through his brokenness, life through his death.
I'd done my best for him;
now he was doing *his* best,
not just for me, but for all.

Silence

Prayer

Lord Jesus Christ,
thank you that though we deserve it so little
you love us so much;
that you value each of us infinitely,
enough to die for.
Thank you for staying true to your chosen path,
despite the hostility you faced,
the misunderstanding you endured,
the pain you suffered
and the darkness you confronted.
In the ugliness that scars the beauty of this world,
the shadow of evil, hatred and death,
teach us that your light shines through
and your love will triumph,
life, now and for all eternity,
being held safely in your hands.

Hymn

Mary, blessed grieving mother

Reading

Matthew 27:57-66

Meditation of the chief priest

It's sorted at last, thank God!
That Jesus fellow silenced for good.
Heaven knows what might have happened had we failed to act,
there would have been hell to pay, mark my words.
You should have seen the crowds that followed him,
heard the things they said.
The Messiah, they shouted,

the son of David,
the one sent to set us free.
We've had enough pretenders already, thank you very much,
and look where they got us:
hopes raised only to be dashed,
followed by brutal and bloody reprisals.
So, you see, we had to stop him,
and we did,
though that weasel Pilate made things harder than they needed to be.
At least he's come up with what we need now –
a guard of soldiers to watch the tomb –
for he knows as well as any
that we can't afford the body to go missing
and his followers spinning some cock-and-bull yarn
about him being alive after all.
No, he's dead alright –
we stayed to the end to make sure of that –
and his body was cold when we sealed it in the tomb.
There's a boulder against it now,
and it would take an army to shift it,
so even his most devoted followers
will have to accept that it's over,
finished,
time to go home.
Jesus is staying put, right where he is,
unless, of course, he can defeat death itself,
and somehow I don't think *that's* likely.
Do you?

Silence

Prayer

Sovereign God,
thank you that when evil had done its worst,
when darkness seemed victorious and death to hold sway,
you were supremely at work.
Thank you that though hatred
appeared to have crushed love
and truth to have been destroyed by falsehood,
even and especially there you were working out your purpose.
Thank you that every effort to thwart your will was futile;
that nothing and no one could conceal the triumph
you won for us in Christ.
Whatever we face,
in life or in death,
teach us that nothing
will ever separate us from your love in him.

Hymn
Come and see

Closing prayer
Lord Jesus Christ,
you were acquainted with grief –
help us to weep over what destroys and denies life.
You were silent before your accusers –
help us to speak for you.
You faced up to darkness –
help us to shed your light.
You took on the forces of evil –
help us to work for good.
You wiped the slate clean –
help us to start again.
You gave your all –
help us to give something back.
You *died* for us –
help us to *live* for you.

Nick Fawcett

The Victim

Preparations
- Place a cross-shaped tree or a cross made of rough branches or wood in a focal position.
- Have plainsong music of the Lamentations of Jeremiah ready to play. For example, Palestrina, *Lamentations of Jeremiah*, I–III.

Introduction
O blackest Friday! The sun hides its light! The earth quakes! Creation weeps! Our Lord and our God, may we alone not remain unmoved.

Today we journey with Jesus into the valley of the shadow of death.

Hymn
The heavenly Word, proceeding forth

Reading
Psalm 22:1-31

Reflection
In the early hours of this morning they brought Jesus to the Jewish High Priest, Caiaphas, who struck him and told his doubters that one man must die on behalf of the nation, to satisfy the Roman authorities who feared a Jewish uprising. The Council pronounce him

guilty and mistreat him. Peter, distraught, wanders around not far away. When asked if he is an associate of Jesus, he denies three times that he knows him. Judas commits suicide. Jesus is taken before the Roman governor, Pilate. Finding no fault in him, Pilate shunts Jesus back to the Jewish king, Herod. He, fearful, prevaricating, insists that this must be a matter for Pilate and sends him back. Jesus is whipped and mocked by Roman soldiers. After attempts to nominate him for a people's pardon fail, Pilate consents to his death. Jesus, with two others also condemned to the same fate of being nailed to two cross beams of wood (sometimes described as a tree), dies slowly of asphyxiation. Pilate has had a placard placed above his head in three languages which says 'The King of the Jews'. Jesus hangs there for six hours; in current terminology, it is between 9.00am and 3.00pm.

During these agonising six hours seven short sentences are wrung from Jesus' lips:

On-screen, display pictures of the crucifixion.

Voice   Father, forgive them, for they know not what they do. *Luke 23:34*

Reflector   He prays for the soldiers who drive nails through his wrists and ankles.

Voice   My God, my God, why have you forsaken me? *Matthew 27:46*

Reflector   He cries as he enters the dark night of the soul, as he falls into the abyss between fallen, rebellious, blinded humanity – a humanity he has assumed – and God whom he eternally is. Physical torment takes its toll. He suddenly discovers that he cannot hear the still, small voice; he has lost his two-way communication within God. His lifeline is not working. He must face the narrow gate of death alone.

Voice   He said to his mother, 'Here is your son!' Then he said to the disciple, 'Behold your mother!' *John 19:26, 27*

Reflector   He is not quite alone. He looks down. Which hurts worse: the pain of being crucified, or the pain of a mother watching her son be crucified, or the pain of a young man whose beloved teacher hangs bleeding before his eyes? He understands their pain in the midst of his own, and tells them to care for each other.

Voice   I thirst! *John 19:28*

Reflector   Time passes slowly. His spring of living water runs dry. He reaches the end of his strength. He is desperately thirsty. Even in his direst need they won't give him so much as a drink of water. Every addict in the world knows how easy it is to satisfy a craving by saying yes to something that will dull you, distort you, demean you. How hard it is to say no. Jesus said no. He never became an addict of people's expectations, not even at death's door.

Voice   Truly, I say to you, today you will be with me in Paradise. *Luke 23:43*

Reflector   A dying thief says, 'Jesus, remember me when you come into your kingdom.' Jesus ignores the cynics standing by – he reassures the thief.

Voice   It is finished. *John 19:30*

Reflector   That's one word in the Greek record. *Tetelestai!* Accomplished! He has rejected temptation and cared for those around him. His duty on earth is complete. He has shown the way God wants us to live. He has bridged the gap. He has won the battle. He has demonstrated the fact that faith and hope and love cannot be destroyed by anything humans can do.

Voice   Father, into your hands I commit my spirit. *Luke 23:46*

Reflector   Like a trusting child, he turns to the Father and takes the next step. He has gone with the divine, sacrificial, cosmic flow of history.
And the earth quaked, and the sun eclipsed.
All creation wept.
And we? Let us mourn with him awhile.

Silence

Music

Pie Jesu *(Andrew Lloyd Webber)*

Hymn

O sacred head, surrounded

Reflection

We have listened to Jesus' seven last sayings from the cross as recorded by the four Gospel writers. He said that if he was lifted up on the cross he would draw all peoples to himself. He still speaks across the shores of time. Let him speak to us in these imagined reproaches of the eternal Son of God who, although not yet revealed as Jesus, had been present to his people long before, as in the Israelites' time in the wilderness (1 Corinthians 10:4b) to the people of the world.

My people, I made you in my likeness,
yet you have marred my image,
degraded body and soul.
I made my children of one blood
to live in families rejoicing in one another,
but you have embittered the races
and divided the peoples.
My people, what wrong have I done to you?
What good have I not done for you? Answer me.

All sing the following refrain to the tune 'Glory be to Jesus' by Friedrich Filitz.
Lord, have mercy on us,
cleanse us from our sins.
Lord, have mercy on us,
turn our hearts again.

I freed you from slavery,
yet you handed me over to death and jeered at me.
I opened the sea before you,
yet you opened my side with a spear!
I fed you in the desert,
guided you with cloud by day and night,
yet you led me to Pilate!
I struck down rulers who would have harmed you,
yet you struck me with a reed.
My people, what wrong have I done to you?
What good have I not done for you?
Answer me.

Refrain

I gave you from the rock living waters of salvation:
you gave me bitter drink and quenched my thirst with vinegar!
I put the sceptre into your hand and made you a royal people:
you crowned me with the crown of thorns!
I made you great by my boundless power:
you hanged me on the gallows of the cross!
My people, what wrong have I done to you?
What good have I not done for you? Answer me.

Refrain

I have come to you in this your land,
yet you have betrayed my sacrifice and spurned my love.
I am your Creator, I have entrusted the land to you,
yet you have violated its laws and misused my creatures.
I entrusted the world to you,
yet you have polluted its air and created the means to destroy it.
My people, what wrong have I done to you?
What good have I not done to you?
Answer me.

Refrain

Intercessions

O King of the Friday,
whose limbs were stretched on the cross,
O Lord who did suffer
the bruises,
the wounds,
the loss.
We stretch ourselves
beneath the shield of your might;
some fruit from the tree of your passion fall on us this night!   *Ancient Irish Prayer; anon*

217

Jesus forsaken,
we pray to you for the forsaken ones of the world –
orphaned children,
lovers spurned,
AIDS victims deserted.

Jesus broken,
we bring to you those suffering
from broken dreams,
broken relationships,
broken promises.

Jesus, defenceless victim,
we bring to you those who are victims
of violence, abuse and false accusation.

Jesus, who has lost everything,
we bring to you those who have lost work,
health or hope.

Jesus, thirsty and destitute,
we bring to you those who are hungry,
homeless and friendless.

Jesus, who looks upon your scattered disciples,
grant your universal Church the grace to stay with you
and walk in the way of the cross.

Jesus who, lifted up on the cross,
draws all peoples to yourself,
look upon the peoples of the world torn apart
through greed and hatred –
and become the source of a reconciling.

Hymn

When I survey the wondrous cross

Blessing

With his task done on the cross
the Saviour's blood forms itself into a stream –
a stream of suffering love that will move the whole world.
And we will flow with the stream.
And we will flow with the stream.

Ray Simpson

The Soldier – You Never Forget the First Time

Matthew 27:27-54; Mark 15:16-39; Luke 23:26-49; John 19:1-37

Opening Prayer

Come, let us watch and wait a while
here in the shadow of the cross.
Let us bring our fears,
our guilts, our troubles,
and at this place declare his love,
and praise the Lord our Saviour.

Hymn

Hail thou once despisèd Jesus

Praise

We adore you, O Christ, and we bless you,
because by your holy cross you have redeemed the world.

Christ was manifested in the body,
vindicated in the spirit,
seen by angels,
proclaimed among the nations,
believed in throughout the world,
glorified in high heaven.

We adore you, O Christ, and we bless you,
because by your holy cross you have redeemed the world.

Anthem 4 Good Friday (Lent, Holy Week and Easter)

Confession
(A brief time of silence)

By your bruised and bloodied body,
forgive us, Lord.
By your thorn-crowned head and spear-torn side,
forgive us, Lord.
By your nail-pierced hands and nail-pierced feet,
forgive us, Lord.
By your cross and cruel throne,
forgive us, Lord.
By your sacrifice and loving gift,
forgive us, Lord.
By your triumph and your victory,
forgive us, Lord.

Reading

Isaiah 53:10-12

Yet it was the will of the Lord to crush him with pain.
When you make his life an offering for sin,
he shall see his offspring, and shall prolong his days;
through him the will of the Lord shall prosper.
Out of his anguish he shall see light;
he shall find satisfaction through his knowledge.
The righteous one, my servant, shall make many righteous,
and he shall bear their iniquities.
Therefore I will allot him a portion with the great,
and he shall divide the spoil with the strong;
because he poured out himself to death,
and was numbered with the transgressors;
yet he bore the sin of many,
and made intercession for the transgressors.

Hymn

O sacred head surrounded

Prayer

Lord Jesus Christ,
whose love for us was shown in the agony of the cross,
may we never take your love for granted;
but filled with love for you
may we seek to serve with courage and compassion
the world for which you died.

Story

You ask me if I'm proud of what I do. I don't know I've ever thought about it like that. I've always known I was going to be a soldier – it's in the blood you might say and if all goes well I expect I shall do my 25 years and retire with a nice little bit of land. That's what my dad did. It's hard mind you, especially the training – twenty miles we have to do, fully loaded, in just five hours, and all that formation practice. I'm not sure I want to still be doing that when I'm 45. I'd rather be in a good fight myself. You've got your mates round you, we know what we're doing and there aren't many who can better the Roman army.

We don't get much fighting out here – not proper battles. We've had a couple of skirmishes but a lot of the time it's more like crowd control. They can get quite excited, the Jews, especially when anything to do with religion is concerned. And that seems to be most of the time. Right touchy lot they are. I was up at Caesarea at the main camp for the first three years. We had one incident up in the Northern area where there were some fanatics going about causing mayhem but we soon got that sorted. They've got no discipline, no organisation. I don't know why they try it on.

It's a bit livelier here in Jerusalem. I've been here a little over a year. Our cohort came to reinforce the garrison for the Festival last year and my century stayed on. It's been all right I suppose. I prefer it in Gaul myself – you get more fighting there. But at least it's not Britain – now there's a cold miserable dump. And have you ever tasted their wine – terrible.

220

I'd been with the same eight blokes in our platoon for two years. We got on pretty well. But I've just been shifted and I'm not sure how I'm going to like it. I know I volunteered – well that's what they call it, but you don't really have a choice. They say it's specialist work – executions. A step up. I'm not sure. They tell me I'll soon get used to it. I've only done one lot so far and I don't think you ever forget the first, do you? Marcellus, he's the centurion, ordered us out just after cock crow. There were two robbers who had already been sentenced and he said there was a possible third. A prisoner had just been brought in by the Jewish leaders – someone they wanted to get rid of. They had been to the Prefect's palace and there was a whole lot of toing and froing from what I could gather. The fourth century got called out when a crowd gathered and started baying and chanting. They wanted Pilate to release a terrorist we'd got locked up, bloke called Barabbas, and to have this other bloke, Jesus, executed instead. Didn't make much sense to me but they had their way in the end. The lads brought him down for the usual scourging. It's painful that. I should know, I had it once for falling asleep on duty. It really cuts you up.

Anyhow, Gallus decided to have some fun. He really does have a wicked sense of humour. He'd heard that this bloke Jesus had claimed to be king of the Jews. Some chance! So we dressed him up, with a purple cloak and all, and Gallus got some thorn twigs and twisted them into a crown and plonked it on his head. It was a right laugh. Then we took him out to start the trudge up to the Skull – it's what they call the place where we do executions. It's a bit of a rocky outcrop really, in an old quarry. But it's a good name.

I didn't like the look of the way this Jesus was walking. He could have pegged out on us which would have made me look a proper fool, this being my first time, so I collared some bloke in the crowd to carry the cross-piece for him. When we got him to the Skull I got the spikes out and we nailed him down. I thought there was going to be all screams and that. There was with the other two. But do you know all he said was 'Father forgive them, they don't know what they're up to.' What kind of thing was that to say? I knew perfectly well what I was doing.

Anyhow we got him hoisted up and offered him some sour wine, but he wouldn't take any. And then it was just a matter of waiting. Apparently there's no telling how long it will take. We got his clothes and divided them between us – a bit of a perk like. The tunic was spare so we threw for it. Didn't get it. I'm never lucky at dice. After about three hours it got really dark. I thought we were going to have a storm. One of the blokes said he felt the earth move but I think it was just a rumble of thunder. There was the usual crowd watching. Even some of the religious leaders came out to have a look and pass comments. They said some of his friends were there but I can't say I noticed.

Anyhow, round about three in the afternoon orders came that out of respect for the Jewish sabbath we should finish them off. We whacked the legs of the two thieves with the iron pole and that put an end to them. But before we got to Jesus he let out this cry, 'It is finished', or something like that, and then he died. So Marcellus told us to give him a poke in the side with a spear just to make sure.

I don't understand Marcellus. He's a long-serving officer. Seen it all. He's been in charge of execution parties for some time. But he just stood there staring at the Jesus fellow. 'That bloke was innocent,' he said. Well what would he know? He could be the son of God for all I care. We'd done our job – got it over in reasonable time and that was that. Proud of it? No I wouldn't say that. But I don't suppose I shall ever forget it.

Take time to reflect on/discuss the story.

Prayers

We pray for all prisoners: for those guilty of crimes,
and those who are innocent;
for those who long for freedom,
and those who cannot face freedom;
for those soon to be released,
and those who will never be released;
for those imprisoned by ignorance, and those imprisoned by guilt;
for those restricted by illness,
and those facing death.
Lord, in your mercy,
hear our prayer.

We pray for all who serve in the armed forces:
for those who face danger,
and those who fear boredom;
for those who seek excitement,
and those who have had too much;
for those who give orders,
and for those who have to obey;
for the injured and the disabled,
for the dying and the grieving.
Lord, in your mercy,
hear our prayer.

The Lord's Prayer

Hymn

We sing the praise of him who died

Blessing

May the power of God surround you,
may the forgiveness of God uphold you,
may the love of God fulfil you.
May the arms of Christ embrace you,
may the welcome of Christ delight you,
may the love of Christ accept you.
May the blessing of God be with you,
upon you, within you and around you,
this day and for evermore.

John Cox

John, the Beloved Disciple – My Dearest Friend

John 19:25-30

Opening prayer

Christ, our Lord and Master,
with towel and water
you show us how to serve.
We worship you.
Christ, our Saviour,
with broken bread and poured out wine
you ask us to remember you.
We worship you.
Christ, our Redeemer, with arms outstretched
and nail-pierced hands
you invite us to love you.
We worship you.

Hymn

Broken for me

Praise

I love the Lord,
for he has heard the voice of my supplication;
because he has inclined his ear to me
on the day I called to him.
I will lift up the cup of salvation.

How shall I repay the Lord
for all the benefits he has given to me?
I will lift up the cup of salvation
and call upon the name of the Lord.
I will lift up the cup of salvation.

I will fulfil my vows to the Lord
in the presence of all his people.
Precious in the sight of the Lord
is the death of his faithful servants.
I will lift up the cup of salvation.

O Lord, I am your servant,
your servant, the child of your handmaid;
you have freed me from my bonds.
I will offer you a sacrifice of thanksgiving
and call upon the name of the Lord.
I will lift up the cup of salvation.

Psalm 116:1, 10-15
(Common Worship)

Confession

(A brief time of silence)

Christ, who has taught us the meaning of service,
forgive us the times we think too much of our own importance.
Christ, who wrestled to do the father's will,
forgive us the times we seek the easy way out.
Christ, who thought of others while in agony on the cross,
forgive us the times we think only of ourselves.

By his victory on the cross
may Christ forgive you and fill you with grace
to follow in his way.

Reading

1 Corinthians 11:23-26

For I received from the Lord what I also handed on to you, that the Lord Jesus on the night when he was betrayed took a loaf of bread, and when he had given thanks, he broke it and said, 'This is my body that is for you. Do this in remembrance of me.' In the same way he took the cup also, after supper, saying, 'This cup is the new covenant in my blood. Do this, as often as you drink it, in remembrance of me.' For as often as you eat this bread and drink the cup, you proclaim the Lord's death until he comes.

Hymn

The head that once was crowned with thorns

Prayer

Loving Lord,
who on the cross showed care
both for your mother and for John,
your beloved disciple,
make us compassionate for the plight of others,
and loving to those in need,
for your name's sake.

Story

We became very close, Jesus and me – but then we were cousins on our mothers' side. Not that I had much to do with him when I was growing up. He was in Nazareth where he took over his father's joinery business and, together with my brother James, I learnt the fishing trade up in Galilee with our father Zebedee. But once he started his preaching and healing we used to see him occasionally and eventually he came and asked us to follow him. It was a bit of a wrench and dad was none too pleased but it seemed the obvious thing to do. There were others from the village like Simon and Andrew who were fishermen as well. Simon was nicknamed Peter and he became the leader among us, after Jesus, but I was always one of the inner group too. Peter and I went with Jesus when he healed Jairus' daughter and also that time on the mountain when he sort of shone with the glory of God. It was a mysterious, breathtaking event – but what a privilege just to be part of it! There was always something special between us.

He asked Peter and me to set up things for him for the Passover – for what turned out to be our last meal with him. There was a house we had stayed in and the owner let us use an upstairs room. So it was there that we gathered. Such a strange evening – full of symbolism and tension, of feeling so close to him, yet fearful at the same time. There were a lot of things he told us – many of them we hardly understood at the time. But it was the things he did which remain so vividly in my memory.

He suddenly took off his coat and grabbed a towel and tied it round his waist and then began to wash our feet – just like the lowest servant. Peter got quite uptight about it, but Jesus spoke in his usual quiet way and persuaded Peter to allow him to do it. It was quite humbling really and it made me remember that time James and I had gone to ask Jesus if we could have the most important seats when he came into his kingdom. It makes me blush with embarrassment now just to think we ever did that. I don't know what we were thinking of. I'm not even sure we knew why we did it. It didn't please the other disciples, I can tell you. And here at our last meal together was our leader doing the meanest of tasks for us. It makes me curl up inside.

As usual I was sitting next to him at the meal and at one point he got very agitated and started talking about being betrayed by one of us. We couldn't believe it. Who on earth would want to do such a thing? We'd all been with him so long. But he persisted. We kept looking at one another, wondering whom he could mean. Peter leant across and nodded at me to ask Jesus whom he meant. 'I'll dip this piece of bread in the sauce and it's the one I hand it to,' was all he said. He passed it to Judas, and he told him to get on with what he had to do. No one else knew what he meant and Judas just left. I had a really bad feeling about things after that.

Jesus broke the bread for us, as he had done so many times before, and he gave the thanks and then passed it round to each of us. 'This bread,' he said, 'is like my body, broken for you. Whenever you eat such a meal together and break the bread, do it in remembrance of me.' At the end of the meal he did the same thing with the wine cup – passing it round after he had given the thanks, and telling each of us to take a drink and to remember it as his blood sealing a new covenant with God. I don't know what I made of it at the time – it was all getting rather emotional for me, this talk of his broken body and poured out blood.

After we had sung the usual psalms he led us out into the night air and we crossed the Kidron valley and went up to one of his favourite places in the olive grove. He asked Peter and James and me to go and watch with him, away from the others. He went on a bit further to pray and it was agony for him. We were so tired we could hardly keep awake – but for him it was like wrestling with God. The sweat poured off him, red with blood.

And that's when they came and arrested him. It was indeed Judas who had betrayed him. The others all ran away but Peter and I followed, keeping our distance, and I got us permission to go into the palace courtyard. Peter went off on his own and eventually I went back to where we were staying.

It was the worst day of my life, that next day when they crucified him. Mary and my mother and one or two others of the women wanted to go, just to be near him. I wasn't too keen. To be honest I didn't think I could bear it, but I couldn't let the women go on their own, so I joined them. I'm glad I did. Mary kept edging nearer and nearer, so by the end we were right up by the cross. It must have been just terrible for her. Not long before Jesus died he looked down and saw us standing there. 'Woman,' he said to her, just the way he often did and he sort of nodded in my direction, 'Woman, here is your son.' And to me he said, 'Here is your mother.' He didn't have to say anything more. I knew what he wanted. I shall look after her just like a son for as long as she needs me. Then he died.

225

It's the sabbath now and we're all together, too numb to know what to do next. I can't believe it's happened. It's like a bad dream and I keep thinking we will wake up and he'll be with us again, like he always was. Only it's not a dream and they have killed my dearest friend, my master, my Lord. I've never loved anyone so much. I can't bear to think he's gone.

Take time to reflect on/discuss the story.

Prayers

Heavenly Father, hear our prayer
and let our cry come unto you.

We pray for the Church,
that its ministers may rightly and reverently
celebrate the mysteries of the Eucharist
and your people know your presence
in the breaking of the bread and in wine outpoured.
Heavenly Father, hear our prayer
and let our cry come unto you.

We pray for forgiveness for all who betray their friends,
their families, their colleagues or themselves.
We pray for arresting officers and local magistrates,
for prison officers and probation officers.
Heavenly Father, hear our prayer
and let our cry come unto you.

We pray for all who watch as loved ones suffer,
for those who are ill-treated and abused,
for those who have no one to care for them
and no one to care for,
the lonely and the anxious the dying and the grieving.
Heavenly Father, hear our prayer
and let our cry come unto you.

We give thanks
for all the benefits you give us
through the death and resurrection of your Son;
keep us faithful in our love for you,
and joyful in the power of your love for us.

The Lord's Prayer

Hymn

My God I love thee

Blessing

May Christ, our crucified Lord,
draw you to himself,
fill you with all hope
and with the assurance of sins forgiven;
and the blessing of God almighty,
the Father, the Son, and the Holy Spirit,
rest upon you and remain with you,
those you love and those you serve,
this day and for evermore.

John Cox

The Way of the Cross

How to pray the Stations

The Way of the Cross, often called the Stations of the Cross, is found in the Catholic, Anglican and Lutheran traditions. It may be used at any time of the year but especially on Fridays in Lent and on Good Friday. It makes a good personal devotion and can be used for meditation using just one or two stations a day or spending time to travel to all of the stations.

The Stations of the Cross began in Jerusalem on the Via Dolorosa (the Sorrowful Way) where pilgrims sought to stop, pray and meditate at various places where tradition said certain events happened. Some of the stations had no basis in Scripture, though they could well have happened, and were used to illustrate the fullness of the saving acts. The non-Scriptural stations are the three falls of Jesus, Jesus meeting his mother, and Veronica wiping his face. The stations were found in artwork or carvings all over Europe by the fifteenth century. Possibly the devotion arose especially for pilgrims who could not hope to travel to Jerusalem. The Stations of the Cross have provided a visual devotion for countless Christians. The number of stations has varied – some would restrict them to the biblically based stations – but usually there are now the fourteen stations.

Above all, it must be remembered that the stations are an act of pilgrimage: this is not an intellectual exercise but an act of devotion. The heart and the imagination have to be able to come into play. The stations are a journey in awareness not only of historical events but also of 'the lamb that was slain before the foundation of the world' (Revelation 13:8); awareness of the presence of the Lord in our lives, in our suffering and in suffering humanity. The Way of the Cross travels through our world and is present wherever someone is betrayed by a kiss or deserted by loved ones; wherever anyone suffers injustice or enters into darkness. Christ is found with the poor and the powerless, with the scorned and rejected. In the midst of all life the Lord is there. The Way of the Cross is a journey with our Lord. It is a journey into the love of God as revealed in his Son Jesus Christ. The crucified one knows our troubles and he is with us always.

We are faced with wonder and mystery. God comes down: the Creator is in the hands of his creation. The Maker of the world is edged out of the world, out of the city, out of lives and on to the cross. He who came to set us free is fixed by nails; he who came to give life is put to death. What is the meaning of all of this? We are to learn that love is his meaning. He comes to us out of love, gives himself in love and love holds him on the cross. The best preparation for us to enter into this wonder and mystery is silence and stillness. We stand before events that the mind can hardly grasp, but the heart can feel. Do not rush the stations; take your time with each one and enter into stillness – stations are where you stop for a while. Pause in the presence and let the power and love of God enfold you, and give your love to him.

Begin the stations with a personal prayer that centres on the presence and love of God. Be still and quiet and give your love to him.

In the saving power of God,
Father, Son and Holy Spirit.

Blessed are you Lord God of our salvation,
in your love for us
you gave us your Son to be our Redeemer.
As we walk the way of the cross,
may we walk with Christ our Lord
and know his great love for us.
As he gave himself for us,
help us to give our life to you,
blessed Father, Son and Holy Spirit.

First station – Jesus is condemned to death

We adore you, O Christ, and we bless you,
because by your holy cross you have redeemed the world.

He was despised and rejected by others; a man of suffering and acquainted with infirmity . . . Surely he has borne our infirmities and carried our diseases . . . He was wounded for our transgressions, crushed for our iniquities; upon him was the punishment that made us whole, and by his bruises we are healed. All we like sheep have gone astray; we have all turned to our own way, and the Lord has laid on him the iniquity of us all. He was oppressed, and he was afflicted, yet he did not open his mouth; like a lamb that is led to the slaughter, and like a sheep that before its shearers is silent, so he did not open his mouth.

Isaiah 53:3-7

The powers of this world are determined to be rid of Jesus.
He challenges their way of life,
their power structures,
their luxury whilst others starve,
their insensitivity towards their fellows,
and for this he is condemned.

The church people are not comfortable with him.
He talks about their dedication.
He questions their lack of mission.
He wants them to love as God loves,
and for this he is condemned.

He came in love and they vent their hatred upon him.
He came to enrich their lives and they strip him and leave him bare.
He came to give life and they condemn him to death.
He sought to set them free and they fix him to a cross of wood.

Jesus, help us to accept you as our Lord and our God.
Increase our sensitivity to your presence in others:
help us to know that as we do it to the least of all we do it to you.

Lord Jesus Christ, who by your cross and passion have redeemed us,
save and help us, we humbly beseech you, O Lord.

Second station – Jesus receives the cross

We adore you, O Christ, and we bless you,
because by your holy cross you have redeemed the world.

'The Son of Man must undergo great suffering, and be rejected by the elders, chief priests and scribes, and be killed, and on the third day be raised.' Then he said to them all, 'If any want to become my followers, let them deny themselves and take up their cross daily and follow me. For those who want to save their life will lose it, and those who lose their life for my sake will save it. What does it profit them if they gain the whole world, but lose or forfeit themselves?'

Luke 9:22-25

Here is the cross.
Take it as if it is yours,
as if you deserved it.
Take upon you the injustice,
the cruelty and the hatred of the world.
Take upon you all the pain and sorrow.

Lord, you give yourself in love –
let me not give a cross to you.
Jesus, we remember all who are forced
to accept suffering as their daily lot,
all who are betrayed by loved ones,
all deserted by their friends,
all who are very much left alone.
In you may they find hope.

Lord Jesus Christ, who by your cross and passion have redeemed us,
save and help us, we humbly beseech you, O Lord.

Third station – Jesus falls for the first time

We adore you, O Christ, and we bless you,
because by your holy cross you have redeemed the world.

Cursed is the ground because of you; in toil you shall eat of it all the days of your life; thorns and thistles it shall bring forth for you; and you shall eat the plants of the field. By the sweat of your face you shall eat bread until you return to the ground, for out of it you were taken; you are dust, and to dust you shall return.

Genesis 3:17-19

The Son of Man is weakened;
a heart is breaking with love.
He came down to lift us up,
and now he descends to the dust.
God and dust mix together.
He humbled himself unto death,
even death on the cross.
Now he crawls in the dust –
see how the dust clings
to him as he arises!
He comes down to the lowest level to raise us up.

Lord Jesus, many are your humiliations:
born in a stable, taken as a refugee,
scorned and rejected, betrayed with a kiss,
denied by a friend, deserted by disciples,
brought down to the dust.
We remember before you
all who suffer humiliation and all who are brought low.

Lord Jesus Christ, who by your cross and passion have redeemed us,
save and help us, we humbly beseech you, O Lord.

Fourth station – Jesus is met by his mother

We adore you, O Christ, and we bless you,
because by your holy cross you have redeemed the world.

Then Simeon blessed them and said to his mother Mary, 'This child is destined for the falling and the rising of many in Israel, and to be a sign that will be opposed so that the inner thoughts of many will be revealed – and a sword will pierce your own soul too.'

Luke 2:34, 35

Mary ought not to have come, but love drew her to him.
This would cost her much pain and sorrow, agony
and awful memories.
Why should this happen to him, to her?
What had either done to deserve this?
There seemed to be no answer.

Pain is not a private thing;
it is shared by loved ones.
If one suffers, all suffer.
Mary experiences the sword that was to pierce her heart.

Lord, we fear that if we love you,
we will be asked to walk the way of the cross.
If we give you our heart,
it will be pierced with the sorrows of the world.

Lord Jesus Christ, who by your cross and passion have redeemed us,
save and help us, we humbly beseech you, O Lord.

Fifth station – Simon of Cyrene is compelled to carry the cross

We adore you, O Christ, and we bless you,
because by your holy cross you have redeemed the world.

They compelled a passer-by, who was coming in from the country, to carry his cross; it was Simon of Cyrene, the father of Alexander and Rufus. Then they brought Jesus to the place called Golgotha (which means the place of a skull).

Mark 15:21, 22

Simon is an African, as Cyrene was what is now Libya.
He had no intentions of doing anything.
He was entering the city from the country.
He is forced to carry the cross.
That day he learnt something that would change him –
for we are told his sons are known by the Church.
Military rule forces its will on people.
People are still compelled to do awful things.
The cross is to be borne in our helping of the least,
in the hungry,
the refugee,
the homeless,
the outcasts.
The Lord calls us to bear one another's burdens.
Lord, as you have given your life for us,
help us to give ourselves to others
and to you.

Lord Jesus Christ, who by your cross and passion have redeemed us,
save and help us, we humbly beseech you, O Lord.

Sixth station – Veronica wipes the face of Jesus

We adore you, O Christ, and we bless you,
because by your holy cross you have redeemed the world.

Hear, O Lord, when I cry aloud,
be gracious to me and answer me!
'Come,' my heart says, 'seek his face!'
Your face, Lord, do I seek.
Do not hide your face from me.

Psalm 27:7-9

Jesus had been badly beaten.
His face is covered with sweat, dust and blood.
He is not a pretty sight.
One in the crowd is moved by his suffering.
She comes forward and stands out from the crowd.
She disregards the danger and the hostility;
she acts on impulse out of love.

It is said that the face of Jesus was captured on the
cloth she used to wipe his face.
She would keep this image in her heart.
She would remember this face,
a face like any other face,
but she had looked into the eyes of God.

The face of God is scarred by thorns,
bloodied by violence.
Lord, how often we defile your image
and mar your likeness.
Forgive us and help us to reveal you to others.

Lord Jesus Christ, who by your cross and passion have redeemed us,
save and help us, we humbly beseech you, O Lord.

Seventh station – Jesus falls for a second time

We adore you, O Christ, and we bless you,
because by your holy cross you have redeemed the world.

My soul clings to the dust;
revive me according to your word.
My soul melts away for sorrow;
strengthen me according to your word.
Let your steadfast love come to me, O Lord,
your salvation according to your promise.
Then shall I have an answer for those who taunt me,
for I trust in your word.   *Psalm 119:25, 28, 41, 42*

Lord, do you never give up?
You are down again –
and we know it will not be for the last time.
How long must you suffer?
How long can your creation defile and degrade you?

Once again you bite the dust for us
and for our salvation.
Dust and divinity mingling together:
dust rising with you when you arise.
Lord, when we attach myself to you, we arise,
for with you is life and life eternal.

Lord Jesus Christ, who by your cross and passion have redeemed us,
save and help us, we humbly beseech you, O Lord.

Eighth station – Jesus meets the women of Jerusalem

We adore you, O Christ, and we bless you,
because by your holy cross you have redeemed the world.

A great number of people followed him, and among them were women who were beating their breasts and wailing for him. But Jesus turned to them and said, 'Daughters of Jerusalem, do not weep for me, but weep for yourselves and for your children. For the days are surely coming when they will say, "Blessed are the barren, and the wombs that never bore, and the breasts that never nursed." Then they will begin to say to the mountains, "Fall on us"; and to the hills, "Cover us." For if they do this when the wood is green, what will happen when it is dry?'

Luke 23:27-31

Only the hardened and the toughest of people
would not be moved,
but many regimes brutalise people.
Some women are openly weeping for Jesus;
their hearts are stirred.

The mothers know a mother's heart must be breaking.
It causes tears to flow.
The sorrow of women for their children
is a great sorrow.

Jesus accepts their sympathy –
but with a warning.
More than tears are needed to change the world.

If they can do this to a just man,
what will they do to others?
If this can be done to the Son of God,
then no one is safe.

Lord, we come to you in sorrow
for the suffering peoples of the world.
Give us the courage and willpower to help where we can.

Lord Jesus Christ, who by your cross and passion have redeemed us,
save and help us, we humbly beseech you, O Lord.

Ninth station – Jesus falls for the third time

We adore you, O Christ, and we bless you,
because by your holy cross you have redeemed the world.

Christ Jesus who, though he was in the form of God,
did not regard equality with God
as something to be exploited,
but emptied himself,
taking the form of a slave,
being born in human likeness.
And being found in human form,
he humbled himself
and became obedient to the point of death –
even death on a cross.

Philippians 2:6-8

There you go, down again.
This is becoming a habit.
You seem to be attached to the dust.

This time it looks as if this is it:
are you still breathing?
Shall we count you out?
We could count you out.

Are you already dead?
How long do you want to lie there:
three days or more?
Death is not far away –
but you rise again.
Lord Jesus, as the dust clings to you as you rise,
may we hold fast to you and to your saving power.

Lord Jesus Christ, who by your cross and passion have redeemed us,
save and help us, we humbly beseech you, O Lord.

Tenth station – Jesus is stripped of his garments

We adore you, O Christ, and we bless you,
because by your holy cross you have redeemed the world.

My God, my God, why have you forsaken me?
Why are you so far from helping me,
from the words of my groaning?
I am poured out like water,
and all my bones are out of joint;
my heart is like wax;
it is melted within my breast;
my mouth is dried up like a potsherd,
and my tongue sticks to my jaws;
you lay me in the dust of death.
For dogs are all around me;
a company of evildoers encircles me.
My hands and feet have shrivelled;
I can count all my bones.
They stare and gloat over me;
they divide my clothes among themselves,
and for my clothing they cast lots.
But you, O Lord, do not be far away!
O my help, come quickly to my aid!   *Psalm 22:1, 14-18*

They have taken all from you.
Now they gamble for the robe your mother gave you.
They take away your dignity and leave you exposed.
They strip you of your humanity
and will take away your life.

There is no Transfiguration,
no white robes,
only bareness;
nothing to shield you from the cross or from mockery.
You are defenceless or so it seems.
Yet in love you allow all this for us.

Lord, strip from us all false pride;
strip away all self-trust;
take away all that keeps us from you.
We remember before you all who are laid bare,
all who have nothing and are counted as nothing.

Lord Jesus Christ, who by your cross and passion have redeemed us,
save and help us, we humbly beseech you, O Lord.

Eleventh station – Jesus is nailed to the cross

We adore you, O Christ, and we bless you,
because by your holy cross you have redeemed the world.

So they took Jesus; and carrying the cross by himself, he went out to what is called The Place of the Skull, which in Hebrew is called Golgotha. There they crucified him, and with him two others, one on either side, with Jesus between them. Pilate also had an inscription written and put on the cross. It read, 'Jesus of Nazareth, the King of the Jews.' Many of the Jews read this inscription, because the place where Jesus was crucified was near the city; and it was written in Hebrew, in Latin and in Greek.

John 19:16-20

Jesus who came to set them free is fixed . . .
to a cross of wood.

Listen to the sound of the nails.
Iron on iron, iron into wood, all resound.
Human flesh does not make much sound,
neither does the Son of Man.

Here is planned cruelty and indignity.
Jesus is hung like a picture –
but not a pretty sight.
Arms are stretched out as if to welcome in an embrace.
This is the cost of your love, of the love of God.
The Christ is poured out for us and for our salvation.

Lord, as you open your arms to welcome us,
let us remember the cost.
By your agony and loneliness,
support us in my troubles.
By your life laid down,
lift us up and bring us to life eternal.

Lord Jesus Christ, who by your cross and passion have redeemed us,
save and help us, we humbly beseech you, O Lord.

Twelfth station – Jesus dies upon the cross

We adore you, O Christ, and we bless you,
because by your holy cross you have redeemed the world.

When it was noon, darkness came over the whole land until three in the afternoon. At three o'clock Jesus cried out with a loud voice, 'Eloi, Eloi, lema sabachthani?' which means, 'My God, my God, why have you forsaken me?' When some of the bystanders heard it, they said, 'Listen, he is calling for Elijah.' And someone ran, filled a sponge with sour wine, put it on a stick, and gave it to him to drink, saying, 'Wait, let us see whether Elijah will come to take him down.' Then Jesus gave a loud cry and breathed his last.

Mark 15:33-37

Can it be that God suffers for us?
Can it be that God dies for us?
The Christ has paid the extreme price of love:
he has laid down his life for us;
through him the darkness is banished.
He has served his Father faithfully even to death,
and in death he has become our Redeemer.
There is no greater love than this.
Lord Christ, our Redeemer,
as you give yourself for us and to us,
help us to give ourselves to you.

Lord Jesus Christ, who by your cross and passion have redeemed us,
save and help us, we humbly beseech you, O Lord.

Thirteenth station – Jesus is taken down from the cross

We adore you, O Christ, and we bless you,
because by your holy cross you have redeemed the world.

When his parents saw him they were astonished; and his mother said to him, 'Child, why have you treated us like this? Look, your father and I have been searching for you in great anxiety.' He said to them, 'Why were you searching for me? Did you not know that I must be in my Father's house?'

Luke 2:48, 49

Once again Jesus returns to his mother's lap.
But there is no joy here: the body is broken
and disfigured.

A sword pierces her own heart.
How long is it since he was last in her arms?

This is a far cry from Bethlehem and Nazareth:
there was so much promise;
it seemed the whole world would follow him.

Now Jesus, her son, is dead.
He came to his own but his own received him not.
The creature has sought to kill the Creator.
What hells are let loose on the world?

Lord Christ,
We remember all who are facing death
or the death of a loved one.
We pray for all who have been killed
through violence or accidents.
Lord, in your death may we find hope.

Lord Jesus Christ, who by your cross and passion have redeemed us,
save and help us, we humbly beseech you, O Lord.

Fourteenth station – Jesus is laid in the tomb

We adore you, O Christ, and we bless you,
because by your holy cross you have redeemed the world.

When evening had come, and since it was the day of Preparation, that is, the day before the Sabbath, Joseph of Arimathea, a respected member of the council, who was also himself waiting expectantly for the kingdom of God, went boldly to Pilate and asked for the body of Jesus. Then Pilate wondered if he were already dead; and summoning the centurion, he asked him whether he had been dead for some time. When he learned from the centurion that he was dead, he granted the body to Joseph. Then Joseph bought a linen cloth, and taking down the body, wrapped it in the linen cloth, and laid it in a tomb that had been hewn out of the rock. He then rolled a stone against the door of the tomb. Mary Magdalene and Mary the mother of Joses saw where the body was laid.

Mark 15:42-47

As the sun goes down,
the Christ is buried in a borrowed grave.

After all the pain and agony he looks at rest:
the whiteness of the linen cloth
helps to hide the wounds and scars.

He lies here like a seed buried in the earth.
This is the winter of the world:
all who love him are left numbed and cold,
exhausted and empty.
At least he has passed beyond it all.

Lord Jesus, come into our darkness,
into our lives sealed against feeling,
into our many deaths.
Help us to know that you are beyond the grave and beckon us to glory.

Lord Jesus Christ, who by your cross and passion have redeemed us,
save and help us, we humbly beseech you, O Lord.

David Adam

The Crucifixion – the Witness of the Scriptures

Different voices should be used for the readings.

Introduction

Let us come to the foot of the cross and watch a while.
Lord, be with us in this time of your agony.
Let us hear the words of Scripture and reflect on their meaning.
Lord, be with us in this time of your glory.
Let us open our hearts to all that Christ achieved in this costly act of self-giving.
Lord, be with us in this time of your victory.

Hymn

When I survey the wondrous cross
or Glory be to Jesus

Reading

Isaiah 52:13–53:12

See, my servant shall prosper;
he shall be exalted and lifted up,
and shall be very high.
Just as there were many who were astonished at him
– so marred was his appearance, beyond human semblance,
and his form beyond that of mortals –
so he shall startle many nations;
kings shall shut their mouths because of him;
for that which had not been told them they shall see,
and that which they had not heard they shall contemplate.
Who has believed what we have heard?
And to whom has the arm of the Lord been revealed?
For he grew up before him like a young plant,
and like a root out of dry ground;
he had no form or majesty that we should look at him,
nothing in his appearance that we should desire him.
He was despised and rejected by others;
a man of suffering and acquainted with infirmity;
and as one from whom others hide their faces
he was despised, and we held him of no account.
Surely he has borne our infirmities
and carried our diseases;
yet we accounted him stricken,
struck down by God, and afflicted.
But he was wounded for our transgressions,
crushed for our iniquities;
upon him was the punishment that made us whole,
and by his bruises we are healed.

All we like sheep have gone astray;
we have all turned to our own way,
and the Lord has laid on him the iniquity of us all.
He was oppressed, and he was afflicted,
yet he did not open his mouth;
like a lamb that is led to the slaughter,
and like a sheep that before its shearers is silent,
so he did not open his mouth.
By a perversion of justice he was taken away.
Who could have imagined his future?
For he was cut off from the land of the living,
stricken for the transgression of my people.
They made his grave with the wicked and his tomb with the rich,
although he had done no violence, and there was no deceit in his mouth.
Yet it was the will of the Lord to crush him with pain.
When you make his life an offering for sin,
he shall see his offspring, and shall prolong his days;
through him the will of the Lord shall prosper.
Out of his anguish he shall see light;
he shall find satisfaction through his knowledge.
The righteous one, my servant, shall make many righteous,
and he shall bear their iniquities.
Therefore I will allot him a portion with the great,
and he shall divide the spoil with the strong;
because he poured out himself to death,
and was numbered with the transgressors;
yet he bore the sin of many,
and made intercession for the transgressors.

A time of quiet reflection during which a suitable piece of music may be played.

Hymn

At the Lamb's high feast we sing *(verses 1-3)*

Reading

Exodus 12:21-27; John 19:14, 16b-22; Revelation 5:12, 13

Then Moses called all the elders of Israel and said to them, 'Go, select lambs for your families, and slaughter the passover lamb. Take a bunch of hyssop, dip it in the blood that is in the basin, and touch the lintel and the two doorposts with the blood in the basin. None of you shall go outside the door of your house until morning. For the Lord will pass through to strike down the Egyptians; when he sees the blood on the lintel and on the two doorposts, the Lord will pass over that door and will not allow the destroyer to enter your houses to strike you down. You shall observe this rite as a perpetual ordinance for you and your children. When you come to the land that the Lord will give you, as he has promised, you shall keep this observance. And when your children ask you, "What do you mean by this observance?" you shall say, "It is the passover sacrifice to the Lord, for he passed over the houses of the Israelites in Egypt, when he struck down the Egyptians but spared our houses."' And the people bowed down and worshipped.

It was the day of the preparation for the Passover; and it was about noon.
So they took Jesus; and carrying the cross by himself, he went out to what is called The Place of the Skull, which in Hebrew is called Golgotha. There they crucified him, and with him two others, one on either side, with Jesus between them. Pilate also had an inscription written and put on the cross. It read, 'Jesus of Nazareth, the King of the Jews.' Many of the Jews read this inscription, because the place where Jesus was crucified was near the city; and it was written in Hebrew, in Latin, and in Greek. Then the chief priests of the Jews said to Pilate, 'Do not write, "The King of the Jews", but, "This man said, I am King of the Jews."' Pilate answered, 'What I have written I have written.'

'Worthy is the Lamb that was slaughtered
to receive power and wealth and wisdom and might
and honour and glory and blessing!'
Then I heard every creature in heaven and on earth and under the earth and in the sea, and all that is in them, singing,
'To the one seated on the throne and to the Lamb
be blessing and honour and glory and might
for ever and ever!'

Agnus Dei
Lamb of God, you take away the sin of the world,
have mercy on us.
Lamb of God, you take away the sin of the world,
have mercy on us.
Lamb of God, you take away the sin of the world,
grant us peace.

Hymn

There is a green hill far away
or On the holy cross I see

Reading

Psalm 69:1-4, 6-8, 13-20; Luke 23:32-43

Save me, O God,
for the waters have come up to my neck.
I sink in deep mire,
where there is no foothold;
I have come into deep waters,
and the flood sweeps over me.
I am weary with my crying;
my throat is parched.
My eyes grow dim
with waiting for my God.
More in number than the hairs of my head
are those who hate me without cause;
many are those who would destroy me,
my enemies who accuse me falsely.

Do not let those who hope in you
be put to shame because of me,
O Lord God of hosts;
do not let those who seek you
be dishonoured because of me,
O God of Israel.
It is for your sake that I have borne reproach,
that shame has covered my face.
I have become a stranger to my kindred,
an alien to my mother's children.
But as for me, my prayer is to you, O Lord.
At an acceptable time, O God,
in the abundance of your steadfast love, answer me.
With your faithful help rescue me
from sinking in the mire;
let me be delivered from my enemies
and from the deep waters.
Do not let the flood sweep over me,
or the deep swallow me up,
or the Pit close its mouth over me.
Answer me, O Lord, for your steadfast love is good;
according to your abundant mercy, turn to me.
Do not hide your face from your servant,
for I am in distress – make haste to answer me.
Draw near to me, redeem me,
set me free because of my enemies.
You know the insults I receive,
and my shame and dishonour;
my foes are all known to you.
Insults have broken my heart,
so that I am in despair.
I looked for pity, but there was none;
and for comforters, but I found none.

Two others also, who were criminals, were led away to be put to death with him. When they came to the place that is called The Skull, they crucified Jesus there with the criminals, one on his right and one on his left. Then Jesus said, 'Father, forgive them; for they do not know what they are doing.' And they cast lots to divide his clothing. And the people stood by, watching; but the leaders scoffed at him, saying, 'He saved others; let him save himself if he is the Messiah of God, his chosen one!' The soldiers also mocked him, coming up and offering him sour wine, and saying, 'If you are the King of the Jews, save yourself!' There was also an inscription over him, 'This is the King of the Jews.'

One of the criminals who were hanged there kept deriding him and saying, 'Are you not the Messiah? Save yourself and us!' But the other rebuked him, saying, 'Do you not fear God, since you are under the same sentence of condemnation? And we indeed have been condemned justly, for we are getting what we deserve for our deeds, but this man has done nothing wrong.' Then he said, 'Jesus, remember me when you come into your kingdom.' He replied, 'Truly I tell you, today you will be with me in Paradise.'

A time of quiet reflection during which a suitable piece of music may be played.

Crucified Lord,
you were insulted and scorned,
reviled and derided,
yet you remained silent.

They pierced you with nails
and fixed you to the cross,
yet you forgave them.

As you hung between criminals,
one asked you to remember him.
You promised him a place in Paradise.

Hymn

Bless the Lord, O my soul
or Father of heaven, whose love profound

Reading

Psalm 22:1-11,14-20; Mark15:33-36

My God, my God, why have you forsaken me?
Why are you so far from helping me, from the words of my groaning?
O my God, I cry by day, but you do not answer;
and by night, but find no rest.
Yet you are holy,
enthroned on the praises of Israel.
In you our ancestors trusted;
they trusted, and you delivered them.
To you they cried, and were saved;
in you they trusted, and were not put to shame.
But I am a worm, and not human;
scorned by others, and despised by the people.
All who see me mock at me;
they make mouths at me, they shake their heads;
'Commit your cause to the Lord;
let him deliver – let him rescue the one in whom he delights!'
Yet it was you who took me from the womb;
you kept me safe on my mother's breast.
On you I was cast from my birth,
and since my mother bore me you have been my God.
Do not be far from me,
for trouble is near
and there is no one to help.
I am poured out like water,
and all my bones are out of joint;
my heart is like wax;
it is melted within my breast;
my mouth is dried up like a potsherd,

and my tongue sticks to my jaws;
you lay me in the dust of death.
For dogs are all around me;
a company of evildoers encircles me.
My hands and feet have shrivelled;
I can count all my bones.
They stare and gloat over me;
they divide my clothes among themselves,
and for my clothing they cast lots.
But you, O Lord, do not be far away!
O my help, come quickly to my aid!
Deliver my soul from the sword,
my life from the power of the dog!

When it was noon, darkness came over the whole land until three in the afternoon. At three o'clock Jesus cried out with a loud voice, 'Eloi, Eloi, lema sabachthani?' which means, 'My God, my God, why have you forsaken me?' When some of the bystanders heard it, they said, 'Listen, he is calling for Elijah.' And someone ran, filled a sponge with sour wine, put it on a stick, and gave it to him to drink, saying, 'Wait, let us see whether Elijah will come to take him down.'

A time of quiet reflection during which a suitable piece of music may be played.

Lord, in our times of doubt,
strengthen the faith within us.
Lord, in times when we feel abandoned,
grant us knowledge of your presence.
Lord, when all seems lost,
search for us and bring us home

Hymn

We sing the praise of him who died
or Come, wounded healer

Reading

Psalm 22:22-31; Luke 23:44-56

I will tell of your name to my brothers and sisters;
in the midst of the congregation I will praise you:
You who fear the Lord, praise him!
All you offspring of Jacob, glorify him;
stand in awe of him, all you offspring of Israel!
For he did not despise or abhor
the affliction of the afflicted;
he did not hide his face from me,
but heard when I cried to him.
From you comes my praise in the great congregation;
my vows I will pay before those who fear him.
The poor shall eat and be satisfied;
those who seek him shall praise the Lord.

May your hearts live for ever!
All the ends of the earth shall remember and turn to the Lord;
and all the families of the nations
shall worship before him.
For dominion belongs to the Lord,
and he rules over the nations.
To him, indeed, shall all who sleep in the earth bow down;
before him shall bow all who go down to the dust,
and I shall live for him.
Posterity will serve him;
future generations will be told about the Lord,
and proclaim his deliverance to a people yet unborn,
saying that he has done it.

It was now about noon, and darkness came over the whole land until three in the afternoon, while the sun's light failed; and the curtain of the temple was torn in two. Then Jesus, crying with a loud voice, said, 'Father, into your hands I commend my spirit.' Having said this, he breathed his last. When the centurion saw what had taken place, he praised God and said, 'Certainly this man was innocent.' And when all the crowds who had gathered there for this spectacle saw what had taken place, they returned home, beating their breasts. But all his acquaintances, including the women who had followed him from Galilee, stood at a distance, watching these things.

Now there was a good and righteous man named Joseph, who, though a member of the council, had not agreed to their plan and action. He came from the Jewish town of Arimathea, and he was waiting expectantly for the kingdom of God. This man went to Pilate and asked for the body of Jesus. Then he took it down, wrapped it in a linen cloth, and laid it in a rock-hewn tomb where no one had ever been laid. It was the day of Preparation, and the sabbath was beginning. The women who had come with him from Galilee followed, and they saw the tomb and how his body was laid. Then they returned, and prepared spices and ointments.

On the sabbath they rested according to the commandment.

A time of quiet reflection during which a suitable piece of music may be played.

Father, in the darkness we look to you for light.
We place ourselves in your hands.

Father, amidst pain and suffering,
we place ourselves in your hands.

Father, at our end and our departing,
we place ourselves in your hands.

Crucified Christ, go with us,
forgiving Christ, go with us,
forsaken and trusting Christ,
go with us, into the waiting time,
Christ go with us.

All leave in silence.

John Cox

SERMON IDEAS

Temple Curtain Torn

When Jesus breathed his last on the cross, Mark tells us that he gave a loud cry, and the curtain of the temple was torn in two, from top to bottom. To realise the significance of this statement we could start from a long distance away, far from Jerusalem.

Imagine we are here in northern Europe at the time when Jesus was still a child, and we want to get as close as possible to the throne of God upon the Earth. We would have to travel all the way across Europe by land or sea, or both, and find our way to the Holy Land. The journey would be difficult and dangerous. Then, having reached the Holy Land, we would have to find our way to Jerusalem.

Having reached Jerusalem, we would find the whereabouts of the temple fairly easily, since it must have been the biggest non-military building in the whole city, the temple that took 46 years to build. We would be allowed to enter the temple as far as the court of the Gentiles, and that would be that. Even a Jewish woman would only be allowed to enter into one more court, and that would be that for her. A Jewish man could enter one more court, and could share that with the (male) priests. But the Holy Place within the final court was an inner sanctum which only the priests could enter and carry out sacred duties.

Between the Holy Place and the Holy of Holies was a curtain, an opaque veil, shrouding the figure of the cherubim whose wings were the throne of God, where the invisible God dwelt with human beings. Only the high priest or his delegate would dare to pass through that curtain to offer incense.

Hence the significance of the curtain being torn in two from top to bottom: thanks to Jesus having sacrificed his life to proclaim the unconditional love and forgiveness of God his Abba, the way is now open for any child of God, any brother or sister of Jesus, to come into the presence of God without an appointment, without an introduction. Tearing down the curtain cost Jesus his lifeblood, and it is always thanks to Jesus that we have such free access to our loving God: no need to journey miles, no need to reach the Holy Land or Jerusalem, no barriers of gender or qualifications.

We are all first-generation children of God, and God is our Abba, not just our creator or the father of the human race; he is not a distant God. Like little children of God, we will never find our Father too busy to listen to us. Every one of us can say, 'I will never find my Father too busy to listen to me.' The throne of God is there in the heart of each and every one of us, and the door to it is open.

Gerald O'Mahony

The Ultimate Sacrifice

From the sixth to the ninth hour, darkness fell over the whole country. Then, at that ninth hour, Jesus shouted out, 'Eloi, Eloi, lama sabachthani?' which, translated, means, 'My God, my God, why have you abandoned me?' (Mark 15:33, 34)

Nothing takes us more powerfully and directly to the heart of this day than that desolate cry of Jesus from the cross: 'My God, my God, why have you abandoned me?' And no words, on the surface at least, could make it seem more inappropriately named, for what on earth can be good about Jesus feeling so helpless, so hopeless, so utterly bereft and alone? It's as though up to this point, despite everything he'd said, he'd been secretly hoping that God might somehow rescue him; that there might be a last-minute reprieve, a miraculous escape. Hadn't he, after all, cried out in Gethsemane, 'if it be possible, take this cup from me'? Was this, then, a crisis of faith as God failed to step into the breach?

It might seem that way, but the reality couldn't be more different. Yes, Jesus felt isolated, forsaken, and yes, the experience was devastating beyond words, but the way of sacrifice and self-denial was what he had committed himself to following right at the start of his ministry – not simply surrendering his life but taking upon himself the sins of the world, bearing them in his body, accepting the punishment that should have been ours. There on the cross Jesus endured the agony of total separation from God, an agony not just of body but of spirit. Rather than abandon us, he faced what it means to feel utterly abandoned. In order to reconcile us with God, he was estranged. It was the ultimate sacrifice to make possible the ultimate gift: new life, resurrection life, lived for evermore. That's the message of Good Friday. Could any day be more appropriately named!

Nick Fawcett

He Was Dead

Since it was the day of preparation for the Passover, the Jews did not want dead bodies left on the cross during the Sabbath, especially because Passover Sabbath was a day of special import, so they asked Pilate to have the legs of those who had been crucified broken and their bodies removed. Accordingly, the soldiers broke the legs of the first and then the second of those crucified with Jesus, but when they came to Jesus, they saw he was already dead so they did not break his legs. Instead, one of the soldiers pierced his side with a spear. (John 19:31-34a)

Some animals, when faced with danger, make use of a cunning trick. Instead of running or standing up to fight, they play dead, thus confusing their attacker, which is only interested in live prey. To hear some people talk, you might imagine that the crucifixion involved a similar trick. Maybe Jesus wasn't dead, after all, some suggest; perhaps in the coolness of the tomb he regained consciousness, and was subsequently whisked away by his followers under cover of darkness.

It's far-fetched, I know, but some people will believe anything rather than have their preconceptions challenged. The idea of resurrection simply goes against everything they believe or experience. Yet, one look at the Gospels – and at the Gospel of John in particular – leaves us in no doubt about the truth. Jesus was dead, a spear thrust into his side to make doubly certain. He was laid limp and lifeless in a tomb, and a stone rolled against the entrance. Humanly speaking it was over, the end of a wonderful ministry and an unforgettable man. He had shared our life; he had shared our death. If the story was to continue, it was out of human hands – it was down now to God.

Nick Fawcett

Easter Eve – Dealing with Death

Joseph of Arimathea, a respected council member who was eagerly anticipating the dawn of God's kingdom, boldly approached Pilate and asked if he could take away Jesus' body. Uncertain whether

Jesus was dead yet, Pilate summoned the centurion and asked whether and when he had died. On receiving confirmation from the centurion that Jesus was indeed dead, Pilate granted Joseph the body, whereupon Joseph bought a linen cloth, took down the body and used the cloth to shroud it before laying out the corpse in a tomb carved in the rock. Finally, he rolled a stone against the mouth of the tomb. Mary Magdalene and Mary, Joses' mother, saw for themselves where the body was laid. (Mark 15:43-47)

According to Sigmund Freud, it's impossible for us to imagine our own death. How true that is, I'm not sure, but – impossible or not – it's not something any of us like to contemplate. It's a spectre we thrust to the back of our minds and do our level best not to think about if at all possible. Death represents an enemy on so many levels, separating us from loved ones, extinguishing our hopes and dreams, relativising all our striving, plucking us rudely out of this world. And all that is not to mention the actual process of dying which, for many, is perhaps the most daunting prospect of all. No wonder talk of death continues to be a modern-day taboo, studiously and discreetly avoided. Yet, of course, death is one of the few things none of us can avoid. And that's why Holy Saturday, or Easter Eve, is important. Coming as it does between Good Friday and Easter Sunday, it reminds us that God in Christ has shared not just our humanity, not just our life, but also our death.

That's what we remember today: that Jesus was cut down lifeless from the cross and sealed in a tomb. Rigor mortis would have set in, his body left cold and inanimate, an empty shell. And for those who had known and loved him, it was over, nothing left afterwards other than to anoint his body one last time. Only, of course, that was not the final word. What appeared to be the end was in fact merely the beginning, as we will celebrate once more in the days ahead. Rejoice, then, in God's gift of resurrection life, but rejoice also in the knowledge that, however frightening it may seem, however bleak and hopeless, death can be faced with confidence in the knowledge that God has been *there* too and will be with us in and through it.

Nick Fawcett

ALL-AGE SERVICES

Pilate

Background

Pilate was the Roman leader in Jerusalem, and had the difficult task of keeping the peace. He tried to make sure that he didn't upset the Jewish leadership too much, and allowed them quite a lot of power. He also had to make sure that his Roman leaders were happy that he wasn't giving in to the religious people too much. Pilate realised the strength of the chief priests and other religious leaders, and he was wise enough to realise that they could easily get plenty of people on their side. With the information he received from all of the soldiers in the area he also knew that Jesus was getting more and more support as he travelled around the area, and he allowed Jesus to be arrested. Now Jesus was in front of him, and he had to decide what to do. Pilate questioned Jesus, but struggled with him.

Bible

Then Pilate announced to the chief priests and the crowd, 'I find no basis for a charge against this man.'

Luke 23:4

Pilate was in trouble. He realised that the religious leaders really wanted to see Jesus put to death, so after some more confusion he offered the crowd a deal – he would release a criminal called Barabbas in the place of Jesus. Pilate knew this was wrong, but wanted to keep everyone happy!

When Pilate saw that he was getting nowhere, but that instead an uproar was starting, he took water and washed his hands in front of the crowd. 'I am innocent of this man's blood,' he said. 'It is your responsibility!'

Matthew 27:24

The decision was made, the crowd had chosen, and Jesus was sentenced to death. Pilate was left with a deep sense of having allowed something wrong to have happened.

Actions and activities

- *Pilate's Place*

  Think about the part that Pilate plays in the story of Jesus' journey to the cross. Do you think he really wanted to see Jesus put to death? Did he understand why the Jewish leaders wanted him to die? Should he have made a different decision?

- Find out about the Romans and their occupation of the Jewish lands of what we now call Israel. Discover more about what the leaders wore and the lifestyles they enjoyed. Draw what you imagine Pilate and his home looked like.

- *Difficult Decisions*

  Write down on a piece of paper a brief account of a time when you have had to make a really difficult decision. Swap that piece of paper with someone else, and read about their difficult decision.

- Pilate was trying to hold a balance between the Romans and the Jewish leaders. Which of these things do you think he may have had in his mind?:

  > If I don't allow Jesus to be put to death there will be a riot. This will keep the chief priests quiet.
  > I really don't know what to do.
  > I want them to get on with it and not involve me.
  > If I don't calm things down I'll lose my power.

- Pilate washed his hands of the situation. Write down what you think he was trying to do by that action. Do you think it is possible for him to accept no responsibility? Do you think he felt better about the decision after he had washed his hands?

Pausing and Praying

- Consider all the situations where you have power. It may be that your friends do what you say, or you have people who work in a team with you as leader. Think about how Pilate used the power that he had. Was he a good example of a leader? Ask God to make you a strong and honest leader, brave enough to do what you know is right.

- Have a bowl of water and a towel. Make a list of the things you are feeling bad and guilty about. Pray that God will forgive you as you wash your hands and dry them. Remember that we can't wash ourselves clean of guilt, but God can make us clean.

- *Father God, Pilate had so many people to listen to.*
  Help me to listen to people who have wise words and trust in you.
  Pilate had worries about losing some of his own power.
  Help me to think only of what you want, and not what I want.
  Pilate wanted to wash away his feeling of guilt.
  Help me to ask you to forgive me for all the times I go wrong.

  Nick Harding

Jesus on the Cross

Theme

Jesus' death

Scripture

John 18:1–19:42

Resources

NB Some advance planning needed!

- About 10 days before this service, sow a large cress cross *(see note 3)*

You will also need:

- All the equipment for your church's Easter Garden
- Three areas around the church with the following signs and items:

  – *Jesus had a home and a family like us*: objects which might have been in Jesus' home *(see note 1)*

  – *Jesus met ordinary people in ordinary places*: several large sheets of sugar paper, each with a picture of Galilee or old Jerusalem in the middle; lots of local newspapers; scissors and glue-sticks *(see note 2)*

  – *Jesus died on the cross – but that was not the end*: equipment for sowing cress crosses *(see note 3)*

- Music and words
- Stations of the Cross *(see note 4)*
- At the back of church, place a collection of heavy, solid objects, each labelled 'Sorry'. Wrap them in plain paper to disguise them or cover any printing: for example, bricks, large stones, big tins, boxes, pieces of wood. Try to avoid anything which rattles
- A large cross to stand or lie on the floor in front of the altar. Next to it, place:

  – A collection of palm crosses, enough for one each

  – *(Only if using the first Conclusion)* Tea-lights, matches and tapers

Leaders

Minimum: 2
- Leader
- Easter Garden Co-ordinator

Optimum: 7+
- Leader *(Introduction and Conclusion)*
- Easter Garden Co-ordinator(s)
- Activity Leader 1
- Activity Leader 2/Storyteller
- Explorer
- Music Leader
- Prayer Leader

Suggestions for additional music

Beneath the cross
You spoke and worlds were formed
From the falter of breath

Act of Witness

Pilgrimage with the cross.

Many churches make some kind of Good Friday pilgrimage: this one should be explicitly a walk for one and all, advertised in the community as well as in the church. Either pick a local hilltop as your destination and walk there from your church, carrying a large wooden cross between you, or walk from the centre of your community to a local church. At the end of the walk, offer a (well-publicised!) feast of hot cross buns.

Welcome

About 30 minutes before you plan to start the service, invite everyone to help you make the Easter Garden, according to your church's custom. Emphasise hands-on interactivity: it is more important to involve people, especially children, in the creative process than it is to fashion a 'perfect' garden.

Introduction

Welcome to our Good Friday service. Today we will be thinking about Jesus and what happened to him on Good Friday. We will try to answer the question that people often ask: 'Why is Good Friday called "good"?'

Activity 1

Here we have three areas to explore which will help us to think about Jesus' life and death. The first is called, 'Jesus had a home and a family like us,' and it is like the Home Corner which many of you may have in school. Come in and play with the sort of toys Jesus might have played with when he was a boy; try dressing up in the sort of clothes he might have worn.

The second area is called, 'Jesus met ordinary people in ordinary places.' Here are lots of pictures of places which may look exotic to us – but they were places which Jesus would have known as well as we know our local streets and shops. Around each of these pictures, we can stick pictures of our own everyday places and familiar people, by cutting them out of these local newspapers.

The third area is called, 'Jesus died on the cross – but that was not the end.' Here we can plant cress seeds to make crosses which will live and grow.

Take some time now to explore each of these three areas.

Music

My song is love unknown

Activity 2/Storytelling

Now we come to the story of what happened on Good Friday. Jesus was in trouble with powerful people because they were afraid he would take away their power. One of his friends told them where they could find Jesus and he was arrested and taken to the Roman governor of Jerusalem – a man called Pontius Pilate. So our story today begins with Jesus and Pilate, and Pilate has a decision to make: will he let Jesus go, or will he condemn him to death?

The Good Friday story is often told in pictures. These are called the Stations of the Cross and they mark the different stages of Jesus' journey. There are usually fourteen of them, but today we have seven and they are spread all around the church.

Can you find picture number one?
Find the picture and gather round it.
The Roman governor decided that Jesus would have to be killed. Jesus didn't say anything.

251

Can you find picture number two?
Find the picture and gather round it.
Jesus had to carry his big, heavy, wooden cross through the streets.

Can you find picture number three?
Find the picture and gather round it.
The cross was so heavy that sometimes Jesus fell down.

Can you find picture number four?
Find the picture and gather round it.
The soldiers took Jesus' clothes.

Can you find picture number five?
Find the picture and gather round it.
The soldiers nailed Jesus to the cross.

Can you find picture number six?
Find the picture and gather round it.
Jesus said, 'It's finished.' Then he died.

Can you find picture number seven?
Find the picture and gather round it.
Jesus' friends laid his body in the grave.

Exploring

The events of Good Friday are so horrible and sad that people often ask, 'Why is Good Friday called "good"?' It is good because it is all about love. Because Jesus loves us, he wants to be close to us – so he became a human being like us and had all the ordinary, wonderful, difficult and amazing experiences of growing up in this world. So he knows what every bit of life is like because he has been through it, too – and on Good Friday he went through death as well, so he knows what dying is like. He did that to share it all with us, because he loves us.

Because Jesus loves us, he also wants us to be close to God, our Father. The bad things we all do – because we are only human – keep us separated from God. So Jesus gave his life for us so that we can get right with God and be close to him forever.

Music

There is a green hill far away

Prayer action

When he died on the cross, Jesus made it possible for us to leave all our wrongdoing behind us. We need this because the messes we have made and the wrongs we have done can be like a heavy weight, dragging us down. Jesus said he would take these burdens from us; in return, we receive God's forgiveness which gives us a completely fresh start. In preparation for our prayers today, let us all take a moment to think of anything we have done or failed to do which still weighs heavy on our hearts. (Pause.) At the back of the church, there is a pile of heavy weights which represent those things for which we need to say sorry. You are invited to take a weight and leave it at the foot of the cross, as a sign that you have left your burden in Jesus' hands. In return, take away with you this little cross as a sign of God's love and forgiveness.

Give people enough time to think before carrying the weights forward. When all have returned to their seats with a cross, end with the following:

Loving Lord,
may this cross be for us
a reminder that you have taken away all our sins and a sign of your everlasting love for us.

EITHER *(If you are holding an all-age service on Easter Day)*

Conclusion

In many churches on the night before Easter, a vigil is held as people sit quietly in the dark church, waiting for the dawn of Easter Day. We will finish our service today with an opportunity to sit quietly for a time and simply wait. Come forward and light a candle. If you would like to join in the song, the words are simple: 'Jesus, remember me when you come into your kingdom.' The robber who was crucified next to Jesus said this, and we can all ask the same thing: 'Jesus, remember me when you come into your kingdom.'

Turn the lights off, light the candles and after a short period of silence, begin the Taizé chant. Begin quietly, grow louder and then end quietly.

Music

Jesus, remember me

OR *(If you are not holding an all-age service on Easter Day)*

Conclusion

But this cross is not the end of the story. After he died, Jesus came alive again! The good news which we celebrate on Easter Day is the best news ever: death is not the end. Because God loves us so much, he sent Jesus to break down the barrier of death so that after we die, we can follow him into heaven and live forever with God.

Bring forward some cress crosses, including the one you planted earlier.

That is why we made these cress crosses. Take your cross home, water it and watch it grow: let it be a living reminder that God's gift to us at Easter is the gift of life. Let us pray:

Father,
we thank you for your everlasting love which,
through your Son,
has given us everlasting life.

Music

Now the green blade riseth

Notes

1. Jesus had a home and a family like us

This area could include a child's wooden bricks; a sheepskin rug; a block of wood, hammer and nails; wooden bowls and spoons. Also some dressing-up clothes in natural colours and fabrics: tunics, robes, sashes and head-cloths (i.e. traditional Nativity play Shepherd outfits).

2. Jesus met ordinary people in ordinary places

Sources of pictures include websites such as www.bibleplaces.com and www.ancientsandals.com. Tourism and pilgrimage brochures for the Holy Land can also be useful. Suitable pictures are also available on the CD-ROM included with this book.

3. Jesus died on the cross – but that was not the end – sowing cress crosses

You will need:

- small plastic plates (or paper plates covered in tin foil)
- a cotton-wool roll cut into narrow strips
- cress seeds
- a small watering can.

Make the shape of a cross with the cotton wool and dampen it slightly, then sprinkle on some seeds and water lightly. If left on a sunny windowsill and watered regularly, they will sprout within a few days. For the large version, I have used a large disposable tin tray and wider strips of cotton wool. Sow this one fairly densely about 10 days before the service and by Good Friday your cross should be covered with a thick forest of cress.

If you are closing your service with the candlelit vigil rather than the good news of Easter, place this cross where people will be sowing their own; otherwise, save it until the closing prayer.

4. Stations of the Cross

Place these all around the church in a random order, so that people have to hunt for them. If your church does not have its own stations, they can be bought as posters from Christian suppliers and bookshops (e.g. Church House Bookshop). Here I have only used half the Stations, namely:

1st: Jesus is condemned to death.
2nd: Jesus accepts his Cross.
9th: Jesus falls the third time.
10th: Jesus is stripped of his garments.
11th: Jesus is nailed to the Cross.
12th: Jesus dies on the Cross.
14th: Jesus is placed in the tomb.

Claire Benton-Evans

The Cross

Although legally still recognised as a Public Holiday, Good Friday has largely become indistinguishable from any other Friday. Shops open, many employees have little choice about working, and the media barely notice it. Ironically Easter Day is now the only day when trading is prohibited! Sadly the connection between the two is barely recognised in most communities, though logic alone dictates that the resurrection could not have taken place without the crucifixion. But this is the heartland of the Christian faith, and Easter is its principal Feast. The celebration of Palm Sunday leads on to Good Friday as its inevitable culmination and the whole congregation should be involved in this.

Many churches are now finding ways to integrate the traditional observance of the Three Hours' Devotion with worship suitable for all age-groups, essential if younger members are to develop an appreciation of its importance. Young people's leaders sometimes offer a Good Friday 'workshop' of activities which are part of the whole church's observance, and even if the full three hours is rigorously kept, some time should be devoted to worship which encompasses all ages and groups. Our church has tried various patterns, and one that works well is to offer more devotional worship for adults while the children have their own activities for a couple of hours, and then to conclude the occasion with an all-age service centred around various symbols of Jesus' Passion and the events of Holy Week. We also prepare collages made up of newspaper and magazine pictures and headlines relating to suffering and crucifixion, which aim to earth the teaching in contemporary events and issues. All of this needs careful preparation, but is well worth the effort.

It may seem regrettable that a supposedly Christian people can be so ill-informed about and disinterested in the events which shaped our faith, but Good Friday is not about rectifying the information gap. On the Cross Jesus confronted and defeated for ever the evil which has so damaged the world. His final cry, 'It is finished!' referred not to his life, but to the mission he had come to fulfil in obedience to his heavenly Father. As the Church celebrates Easter it shares in the victory of Jesus over sin and death, and its worship is directed at enabling everyone present to know that as their own experience.

Hymns

Traditional

- In the cross of Christ I glory
- It is a thing most wonderful
- On a hill far away
- O sacred head, surrounded
- There is a green hill
- The royal banners forward go

Contemporary

- A purple robe
- I do not know the man
- Mary, blessed grieving mother
- My Lord, what love is this
- There is a Redeemer
- Were you there

Chant
- Jesus, remember me

Children's song
- Lord, you've promised

Readings

Years A, B and C
Isaiah 52:13–53:12
Hebrews 10:16-25 or 4:14-16, 5:7-9
John 18:1–19:42

Confession

Lord Jesus,
though we claim to be your friends
we have often let you down.
We confess that we have turned away
from your suffering,
kept silent when you are mocked and ill-treated,
and pretended we do not know you.
Forgive us and help us, we pray,
and in your mercy
bring us the joy of your salvation,
through Jesus Christ our Lord.

Absolution

May God our Father,
whose Son Jesus Christ has won
the victory over evil and death,
have mercy on you,
pardon and deliver you from all your sin,
and release you from fear
into freedom and peace,
through Jesus Christ our Lord.

Prayer

As our Saviour lays down his life for us
on the cross,
we recognise him as the Redeemer of all saying,
Lord, hear our prayer,
and let our cry come to you.

We thank you, Lord, that on the cross
you willingly forgave those who hated you
and condemned you to death.

Please help those who exploit others
for personal gain
to realise that only in accepting your love
will they find true satisfaction.
Especially we pray for . . .
Lord, hear our prayer,
and let our cry come to you.

We thank you, Lord, that on the cross
you showed compassion and care.
Please help those who seek to share your love
with the needy, lonely and suffering
wherever they are in the world,
and give them strength and encouragement in their service.
Especially we pray for . . .
Lord, hear our prayer,
and let our cry come to you.

We thank you, Lord, that on the cross
you showed mercy and forgiveness
to the penitent thief
who recognised you as King.
Please help those who feel rejected
or unworthy of your love
to know that you accept them as they are
and give them true peace.
Especially we pray for . . .
Lord, hear our prayer,
and let our cry come to you.

We thank you, Lord, that on the cross
you obeyed your Father even to death.
Please help us who follow in your footsteps
to demonstrate in our lives
your willing obedience and selfless love.
Especially we pray for . . .
Lord, hear our prayer,
and let our cry come to you.
As you have loved us,
so may we love one another,
that all people will know we are your disciples
and be drawn to you as Saviour and King.
In your name we ask this.

All-age address

The basis of this address comes from *For All the Family* (Kingsway, 1984), a pioneering book of ideas for all-age talks.

Beforehand take either an acetate sheet for an OHP or a large square piece of card, and on it draw a cross, with the lengths of both lines equal. To begin, hold this up and slowly rotate it through 45 degrees, asking as you do so what this symbol might mean. Four answers are likely to emerge.

1) In mathematics it's either an addition sign, or, if turned round, a multiplication sign, both of which indicate an increase in value. Emphasise that God doesn't regard us as valueless, but that without him our lives can't be as fulfilled or purposeful, because he created us for himself. Jesus said he came so that we might 'have life in all its fullness'. When we respond to his love, accept his forgiveness and follow his ways, we find the Cross gives our lives a new 'value' – eternal life.

2) A cross is also used by teachers to indicate when a question's been answered wrongly. A card with a simple miscalculation marked as wrong will help make the point more effectively. No one likes to get things wrong, but we need to be told, so that we can learn how to put it right next time. The cross tells us we've got something wrong – unkind words, selfish actions, unpleasant thoughts. On our own we haven't got a hope of doing anything about it. We'd much prefer not to admit we're wrong and need help, but nothing will change unless we do. The cross does far more than tell us we are wrong. Because Jesus was the only person who did get it right, God accepts us through him, just as we are, forgives us for all we've done wrong and gives strength to live for him from then on.

3) Another use of the cross symbol is at the end of a letter or on a Valentine's card. We might write, 'I love you. xxxxx' – here you could display the inside of a card with a couple of red hearts and a suitable inscription. The cross is a sign of Jesus' great love for us, too. There's nothing he would not to bring us back to himself, even death as a criminal. When someone says they love us, we want to see some evidence that they mean it (you could produce a box of chocolates or a bunch of flowers). God didn't just say he loves us – the cross proves it beyond doubt.

4) Finally display on a card a red triangle with a cross inside. Someone may already have mentioned its use to mark a crossroads. When we come to one, we know we have to make a decision about which way to go and if we are not sure we consult an atlas. The cross of Jesus forces us into deciding which way we're going in our lives. We choose to go our own way or to follow him. He doesn't force us because he wants us to make our own minds up, but when we see his cross we're faced with a decision we can't avoid.

Stuart Thomas

'Truly This Was the Son of God'

Moving out of our churches on Good Friday to join in shared worship in our local areas is a powerful opportunity for mission and outreach. So many people have only a very vague idea of who Jesus is, and few would know why this Friday is called Good. For many, a telling of the Good Friday story as part of this worship will be a fresh event, and a 'churches together' storytelling will also give Christians the opportunity of hearing it in a new way.

Shared preparation

The idea is that, after processing through the town centre, everyone gathers in a public area, each person with a copy of the script. From within each church, groups take responsibility for preparing symbols and sound effects to be used, and in the telling all these sound effects and symbols are scattered throughout the gathering, so no one is far from them. People gather in small circles of up to 20 people, around a central space.

Advertise the event in the local press, inviting people to come to listen. They join the circles, so that there is at least one set of sound effects in each circle.

Symbols and sound effects

Each church brings one each of the following, prepared by different age groups. I have given suggestions for how the sounds might be made, but do use the ideas of the group to come up with whatever seems most effective.

The betrayal: A pouch with 30 silver coins, which is shaken at the first * in the story and then, at the second *, it is opened and the coins thrown out on the ground. (Coins can be made from card covered in foil, or you could use metal disks.)

The arrest: The sound of metal clashing on metal (cutlery, metal umbrella spokes) and metal chains clinking. The sound of footsteps running (a flat bowl of gravel and blocks of wood stamped into them by several people at once). Shouts of soldiers.

Peter's denial: The sound of a fire (crackling paper). The sound of a cock crowing (someone can make this sound).

Pilate washes his hands: A bowl and a jug of water. Pour the water into the bowl and wash your hands in it noisily.

The flogging: Whips of rope flung several times against the ground.

The crown of thorns: Woven hawthorn or bramble (using thick gardening gloves) held up at the appropriate time and then placed in the centre of each circle of people.

The cross: Two large pieces of wood and some rope which is used to lash them together. The sign 'Jesus of Nazareth, King of the Jews' is on a nail which is hammered in.

The crucifixion: Nails are hammered into wood.

The dice: Two big dice are made and rolled. (Cube boxes covered with paper, and spots stuck or painted on.)

The curtain of the temple: Some heavy fabric, already cut to start off a rip. It is ripped strongly apart.

Earthquake: Large metal tray or sheet of heavy card, rattled.

The Story

Men and boys	About 2000 years ago in Bethlehem, Jesus was born. When he was about 30 years old Jesus travelled for two or three years around the areas of Galilee and Jerusalem, announcing the kingdom of God.
Women and girls	Many were healed by him, many forgiven, and many given new hope in God because of what Jesus said and did.

All	Huge crowds would seek him out wherever he went, and Jesus was well known for his compassion and his wisdom. He was also well known for speaking out the truth, even when the truth wasn't comfortable to hear. That made him enemies as well as followers.
A man	Jesus had gathered a group of twelve disciples and trained them. Judas, one of these close friends, went to the Roman authorities and offered to betray Jesus to them. They paid him thirty pieces of silver for the information. * After Jesus' death Judas was horrified by what he had done, and threw the money down at their feet before committing suicide. *
A woman	Another of Jesus' disciples, called Peter, had promised Jesus he would never let him down or desert him, whatever happened. But Jesus had looked at him and told him that before the cock crowed, Peter would have denied him three times.
A child	Peter was sure Jesus was wrong about that.
All	Led by Judas, the soldiers found Jesus praying among the olive trees in the darkness of Thursday evening. Judas greeted Jesus with a kiss, to show the soldiers which one he was, and they arrested him. * All Jesus' disciples ran away.
Men and boys	The soldiers dragged him before Caiaphas, the High Priest, to face his accusers. They were all making false statements against him. Peter crept into the courtyard to find out what was happening. It was cold, and there was a fire burning there. *
Peter	As Peter stood getting warm by the fire, a servant girl came out and said:
A woman	'You also were with Jesus the Galilean.'
Peter	Peter denied it. 'I don't know what you're talking about!' he said. Another servant girl noticed him and told the bystanders:
A woman	'This man here was with Jesus of Nazareth!'
Peter	Peter denied it again. 'I swear I don't know the man!' he said. Then one of the bystanders came up to him.
A man	'You certainly are one of them – your accent gives you away!'
Peter	Peter swore blind that he didn't know Jesus at all. And just then the cock crowed: and Jesus turned his head and looked straight at him. Peter suddenly remembered his promise, and what Jesus had said, and he felt terrible. He went out into the darkness, broke down and wept bitterly.
Women and girls	Those who were holding Jesus were mocking him. Jesus had a reputation for being a prophet, so they blindfolded him and then hit him, calling out:
Men and boys	'Go on, Prophet, prophesy! Who is it who struck you that time?'

Women and girls	On Friday morning they brought Jesus to the Council, and started questioning him.
A man	'If you are the Messiah, then tell us.'
Jesus	Jesus replied, 'If I tell you, you won't believe me. But I'll give you a clue – from now on the Son of Man will be seated at the right hand of God.'
All	At that, all of them started asking, 'So you are the Son of God, then?'
Jesus	Jesus was careful how he replied. He said, 'You say that I am.'
All	'That settles it,' they said. 'What other evidence do we need? We've heard it from his own lips!' And they brought Jesus to the Roman governor of the time – Pontius Pilate.
Pilate	When Pilate heard Jesus was from the Galilee region, he sent him off to Herod. Herod and his soldiers treated Jesus with contempt and sent him back to Pilate. But Pilate could find no offence he was guilty of, because Jesus was innocent. The crowds were all shouting for Jesus' death.
All	'Crucify him! Crucify him!'
Pilate	Pilate could see a riot was brewing, which was the last thing he wanted. He took some water * and in full sight of the crowds he washed his hands, shouting, 'I am innocent of the blood of this just man. See to it yourselves!' He had Jesus flogged * and then handed him over for death by crucifixion.
Men and boys	The soldiers stripped Jesus and put a scarlet robe on him, pushing a crown made of thorns * down over his head. They put a reed in his hand and pretended to bow down as if to a king, saying 'Hail, O King of the Jews!' And they spat on him and hit him.
Women and girls	Then Jesus was led away through the streets of Jerusalem, staggering from the beatings and carrying the cross * for his own execution. When he had fallen a couple of times they made a visitor to the city help carry the cross. All along the way the crowds watched him pass. Some were jeering at him, some crying. His mother was there, helpless.
Men and boys	They went out of the city to a hill called The Skull, where they nailed * Jesus to the cross by his hands and feet, and hoisted the cross into a slot in the rock so it stood upright. The soldiers threw dice * to win his clothes, and then they sat down to watch him die. The charge against him was fixed above his head:
All	'Jesus of Nazareth, King of the Jews.'
A few men	That didn't please the High Priests at all. They said, 'The whole point is that he pretended to be the King of the Jews – and that's blasphemy, punishable by death!' But no one changed the sign.
All	People passing by would call out, 'He saved others, but he can't save himself, can he?' or 'Come down from that cross – then we'll believe you!'

Jesus   Jesus was praying, 'Father, forgive them – they don't understand what they're doing.'

Men and boys   On either side of Jesus were bandits, also being crucified to death. One of them was cursing him, but the other asked, 'Lord, remember me when you come into your kingdom.'

Jesus   And Jesus said to him, 'I promise you, this very day you will be with me in Paradise!'

Women and girls   When it got to midday, there was darkness over the whole country for three hours, and at three o'clock in the afternoon Jesus cried out with a loud voice:

Jesus   'Father, into your hands I commend my spirit!' And he breathed his last, and died.

All   And the curtain to the holy of holies in the temple was suddenly ripped in two,* from the top to the bottom, and the earth shook and rocks were split apart. *

Centurion   When the centurion saw the way Jesus died, he said, 'Truly this man was God's Son.'

Men and boys   The soldiers came to speed up the dying by breaking the legs of the people being crucified, but when they came to Jesus he was already dead – they checked by piercing his side and found the blood had already separated into the blood and water of death.

Women and girls   Many women were there, watching from a distance, and Joseph of Arimathea, a rich man, and a disciple of Jesus, asked the authorities for the body.

Men and boys   Joseph took the body of Jesus down from the cross, wrapped it in a clean linen cloth and laid it in his new tomb in the rock. A great stone was rolled across the entrance to seal it.

All   So Jesus was laid to rest on Friday evening, as the Sabbath was beginning.

A child   But death could not hold the Lord of life. By Sunday, Jesus was alive again in a whole new way, and he has been alive ever since.

All   We believe that Jesus, who died on the cross that day, is the Son of God, and we worship him as Lord and Saviour.

Susan Sayers

At the Foot of the Cross

Resources

- A large piece of card or strip of lining paper which has been marked as if with paving stones or cobbles
- A large wooden cross, standing on the 'stones'
- Felt pens.

Leader

Jesus asked his friends to wait up with him on the night he was arrested, but they fell asleep. Just before Easter, many churches hold a night vigil as a way of watching and waiting through the night with Jesus. Our Good Friday prayers today will offer a sign that we, too, are waiting at the foot of the cross with Jesus – waiting through the darkness for the good news of Easter morning. In your own time, come forward and write your name or make your mark on one of these stones at the foot of the cross, as a sign that you are here.

Prayer action

Allow enough time for everyone to make a mark. Children may well want to draw as well as write.

Closing prayer

Self-giving Lord,
we have nothing to offer you but ourselves.
May our names written here remind us
that we are here with you this Easter,
and that you are always here with us.

Claire Benton-Evans

The Soldiers

Background

The soldiers who were in Jerusalem at the time of Jesus were working for many different people! Their job was to keep the peace, and most of the time there was an uneasy peace in the area, even though many people wanted to get rid of the Roman army.

The Romans were occupying the land, and wanted to make sure that there was peace by not upsetting the religious leaders too much. King Herod had his own army, and used it to protect himself and to remind the Romans that they were unwelcome there! The chief priests and religious leaders also had their own soldiers who carried out their work and protected their riches.

Soldiers were responsible for arresting Jesus, moving him from place to place as he was questioned and tortured. Soldiers also did all they could to make the final hours of Jesus really tough.

Then the governor's soldiers took Jesus into the Praetorium and gathered the whole company of soldiers round him. They stripped him and put a scarlet robe on him, and then twisted together a crown of thorns and set it on his head.

Matthew 27:27-29

The soldiers taunted Jesus and called him names before making sure that he was taken up the hillside to the Place of the Skull, Golgotha, and nailed to the cross. As Jesus slowly died on the cross the soldiers shared out his few possessions between them, and waited for his death. Yet even then Jesus was at work, and as the sky went black and the earth shook, Roman soldiers looked on, amazed.

When the centurion and those with him who were guarding Jesus saw the earthquake and all that had happened, they were terrified, and exclaimed, 'Surely he was the Son of God!'

Matthew 27:54

Actions and Activities

- What would it have been like to be a soldier at this time? Do you think it was good to have the weapons and authority to arrest people? Do you think it was safe? How long do you think soldiers would have lived?

- What do you think the soldiers would have said to Jesus as they put the crown of thorns on his head and mocked him? Write down some of the phrases you think can of, and then have a go at drawing the scene of Jesus being tortured.

- *Orders*

  Soldiers have to promise that they will obey the orders of their leaders. In pairs play a simple game, with one person telling the other what to do, and then swapping over so that everyone gives the orders, and everyone has to obey!

- You are a soldier being ordered to go to the quiet Garden of Gethsemane and arrest Jesus. You are not sure whether you should do this. What questions would you ask your commanding officer? What would you do if you really didn't think it was the right thing?

- The centurion, one of the Roman army leaders, was amazed by the death of Jesus and realised that he really was the Son of God. Imagine you are that centurion. What would you do after seeing Jesus die on the cross and realising that he was so special? Who would you tell about how you felt?

Pausing and Praying

- Find out about places in the world where soldiers are fighting now. Ask God to bring peace to countries and lands that are struggling, and keep armies and soldiers safe. Ask God to be with all soldiers.

- The soldiers had to do as they were told, even though some of them may not have liked doing it. Write a prayer asking God to help you to speak up and do the right thing when you are told to obey orders.

- *When I see bad things happening in my work or my school,*
  may I be a soldier for God, willing to do what is right.
  When I see people who need help and friendship,
  may I be a soldier for God, willing to do what is right.
  When I am feeling lost and tired,
  may I be a soldier for God, willing to do what is right.
  When I am tempted to do what I know is wrong,
  may I be a soldier for God, willing to do what is right.

Nick Harding

The Prisoners

The scene is a prison cell somewhere east of Skegness. Two prisoners are passing the time away (before it passes away completely) with a bit of chat and the occasional smile.

They are feeling less than happy about their predicament but are puzzled by another prisoner who left a few moments ago. Why was he so calm? Why wasn't he terrified at the prospect of being tortured and strapped to a cross? Wasn't he worried about getting splinters? Before they have time to chat any further, a guard comes along to take them on a little walk through the town and up a hill, where they will be given a lift up so that they can admire the view. You never know, they might meet up with that guy they met earlier.

Characters

Two petty crooks whose expertise and cunning are only rivalled by a bag of jelly babies.

Scene

Inside a prison cell. Shadows of bars fall across the two prisoners' faces. Sitting nervously, they cast glances about them. Not sure what will happen next they both sit hunched-up.

Props

Two benches or small seats. Chains around the hands and legs of the crooks. A projector or spotlight to project the shadows of bars.

Convict	*(looks around nervously; looks sideways at Villain)* What are you in here for?
Villain	*(doesn't look at Convict)* It's a bit embarrassing really.
Convict	You don't look like a bloke who can get embarrassed easily. Not with a haircut like that.
Villain	*(looks at Convict)* You can talk. Looks like you got dressed with whatever you found on the washing line.
Convict	*(sniffs)* I did.
Villain	Must have been in a bit of a hurry, then.
Convict	I was, mate. Matter of life and death.
Villain	*(folds arms across chest)* Well it certainly is now.
Convict	What?
Villain	Life and death. I hope you enjoyed what you had because there doesn't seem much hope of extending your life insurance policy.
Convict	Insurance salesmen! Bunch of robbers. It's them who should be in here, not law-abiding citizens like me and you.
Villain	Not quite law-abiding. Perhaps a citizen who's got a different interpretation of the law to some. A kind of flexible approach. I like to bend it my way.
	Both characters remain quiet for a few moments. In the background can be heard the sounds of shouting, a cell door is slammed shut and chains rattle.
Convict	*(shakes head slowly from side to side)* So anyway, what are you in here for?
Villain	Joyriding.
Convict	Joyriding! Is that all? How on earth did you get caught?

Villain   Couldn't get the donkey to wake up.

Convict   And some early morning guard nabbed you then?

Villain   No. I went to fetch some carrots from the local store.

Convict   And then you got nabbed? Isn't that breaking and entering?

Villain   No, well yes, technically. You see, I suddenly remembered I hadn't had any breakfast, so I munched my way through the fruit section and then moved on to the deli counter.

Convict   And then what?

Villain   I fell asleep.

Convict   And then you felt the long arm of the law prod you into consciousness?

Villain   No, it was the storekeeper's wife with her broom.

Convict   *(winces)* Ooh, that could have been nasty. So, how come you got done for joyriding?

Villain   I tried to make my getaway on the donkey. *(faint sound of hooves 'clip-clop' on stone road)* I had to escape.

Convict   So would I, mate, with a broom about to interfere with my anatomy. Anyway, that's still not joyriding, merely trying to escape from a severe bout of broomitis.

Villain   It's called joyriding when the donkey races off like lightning with me hanging on to its tail. Up-ended six priests, two tax collectors and a soothsayer before they caught me. So, what's your story?

Convict   I'm in for domestic violence.

Villain   Can't you sort out your domestic squabbles in private?

Convict   Wish I could. They put me in here for my own protection. You haven't seen the wife. Muscles the size of temple pillars. Makes me shudder to think. *(looks nervously around)*

Villain   Still, a bit steep putting you in here over a tiff.

Convict   That's what I tried to tell them. But some bright spark recognised me from a wanted poster.

Villain   What you wanted for then, throwing a tantrum in the bath?

Convict   Blind Bartimaeus.

Villain   But he is blind!

Convict   I just thought it was his nickname. You know, sort of turns a blind eye to things.

Villain   He definitely did that.

Convict   Bit of bad luck that, really.

Villain   Yeah. Still, not so unlucky as the bloke who was in here earlier.

Convict   Who was that, then?

Villain   Some religious teacher who got caught up in a bit of politics.

Convict   Politics. It'll be the death of us.

Villain   It will, mate, take my word for it. But this bloke, he sounded an OK sort of guy. I heard he was some sort of teacher. Upset a few of the local big noises but his heart was in the right place.

Convict   Bet he was really narked at being thrown in here and then put on trial.

Villain   Now, that's the funny thing. He didn't seem to mind, sort of expected it. Didn't hold a grudge.

Convict   I heard he did a lot of amazing things. Someone told me he even healed Blind Bartimaeus.

Villain   He'll have to get another nickname now.

Convict   He might make a better look-out though.

Villain   Yeah, at least things are looking up for him.

Convict   I think things will be looking up for us soon. *(looks in the direction of the light projecting image of prison bars)*

Villain   Yeah, looking up at a great chunk of wood waiting for our attention.

Convict   Oh well, beats work.

Sound of another cell door being slammed and loud footsteps echo along the corridor. A key is heard turning in the lock and a cell door creaks open.

Villain   Talking of beating, here comes that guard with the welcoming snarl.

Summary

At his trial, Jesus must have felt that the whole world was against him. There were those who openly opposed him and had done everything they could to silence a voice that threatened to disrupt their egocentric lifestyles. There were those people who wanted to dispose of a voice that openly criticised their religious activity (an activity which said more about their devotion to themselves and rituals than their devotion to God). And there were those who wept. They wept because they felt a sense of loss, a sense of defeat and a sense of betrayal. They felt betrayed by those followers of Jesus who faded into the background when things began to get tough. They felt betrayed by their own emotions which had hoped for so much and now saw all their desires crumble under a whip. But the one who was betrayed and had suffered the biting lashes of rejection wouldn't have chosen any other way. This was the way forward, the way chosen by his Father.

The crucifixion was a barbaric form of punishment. The suffering and obvious pain were all part of a process designed to act as a warning to anyone who had thoughts of rebellion against the system.

When the person to be crucified reached the place of crucifixion, the T-shaped cross (there was no extended top piece so that the person had nowhere to rest their head) was placed upon the ground and the person's arms were stretched out across the bar and their hands nailed to the wood. The feet were fastened to the upright. About halfway up the cross was a piece of wood called the 'saddle'. This was designed to take the weight of the victim so they didn't tear their hands from the nails. The 'cross' was then lifted into a socket which kept the person's feet about a metre above the ground.

Dragging the heavy wooden cross through the streets (often going the long way round) and the subsequent nails and lifting into position were excruciatingly painful but not designed to kill the victim immediately. The victim was left to die of a mixture of pain, thirst and starvation.

Pete Townsend

Jesus Suffered for Us (an all-age talk)

Ask two people to come out and stand at least three metres apart. Ask one of the people to walk down to reach the other. Was there any problem in that? (Hopefully not.) Now ask both people to get to you, only this time with one condition – they mustn't move. Can they do it? (No, it's impossible.) If they want to get across to reach you they will have to go on a journey to do it. Is the journey easy or difficult? (They can try it to find out.) They probably did that with no trouble at all.

But suppose the journey is made very difficult? (Tie all four ankles together with a scarf and walk away from them.) Can they get to me now? (Let them try.) As they are moving along explain that they can certainly do it, but only by using a lot more effort, and with quite a struggle. Stop them halfway and explain how being crucified was like a terrible journey that Jesus had to make to rescue us. In the middle of his journey people shouted at him to come down from the cross and save himself from the suffering.

Ask the people if they would be capable of untying the scarf and walking free. Jesus could have come down from the cross, so why didn't he? He died on the cross because there wasn't any other way to rescue us apart from accepting all the chains of our sin and carrying them for us, even though it made his journey so difficult. So instead of opting out, he carried on (the people can carry on too) until the journey was finished and we can all be set free (untie the legs of the volunteers).

Susan Sayers

RESOURCES

Good Friday

Good Friday is the Friday of Holy Week, when Christians remember the crucifixion of Christ. The name may be derived from 'God's Friday' in the same way that 'Goodbye' is derived from 'God be with ye'.

All four Gospels carry an account of the crucifixion, and each one gives a differing emphasis. The four Gospels all agree on the timing: midday until three o'clock on the day before the Sabbath. The Jewish authorities were very disturbed over Jesus' teachings and wanted to stamp out what they saw as blasphemy. They didn't have the authority to execute Jesus and so had to resort to the Roman Governor, Pontius Pilate. It is these events leading up to Jesus' death and burial that form the focus of Good Friday worship.

At the point of death, Jesus cried out, 'It is finished!' This was not a cry of defeat but rather a shout of triumph. He had accomplished what he came to do – that is, to redeem humanity. On the cross at Calvary, Jesus completed the task from which he prayed to be delivered in the garden of Gethsemane.

There is usually no celebration of the Eucharist on Good Friday. In many churches, a prayer service is held from midday to 3pm, known as the Three Hours' Devotion, and is sometimes based around the seven last words of Jesus. No single Gospel contains all seven last sayings, and readings are taken from all four Gospels. Some three-hour services are a conflation of Matins, Ante-communion (using the Reserved Sacrament in high church parishes) and Evensong.

A service of 'The Stations of the Cross' is often observed, either in the church or outside at 3pm. The 'stations' are usually pictures or carvings which represent incidents in the journey made by Jesus from his being condemned to death by Pilate to his being placed in the tomb of Joseph of Arimathea. Prayers and meditations are made at each station.

In many places, Christians of all traditions come together to take part in a Procession of Witness. They carry a cross through the streets of the community as a silent witness to the importance of the day. Stops are made at strategic points on the procession where Bible readings or an address may be given, or a hymn may be sung.

David Schofield

Imagine

Imagine you are one of those in the crowd that has followed the path of Jesus to the place called Golgotha. You have watched thus far in horror, but now you close your eyes, unable to look any more at the scenes unfolding before you, yet you cannot block out the sounds of what is happening; sounds which are equally if not more dreadful. The ringing of the hammer as it drives the nails mercilessly through the flesh of Jesus. The involuntary gasps of agony as the cross is lifted up and those skewered hands and feet begin to tear under his weight. The raucous jeers of the crowd as they gather round to gloat, mingled with the sobs of women close by, their hearts close to breaking. Surely it will be over soon? Nothing can be

269

worse than this! And then it comes, the most terrible, haunting sound of all; a cry of such torment, such desolation, that your blood runs cold: 'My God, my God, why have you forsaken me?' And suddenly you realise, for the first time, just how much this man dying before you has gone through; the full extent of his suffering, the wonder of his sacrifice. Today, as best we may, we stand by that cross again. We listen, we watch, we marvel!

Nick Fawcett

Jesus – Threat to the Authorities

The crucifixion of Jesus with two criminals was not a mere coincidence. By positioning Jesus between the two criminals the authorities were attempting to make a statement. First, that Jesus was no more than a common criminal, a thief or con artist. Second, a crown of thorns and a placard declaring him to be a king was intended to imply that he was nothing more than a leader of other criminals, a self-professed lord and liar.

Jesus is mocked by three groups of people. The leaders, or Jewish rulers, mock him with a sense of relief. To them, Jesus posed a threat, a constant thorn in their side who reminded them of their duty to God and to the community. It came as a huge sense of relief to the authorities when Jesus was 'put in his place' and humiliated. It was a public statement that implied Jesus had been judged by the real leaders and found to be a fraud whose followers were nothing more than a bunch of no-hopers.

The soldiers had mocked Jesus by again questioning his ability to do anything about his situation. To the soldiers, a leader was someone to be respected, someone who held authority and whose orders were obeyed. They despised someone who claimed to have authority but who received nothing more than public disgrace.

The two criminals who were crucified with Jesus mocked him because it appeared that he'd been brought down to their level. To be crucified with them meant he was no better than them and was someone who wasn't clever enough, or powerful enough, to avoid the punishment of a common criminal.

Almost immediately the criminals realised that an innocent person was being crucified. One of the criminals understood that Jesus was taking the blame for the crimes of other people.

A little while later a Roman officer began to praise God after recognising that Jesus was everything he claimed to be. And it wasn't long before the authorities realised that their attempt to kill Jesus was nothing more than a fulfilment of everything Jesus had said would happen. Their mockery died as Jesus rose from the dead.

Why was Jesus considered to be such a threat to the religious authorities?

For a short time the religious authorities welcomed the words that initially John the Baptist and then Jesus used to encourage people to a faith in God. But, it wasn't long before they realised that Jesus considered them, the religious leaders, to be as far from a real relationship with God as anyone else. Even more worrying was the fact that Jesus didn't encourage the people to go through the religious procedures and customs considered so important by the religious leaders. In fact, Jesus pointed out the hypocrisy of the religious leaders who abused their positions of power for their own selfish reasons. Little wonder that the religious leaders thought they'd be better off with Jesus dead.

Pete Townsend

The Trial

When Jesus Christ was tried in Palestine,
two charges were considered by the courts:
first, that he posed a threat to Church and God;
second, he was a danger to the State.
But neither accusation could they prove,
and Christ's conviction was unjustified.

What did those giants have to fear from him –
the Son of David, armed with nought but love?
Do priests and temples, kings and empires shake
before the man whose crown is twisted thorns?

Yet maybe Caiaphas and Pilate knew
that Jesus had a greater strength than theirs:
a message set to win the common heart
and shake the unjust powers from their thrones;
a Spirit which would fire the human soul
and burn away the dross of inborn sin;
a love to bear all suffering and wrong
and build a kingdom out of truth and good.

The influence of Jesus on this world
cannot be measured, nor is yet complete;
for whereas those who tried him are long gone,
his living presence stirs our spirits still.
And though our Lord seemed helpless, when he stood
in mocking robe of purple stained with red,
it is not he who stands on trial now,
but Church, and State, and every mortal soul.
And though he is a king, he does not rule
by force of arms, or wealth's persuasive power;
but by the seeming weakness of his love,
he gains an entrance to the human heart.
As he himself declared, it is the meek
to whom God, in his pleasure, gives the earth.

Peter Dainty

The Ultimate Sacrifice

Read

From the sixth to the ninth hour, darkness fell over the whole country. Then, at that ninth hour, Jesus shouted out, 'Eloi, Eloi, lama sabachthani?' which, translated, means, 'My God, my God, why have you abandoned me?'

Mark 15:33, 34

271

Ponder

Nothing takes us more powerfully and directly to the heart of this day than that desolate cry of Jesus from the cross: 'My God, my God, why have you abandoned me?' And no words, on the surface at least, could make it seem more inappropriately named, for what on earth can be good about Jesus feeling so helpless, so hopeless, so utterly bereft and alone? It's as though up to this point, despite everything he'd said, he'd been secretly hoping that God might somehow rescue him; that there might be a last-minute reprieve, a miraculous escape. Hadn't he, after all, cried out in Gethsemane, 'if it be possible, take this cup from me'? Was this, then, a crisis of faith as God failed to step into the breach?

It might seem that way, but the reality couldn't be more different. Yes, Jesus felt isolated, forsaken, and yes it was devastating beyond words, but this was what he had committed himself to doing right at the start of his ministry – not simply surrendering his life but taking upon himself the sins of the world, bearing them in his body, taking upon himself the punishment that should have been ours. There on the cross Jesus endured the agony of total separation from God, an agony not just of body but of spirit. Rather than abandon us, he faced what it means to feel utterly *abandoned*. In order to reconcile with God, he was estranged. It was the ultimate sacrifice to make possible the ultimate gift: new life, resurrection life, lived for evermore. That's the message of Good Friday. Could any day be more *appropriately* named!

Ask yourself

Do the physical sufferings of Christ cause you to forget what he went through spiritually? Have you appreciated the extent of his sacrifice? Have you made your own the relationship with God that he made possible?

Pray

Lord Jesus Christ, I marvel at your willingness to endure thorns pressed into your head, a whip cutting into your back, nails hammered into your hands and feet, and your body stretched and broken upon a cross. Yet, still more, I marvel at what you were ready to suffer spiritually: the awfulness of being estranged from the Father having previously lived every moment at one with him; of feeling abandoned, hopeless, utterly alone; of carrying the world's sin on your shoulders though you alone were without sin. Thank you for what you achieved through that sacrifice – for accepting the punishment that was mine so that I might share the life that is yours.

Remember

Christ suffered and died for sins once for all, the righteous offering himself for the unrighteous, in order to bring you to God.

1 Peter 3:18a

Close

For bringing me close to God through being made far from him, for reconciling me through being estranged, Lord, receive my grateful praise.

Nick Fawcett

Crucifixion – a Sketch

As the great drama of Holy Week nears its close, Jesus takes up his cross and is lifted up as he had predicted. Around it gathers a representative selection of humanity whose counterparts are with us today: close at hand the true believers and the critics, further away the disinterested passers-by and, somewhere in between, those – like Simon the sign-writer – who just can't make up their mind about Jesus of Nazareth, King of the Jews.

Bible source

John 19:16-30

Performance time

Six minutes with reading

Characters

Reader
Simon – a sign-writer
Scene setter
Baruch – a trader

Scene setter

Simon stands Right of centre, looking out over the audience. Baruch is off Left. If possible the scene should be in darkness while the Reader, spotlit, is on stage.

The Reader enters and takes centre stage.

Reader Finally Pilate handed him over to them to be crucified. So the soldiers took charge of Jesus. Carrying his own cross, he went out to the place of the Skull (which in Aramaic is called Golgotha). Here they crucified him, and with him two others – one on each side and Jesus in the middle.

Pilate had a notice prepared and fastened to the cross. It read: JESUS OF NAZARETH, THE KING OF THE JEWS. Many of the Jews read this sign, for the place where Jesus was crucified was near the city, and the sign was written in Aramaic, Latin and Greek. The chief priests of the Jews protested to Pilate, 'Do not write "The King of the Jews", but that this man claimed to be king of the Jews.'

Pilate answered, 'What I have written, I have written.'

When the soldiers crucified Jesus, they took his clothes, dividing them into four shares, one for each of them, with the undergarment remaining. This garment was seamless, woven in one piece from top to bottom.

'Let's not tear it,' they said to one another. 'Let's decide by lot who will get it.' This happened that the Scripture might be fulfilled which said, 'They divided my garments among them and cast lots for my clothing.' So this is what the soldiers did.

Near the cross of Jesus stood his mother, his mother's sister, Mary the wife of Clopas, and Mary Magdalene. When Jesus saw his mother there, and the disciple whom he loved standing near by, he said to his mother, 'Dear woman, here is your son,' and to the disciple, 'Here is your mother.' From that time on, this disciple took her into his home.

Later, knowing that all was now completed, and so that the Scripture would be fulfilled, Jesus said, 'I am thirsty.' A jar of wine vinegar was there, so they soaked a sponge in it, put the sponge on a stalk of the hyssop plant, and lifted it to Jesus' lips. When he had received the drink, Jesus said, 'It is finished.' With that, he bowed his head and gave up his spirit.

The Reader exits.

The scene lights up. Baruch enters carrying a bag over his shoulder. He is about to pass upstage but notices Simon and comes over to stand beside him, putting his bag on the ground.

Baruch	Another execution! One would think the Romans had enough blood on their hands already.
Simon	*(turns to him, speaking softly)* It is not wise to criticise the Romans, friend. Particularly at this time when revolt is in the air.
Baruch	Oh, revolt is always in the air somewhere in the great empire. Here, in my own country, even in Rome itself, I hear. But nothing ever comes of it. People are fatalistic. If it were not Rome it would be another great power. The devil you know . . . *(he laughs)* Besides, they bring civilisation of a sort – plumbing and circuses. *(they both laugh)*
Simon	What is your business, friend?
Baruch	Oh, spices, perfumes, nard. *(he taps the bag)* Always in demand at these festivals. I follow the crowds from one city to another. And you?
Simon	A sign-writer. You can see an example of my work up there. *(points)* Above that cross in the centre of the three.
Baruch	*(peering up)* I commend your skill, my friend. Finely written. I can read the Greek and Latin – but not the . . .
Simon	Aramaic.
Baruch	Ah yes. Aramaic. What does it say? The King of the Jews. King of the Jews? Surely they are not crucifying your king?
Simon	To tell you the truth, I don't know who they're crucifying. The man, Jesus of Nazareth he is called, was a teacher and healer. There are many such as he in our country. For the past three years he has been travelling around with a small group of followers. The common people loved him; called him a prophet, perhaps Elijah come back to us. Some even believed he was Messiah.
Baruch	Messiah? Is that a king?

Simon	Of a kind, yes. Our holy scriptures promise that one day Messiah will come and put all things right. He is to be of the house of David and he will rule over his people for ever, from this city of Jerusalem, the holy city.
Baruch	*(points)* Listen, your king cries out. He is thirsty. Ah, they are putting some wine on a sponge and raising it to his lips. *(pause)* He drinks.
Simon	It will be wretched stuff. Not fit for a king.
Baruch	But fit for a criminal. For only criminals are crucified by the Romans, are they not? Criminals and slaves.
Simon	Pilate could find no crime against him. He wanted to let him go. But the scribes and the Pharisees had it in for him. They've been against him from the start, ever since he said he could forgive sins.
Baruch	Forgive sins! But in your religion – forgive me if I am wrong – sins can only be forgiven by God.
Simon	Exactly. So he was saying, in what he did and what he said, that he was Messiah, in the Greek Christos, he who should come. And they wouldn't have that. Nor, in the end, would the people. And nor, so I've heard, would his followers. Everyone has denied or deserted him.
Baruch	And what about Rome?
Simon	Oh, as I say, Pilate would have let him go but in the end the religious lobby had its way. He couldn't afford to offend them again. But that sign of mine is his way of getting his own back. Jesus of Nazareth, the king of the Jews. You should have seen the look on those high priestly faces when the soldiers tacked that up! Stuck in their craw it did.
Baruch	He speaks again. I can't quite hear. His head drops. The women there cry out. It is the end for your king, my friend.
Simon	Yes, I suppose it is. It's funny, you know, I never thought it would come to this. Even when he was being lashed. Even when he was on the cross. I half expected him to come into his own. To come down from the cross and prove his enemies wrong.
Baruch	*(puts a hand on Simon's shoulder)* No, my friend. The only way your king will come down from that cross is for burial. Who knows, he might even be a good customer for me. *(pats his bag)* Speaking of which I must be going. *(looking up)* It's getting quite dark. Goodbye, my friend. May your God be with you.
Simon	Goodbye. May you prosper. *(turns back to look for the last time)* Jesus of Nazareth, The King of the Jews. Fair writing under pressure, though I say it myself. But who were you? Preacher? Teacher? Healer? False prophet? Not Messiah at any rate. No son of God would finish up dead on a Roman cross. *(turns to walk off Right)* That's only for criminals – and slaves. *(exits)*

Blackout.

Peter Jackson

All Right, So My Motives Were Mixed – Judas Iscariot

But Judas Iscariot, one of his disciples (the one who was about to betray him), said, 'Why was this perfume not sold for three hundred denarii and the money given to the poor?' (He said this not because he cared about the poor, but because he was a thief; he kept the common purse and used to steal what was put into it.)

John 12:4-6

Meditation

All right, so my motives were mixed,
more about my pockets than the needs of the poor,
but I had a point, didn't I – give me that.
Remember, that perfume of Mary's was expensive stuff:
not just the price of a couple of days' wages
but something you'd have to save up for over weeks,
even months.
Think of the difference it could have made to people's lives –
the food it could have put on someone's table,
clothes on a child's back –
and there she was pouring it out in one sentimental gesture,
the whole lot wasted in an instant.
It was criminal,
profligate –
that's how I saw it,
and if *she* saw no better use for it
then, believe me, *I* did!
But far from reprimanding her, as I expected,
Jesus turned on me as though *I* were the one in the wrong.
What was up with him?
Didn't he care about the poor?
Of course he did, more than anyone,
but he realised, even if no one else did,
that he had to face death to bring others life –
and Mary, even if unwittingly,
was anointing his body for burial.
He cared all right,
not just for the poor but for everyone,
even a worthless wretch like me:
enough to give his all to make real change
possible in our broken world.
What was I thinking of to send him to his death?
I must have been mad!
But, you see, despite the rumours of me thieving,
I genuinely wanted to help my people,
and I foolishly believed Jesus was leading them astray –
only, of course, I couldn't have been more wrong.
He offered his life to give hope to all,
no price too high to pay.
So if you care,

really care,
about those in need,
how much are *you* willing to give in turn?

Prayer

Loving Lord,
teach us to give generously,
to others and to you;
to use the resources you put at our disposal in your service,
striving in some small way to build a better world,
bringing your kingdom closer here on earth.
Help us to love you more truly
and to show that love in both our worship and service,
reaching out where we can to those in need.
Through responding to them
may we respond also to you.

Nick Fawcett

I Could Find No Case against Him – Pontius Pilate

Pilate went out again and said to them, 'Look, I am bringing him out to you to let you know that I find no case against him.' So Jesus came out, wearing the crown of thorns and the purple robe. Pilate said to them, 'Here is the man!' When the chief priests and the police saw him, they shouted, 'Crucify him! Crucify him!' Pilate said to them, 'Take him yourselves and crucify him; I find no case against him.' The Jews answered him, 'We have a law, and according to that law he ought to die because he has claimed to be the Son of God.' Now when Pilate heard this, he was more afraid than ever. He entered his headquarters again and asked Jesus, 'Where are you from?' But Jesus gave him no answer.

John 19:4-9

Meditation

I could find no case against him,
no charge to answer.
He wasn't a rebel, urging revolt,
nor some usurper with designs on power –
his intentions, in terms of this world,
clearly harmless, albeit misguided.
He'd hurt no one,
wronged no one,
yet clearly he'd caused offence,
for those infernal scribes and Pharisees,
with their never-ending rules and regulations,
wanted him dealt with:
not just punished or imprisoned,
but dead.
That wouldn't have bothered me in the usual run –
what's one less troublemaker? –

but this Jesus fellow unnerved me from the start.
Those eyes of his!
Those quiet yet assured replies!
They threw me completely,
seeming to say *my* fate was in *his* hands,
rather than *his* in *mine*.
Where was he from, I wondered?
Who could he be?
A visitor from the gods?
And as that alarming thought took hold,
I tried to set him free.
But it was hopeless,
the pack having scented the kill,
and the harder I pleaded his cause
the louder they bayed for blood.
I gave in, eventually.
What choice did I have?
Rather his neck on the line than mine.
But I've not slept easy since,
that gentle innocent face of his haunting my dreams.
I found no case against him,
yet sent him to his death,
and I'm just hoping now that he's not who he claimed to be –
king of another world –
for if he was, I fear one day another verdict may be delivered . . .
in a case against me.

Prayer

Suffering Saviour,
for receiving the sentence that is ours,
facing the punishment that is ours,
bearing the sin that is ours,
enduring the death that is ours,
we worship you.
Receive the thanks, praise, worship and service
that is rightfully *yours*, and, in your mercy,
help us to receive the victory you have won
and to walk each day in newness of life,
cleansed,
renewed,
forgiven.

Nick Fawcett

By Way of Betrayal

Matthew 21:1-11; Matthew 26:14–27:66

Why did he ask, Judas?
Why did he ask, 'Surely not I, Lord?'

He knew very well he was going to betray Jesus:
unless he didn't see it as betrayal.

Misunderstanding,
frustration at his Lord's failure
to deliver: whatever.
The disciples' treasurer
sold their greatest asset down the river.

Just the first
of a long line of betrayals

Gethsemane.
Why did he ask the disciples to pray with him?
He might have known they would fall asleep
yet he had human need . . .

Three times he came and found them there,
those three whom he had awakened
to new life,
preferring sleep to prayer.
Betrayal.

And when at last
the time came – maybe they were blasé,
no one had been able to lay hands on him before –
the time of his arrest,

all of those with whom he had just shared bread,
all of them,
all who counted themselves so privileged
to be his closest followers, fled.
Betrayal.

So bring him to trial!
But on what grounds?
Find a witness who will quote his claim
to pull down, and rebuild the temple?

Quote, or misquote?
He never uttered such a threat: spoke rather
of himself. And such a charge, even if accepted,
would not secure the Roman vote

needed for execution, as Caiaphas well knew;
master of intrigue, wily fox
using and abusing
power for his own ends –

having failed to dish the dirt
on Jesus, puts him under oath,

against the law,
making the living God swear to his own hurt.
Betrayal.

Meanwhile, outside
Peter is also swearing;
as we do, so many of us
whenever we're put on the spot;

faced with accusation, he fumbles
for words, finds the wrong ones.
Flustered, fearful,
the one whom Jesus called the Rock, crumbles.
Betrayal.

From a man with a reputation
like Pontius Pilate
you wouldn't, of course, expect grace
(or that he'd take any notice of his wife)

so, failing to restore
his conscience alongside his career
he washes his hands; one man's weakness
undermines the strength of Roman law.
Betrayal.

From a Gentile,
understandable indifference;
from the Jewish priests and elders
uncomprehending enmity:

threading the crowd, sowing the seed,
incitement to religious hatred,
demanding a barbarian death
none would normally have agreed.
Betrayal.

And what is it about a crowd
that makes it so malleable,
so apt to park its mind,
become a loud mob?

So soon, to abandon the palm
and the shouts of 'Hosanna!'
So soon, to cry 'Crucify!'
to sing such a different psalm.
Betrayal.

Faced with the two,
Jesus of Nazareth and Jesus Barabbas:
what's in a name? Both fight for freedom
and both are 'sons of the father':

one is a common criminal,
commonly understood, fighting a common cause;
the other, an uncommon prophet
delighting, disturbing ...

How is the crowd to be wise
as to which son, which father,
which freedom they'd rather have?
So one Jesus is saved, as his Saviour dies;

with well-deserved punishment waived
did Barabbas – do I? – find a different freedom?
One Jesus crucified on the other's cross
dying my death, and I am saved?

All this betrayal, then.
Not so much tragic irony as long-held plan?

I am Judas;
I am Peter; I am a sleepy disciple;
I am a false witness; I am priest and people;
I am the fickle crowd.

The very fact
that we cannot be trusted
to be courageous, loyal, wise, true
establishes the reason

for such a plan, and that its instrument
is treason:
therein lies its irony
its poetry, its grace.

Sheila Walker

Friday

It was bad Friday on Golgotha hill
when they set up a cross in order to kill.
They nailed through the hands
and they nailed through the feet
of the man of love to whom life was sweet;
and his blood washed away
in the tears of the rain,
and the very earth shook
with the shame of his pain.
It was bad Friday on Golgotha hill
when they set up a cross in order to kill.

It was bad Friday on Golgotha hill,
when they murdered a man for doing God's will.
His tongue was dry
and his throat was hoarse,
but the clamour of men
was strident and coarse;
and black was the earth
and black was the sky
when the Truth was stretched
on a cross to die.
It was bad Friday on Golgotha hill
when they murdered a man for doing God's will.

It was bad Friday on Golgotha hill,
when the voices of love and of truth were still.
And a duty was done
for the good of the state
outside the respectable city gate;
and the world was ruled
for those six evil hours
by the pride and the greed
of corrupt human powers.

It was bad Friday on Golgotha hill
when the voices of love and of truth were still.
But now we can see with a clearer eye
the power of a man who was ready to die.
For the light that was hid
and the life that was lost
have won for the world,
at a measureless cost,
the ultimate triumph
of truth and of good
against all the worst tortures of iron and wood.
So that bad Friday on Golgotha hill
became Good Friday then,
and is Good Friday still.

Peter Dainty

The Burial

Jesus is not buried by his enemies,
but by his friends –
not by Caiaphas and Pilate,
but by Joseph and Nicodemus;
not by atheists and unbelievers,
but by those who love him.

It is his followers who seek
to lay him reverently to rest.
They bury him deep
under mountains of tradition,
safely entomb him
in the narrow coffin of religion.

They wrap him up tight
in the protective shroud of dogma,
preferring funereal ritual
to resurrection joy,
and a dim religious light
to the eye-stinging brightness
of God's good morning.

The tears are genuine,
and the precious ointment of fine words,
preserving the fragrant memory
of a mummified saviour.
But the heavy stone
they roll across the tomb is the stone of fear –
fear of the living God.

God-in-a-box
is not as disturbing
as God in the world.

Yet they may as well try
to bury the wind,
for he is free and alive,
and his devoted guardians
cannot hold him down,
however grave their intentions.

Peter Dainty

ABOUT THE CONTRIBUTORS

DAVID ADAM was the Vicar of Lindisfarne, off the Northumbrian coast, for thirteen years until he retired in March 2003. His work involved ministering to thousands of pilgrims and other visitors. He is the author of many inspiring books on spirituality and prayer, and his Celtic writings have rekindled a keen interest in our Christian heritage.

CLAIRE BENTON-EVANS writes exclusively for Kevin Mayhew. She is the author of many resource books for church leaders working with children, including two popular series, *Allsorts Worship* and *All-sorts Prayer*. She studied English at Oxford before teaching English and Drama in London, Devon and Cornwall. Her writing for schools includes *What's the Story?* – a collection of Bible assemblies – and the *Beastly Bible Stories* series. Claire regularly trains clergy, head teachers and school governors in children's spirituality; she also enjoys leading Beastly Bible Stories school events. She lives with her family in the Scottish Borders, where she works as the Youth and Children Officer for the Diocese of Edinburgh.

RUPERT BRISTOW, a Reader in Trinity Benefice, Folkestone, is the author of seven books of prayers for Kevin Mayhew and was Director of Education for Canterbury Diocese from 1995 until his retirement in 2008. He has taught on VSO in Rwanda, was the second Director of the UK Council for Overseas Student Affairs, and then Dean of Student Services at London South Bank University. He has also been a specialist adviser to a House of Commons select committee, edited and written for various educational publications and chaired Kent SACRE (Standing Advisory Council for Religious Education). He is an Honorary Fellow of Canterbury Christ Church University and is currently a governor of East Kent College and a member of the Discipleship and Spirituality Resource Group in Canterbury Diocese.

JOHN COX was ordained to a curacy in the diocese of Liverpool in 1968. He spent a second curacy in an inner-city ex-slum parish in Birmingham and became rector in the same parish. After a five-year period at Church House, Westminster where he was Senior Selection Secretary, helping to select ordinands, he was made Canon Treasurer at Southwark Cathedral and Diocesan Director of Ordinands and Post-ordination training. Following four years as Vicar of Roehampton he moved to become Archdeacon of Sudbury in the Diocese of St Edmundsbury and Ipswich in 1995. When he retired in 2006 he was asked to be the part-time Diocesan Director of Education, a job he did for nearly four and a half years before retiring for a second time. It has been during these retirement years that John has been writing for Kevin Mayhew.

PETER DAINTY was ordained in 1963 after studying church history whilst training for the Methodist ministry, and ministered in two circuits (Brigg and Pontefract). He moved to Bury St Edmunds in 1971 to teach at Culford School (an independent Methodist co-educational boarding and day school) where he stayed until his retirement in 2001. From 1973 - 1993 he was a non-stipendiary minister at a small church in Bury St Edmunds. Peter has worked part-time as an editor for Kevin Mayhew and has published many books and anthologies, as well as six gift books for special occasions, all of which include his own prayers.

NICK FAWCETT was brought up in Southend-on-Sea, Essex and trained for the Baptist ministry at Bristol and Oxford, before serving churches in Lancashire and Cheltenham. He subsequently spent three years as a chaplain with the Christian movement Toc H, before focusing on writing and editing, which he continues with today, despite wrestling with myeloma, a currently incurable cancer of the bone marrow. He lives with his wife, Deborah, and two children – Samuel and Kate – in Wellington, Somerset, worshipping, when able, at the local Anglican church. A keen walker, he delights in the beauty of the Somerset and Devon countryside around his home, his numerous books owing much to the inspiration he unfailingly finds there. Nick has had over 130 books published by Kevin Mayhew.

MICHAEL FORSTER grew up in an Anglican vicarage, trained for the Baptist ministry at Regent's Park College, Oxford, and later transferred to the United Reformed Church. He has served a variety of churches as minister, and as a whole-time chaplain in a mental health and learning disability NHS Trust. During his training, Michael became attracted to the work of the psychologist Carl Rogers and later gained a post-graduate diploma in counselling and psychotherapy. Michael is perhaps best known in the churches as a writer of hymns and other worship material. Now retired, his main activities are writing and cabinetmaking. The rest of his time he is busy doing nothing – a duty sadly neglected for far too long.

NICK HARDING is currently Children's Ministry Adviser for the Church of England in Nottinghamshire, as well as being a magistrate, a member of General Synod, and he speaks at conferences throughout Britain and Ireland. Nick has written a range of resource books for those who work with children and has a particular interest in how all-ages can work together. He has led all-age worship and seminars at Spring Harvest for many years, is married to Clare, a headteacher, and has two grown-up sons.

JOHN HARDWICK is well known as a creative Christian communicator whose aim is to present the Christian faith in an exciting and relevant way. He is a juggler, singer-songwriter, storyteller and puppeteer. John travels widely but also works locally leading primary school assemblies and events for local churches.

MARY HATHAWAY is the author of *A Word for All Seasons: Reflections, Meditations and Prayers for the Church Year* published by Kevin Mayhew, for use in public worship, house groups and other small gatherings, but also suitable for individual use.

PETER JACKSON is a writer, editor and lay preacher. A published author of business communication books, he has also written plays and sketches for schools and church groups. Several of his books of sketches have been published by Kevin Mayhew, including *The Star and the Stable, Acts of Faith, The Coming King* and *Footsteps to Glory.*

GERALD O'MAHONY was born in Wigan, Lancashire, and at the age of 18 joined the Society of Jesus (the Jesuits). He was ordained priest at the age of 30 and since then has worked in two main areas: ten years as an adviser to teachers of religious education in the Archdiocese of Liverpool, and thirty years as a retreat director and writer at Loyola Hall Jesuit spirituality centre.

SUSAN SAYERS is a teacher by profession, was later ordained a priest in the Anglican Church and, before retirement her work was divided between the parish of Southend-on-Sea, the local women's prison, writing, training days and retreats. Susan is the author of many popular resource books for the church including our ever-popular *Living Stones* and *Confirmation Experience* ranges. Her most recent publication for Kevin Mayhew is *The Holy Ground Around You, Reflective services for taking the church outside.* Through the conferences and workshops she is invited to lead, she has been privileged to share in the worship of many different traditions and cultures.

DAVID SCHOFIELD is a retired Anglican priest who served all his thirty-two years of ministry in the Diocese of Lincoln. David's first book for Kevin Mayhew, *Troubled Water*, is his account of how he dealt with his cancer. David was diagnosed in June 2008 with myeloma and since then has sought to try and make sense of his illness and bring something positive from it. His second book, *The Everlasting Arms*, is an introduction to bereavement care and funeral practice.

RAY SIMPSON is a Celtic new monastic for tomorrow's world, a lecturer, consultant, liturgist, and author of some 30 books. He is the founding guardian of the international Community of Aidan and Hilda (www.aidanandhilda.org) and the pioneer of its e-studies programmes. He is an ordained member of the Christian church and lives on the Holy Island of Lindisfarne. His website is www.raysimpson.org

KEN TAYLOR is a retired Methodist minister from Yorkshire. He is the author of *Sunday by Sunday (Volumes 1 and 2): Meditations and resources for all appointed Gospel readings Years A, B and C, Cradle of Hope* and *Tried and Tested Talks for Children*, all published by Kevin Mayhew.

STUART THOMAS was ordained in 1987 and has served in Guildford Diocese for the whole of his ministerial career. After a curacy in Guildford and a first incumbency in Churt, he spent almost 20 years in Ewell, where the ecumenical Ruxley Church was opened in 2013. In 2014 he moved to become Rector of Frimley (still in Surrey!). He has been Diocesan Ecumenical Officer and Rural Dean of Epsom, and is an Honorary Canon of Guildford Cathedral. Stuart has been involved in liturgy and training for most of his ordained life, with a particular focus on liturgical music, on which he recently completed a thesis. As well as his books for Kevin Mayhew, has also written a number of hymns.

PETE TOWNSEND's literary career began as a furniture salesman. After three years of University, he began teaching at a local Further Education College. With a brief sojourn as Head of Department in a Secondary school, and studying for a post-graduate diploma, a decision was made to indulge his passion for writing and playing music. He has written two novels, in excess of twenty educational books and contributed to numerous revision guides and magazines.

SHEILA WALKER is an assistant curate, working with four village churches in East Devon, and in addition, she is a part-time librarian. She has also worked as a French teacher, editor and careers adviser. For Kevin Mayhew, Sheila has written the successful resource book *Contemporary Reflections for Praying and Preaching* which covers Church Years A to C.